THE
APPLIED AI AND NATURAL LANGUAGE PROCESSING
WORKSHOP

Explore practical ways to transform your simple projects into powerful intelligent applications

Krishna Sankar, Jeffrey Jackovich, and Ruze Richards

THE APPLIED AI AND NATURAL LANGUAGE PROCESSING WORKSHOP

Authors: Krishna Sankar, Jeffrey Jackovich, and Ruze Richards

Reviewers: Ridhima Garg, Sasikant Kotti, Ankit Malik, Sagnik Pal, Robert Ridley, and Dr. Priyanka Singh

Managing Editor: Pournami Jois

Acquisitions Editors: Sneha Shinde, Anindya Sil, Archie Vankar, and Karan Wadekar

Production Editor: Shantanu Zagade

Editorial Board: Megan Carlisle, Mahesh Dhyani, Heather Gopsill, Manasa Kumar, Alex Mazonowicz, Bridget Neale, Dominic Pereira, Shiny Poojary, Abhishek Rane, Brendan Rodrigues, Erol Staveley, Ankita Thakur, Nitesh Thakur, and Jonathan Wray

First published: July 2020

Production reference: 1240720

ISBN: 978-1-80020-874-2

Published by Packt Publishing Ltd.

Livery Place, 35 Livery Street

Birmingham B3 2PB, UK

EXPERIENCE THE WORKSHOP ONLINE

Thank you for purchasing the print edition of *The Applied AI and Natural Language Processing Workshop*. Every physical print copy includes free online access to the premium interactive edition. There are no extra costs or hidden charges.

Figure A: An example of the companion video in the Workshop course player (dark mode)

With the interactive edition you'll unlock:

- **Screencasts**: Supercharge your progress with screencasts of all exercises and activities.

- **Built-In Discussions**: Engage in discussions where you can ask questions, share notes and interact. Tap straight into insight from expert instructors and editorial teams.

- **Skill Verification**: Complete the course online to earn a Packt credential that is easy to share and unique to you. All authenticated on the public Bitcoin blockchain.

- **Download PDF and EPUB**: Download a digital version of the course to read offline. Available as PDF or EPUB, and always DRM-free.

To redeem your free digital copy of *The Applied AI and Natural Language Processing Workshop* you'll need to follow these simple steps:

1. Visit us at https://courses.packtpub.com/pages/redeem.

2. Login with your Packt account, or register as a new Packt user.

3. Select your course from the list, making a note of the three page numbers for your product. Your unique redemption code needs to match the order of the pages specified.

4. Open up your print copy and find the codes at the bottom of the pages specified. They'll always be in the same place:

EXERCISE 4.02: PERFORMING MISSING VALUE ANALYSIS FOR THE DATAFRAMES

In this section, we will be implementing a missing value analysis on the first DataFrame to find the missing values. This exercise is a continuation of *Exercise 4.01, Importing Data into DataFrames*. Follow these steps to complete this exercise:

1. Import the **missingno** package:

```
# To analyze the missing data
!pip install missingno
import missingno as msno
```

2. Find the missing values in the first DataFrame and visualize the missing values in a plot:

```
# Missing Values in the first DataFrame
msno.bar(dataframes[0],color='red',labels=True,sort="ascending")
```

A B 2 1 C

**Figure B: Example code in the bottom-right corner, to be used
for free digital redemption of a print workshop**

5. Merge the codes together (without spaces), ensuring they are in the correct order.

6. At checkout, click **Have a redemption code?** and enter your unique product string. Click **Apply**, and the price should be free!

Finally, we'd like to thank you for purchasing the print edition of *The Applied AI and Natural Language Processing Workshop*! We hope that you finish the course feeling capable of tackling challenges in the real world. Remember that we're here to help if you ever feel like you're not making progress.

If you run into issues during redemption (or have any other feedback) you can reach us at workshops@packt.com.

Table of Contents

Chapter 2: Analyzing Documents and Text with Natural Language Processing   41

Chapter 6: Computer Vision and Image Processing 223

Appendix 275

Index 353

PREFACE

ABOUT THE BOOK

Are you fascinated with applications like Alexa and Siri and how they accurately process information within seconds before returning accurate results? Are you looking for a practical guide that will teach you how to build intelligent applications that can revolutionize the world of artificial intelligence? *The Applied AI and NLP Workshop* will take you on a practical journey where you will learn how to build **Artificial Intelligence** (**AI**) and **Natural Language Processing** (**NLP**) applications with **Amazon Web Services** (**AWS**).

Starting with an introduction to AI and machine learning, this book will explain how Amazon S3, or Amazon Simple Storage Service, works. You'll then integrate AI with AWS to build serverless services and use Amazon's NLP service Comprehend to perform text analysis on a document. As you advance, the book will help you get to grips with topic modeling to extract and analyze common themes on a set of documents with unknown topics. You'll also work with Amazon Lex to create and customize a chatbot for task automation and use Amazon Rekognition for detecting objects, scenes, and text in images.

By the end of *The Applied AI and NLP Workshop*, you'll be equipped with the knowledge and skills needed to build scalable intelligent applications with AWS.

AUDIENCE

If you are a machine learning enthusiast, data scientist, or programmer who wants to explore AWS's artificial intelligence and machine learning capabilities, this book is for you. Although not necessary, a basic understanding of AI and NLP will assist with grasping key topics quickly.

ABOUT THE CHAPTERS

Chapter 1, An Introduction to AWS, introduces you to the AWS interface. You will learn how to use Amazon's Simple Storage Service as well as test the NLP interface with the Amazon Comprehend API.

Chapter 2, Analyzing Documents and Text with Natural Language Processing, introduces the set of AWS AI services and the emerging computing paradigm that is serverless computing. You will then apply NLP and the Amazon Comprehend service to analyze documents.

Chapter 3, *Topic Modeling and Theme Extraction*, describes the basics of topic modeling analysis and you will learn how to extract and analyze common themes using topic modeling with Amazon Comprehend.

Chapter 4, *Conversational Artificial Intelligence*, talks about the best practices in the design of conversational AI and then proceeds to show you how to develop bots using Amazon Lex.

Chapter 5, *Using Speech with the Chatbot*, teaches you the basics of Amazon Connect. You will program for voice interaction with a chatbot as well as create a personal call center using Amazon Connect and your own phone number to interact with your bots.

Chapter 6, *Computer Vision and Image Processing*, introduces you to the Rekognition service for image analysis using computer vision. You will learn how to analyze faces and recognize celebrities in images. You will also be able to compare faces in different images to see how closely they match each other.

CONVENTIONS

Code words in text, database table names, folder names, filenames, file extensions, pathnames, dummy URLs, user input, and Twitter handles are shown as follows: "Here, the selected bucket name is **known-tm-analysis**, but you will need to create a unique name."

A block of code is set as follows:

```
filename = str(text_file_obj['s3']['object']['key'])
print("filename: ", filename)
```

Words that you see on the screen, for example, in menus or dialog boxes, also appear in the text like this: "From the menu panel on the left-hand side of the screen, select the **Routing** menu."

New terms and important words are shown like this: "The machine learning algorithm that Amazon Comprehend uses to perform topic modeling is called **Latent Dirichlet Allocation (LDA)**."

CODE PRESENTATION

Lines of code that span multiple lines are split using a backslash (\ ). When the code is executed, Python will ignore the backslash, and treat the code on the next line as a direct continuation of the current line.

For example:

```
history = model.fit(X, y, epochs=100, batch_size=5, verbose=1, \
                    validation_split=0.2, shuffle=False)
```

Comments are added into code to help explain specific bits of logic. Single-line comments are denoted using the # symbol, as follows:

```
# Print the sizes of the dataset
print("Number of Examples in the Dataset = ", X.shape[0])
print("Number of Features for each example = ", X.shape[1])
```

Multi-line comments are enclosed by triple quotes, as shown below:

```
"""
Define a seed for the random number generator to ensure the
result will be reproducible
"""
seed = 1
np.random.seed(seed)
random.set_seed(seed)
```

SETTING UP YOUR ENVIRONMENT

Before we explore the book in detail, we need to set up specific software and tools. In the following section, we shall see how to do that.

SOFTWARE REQUIREMENTS

You'll also need the following software installed in advance:

1. OS: Windows 7 SP1 64-bit, Windows 8.1 64-bit or Windows 10 64-bit, macOS, or Linux

2. Browser: Google Chrome, latest version

3. An AWS Free Tier account

4. Python 3.6 or above

5. Jupyter Notebook

INSTALLATION AND SETUP

Before you start this book, you will need an AWS account. You will also need to set up the AWS **command-line interface** (**CLI**), the steps for which can be found below. You will also need Python 3.6 or above, pip, and an AWS Rekognition account for the book.

AWS ACCOUNT

For an AWS Free Tier account, you will need a personal email address, a credit or debit card, and a cell phone that can receive a text message so that you can verify your account. To create a new account, follow this link: https://aws.amazon.com/free/.

A WORD ABOUT AWS REGIONS

AWS servers are distributed across the globe in what AWS calls Regions. The number of Regions has grown since AWS first started, and you can find a list of them all at https://aws.amazon.com/about-aws/global-infrastructure/regions_az/. When you create an AWS account, you will also need to choose a Region. You can find your Region by going to aws.amazon.com and selecting `AWS Management Console`:

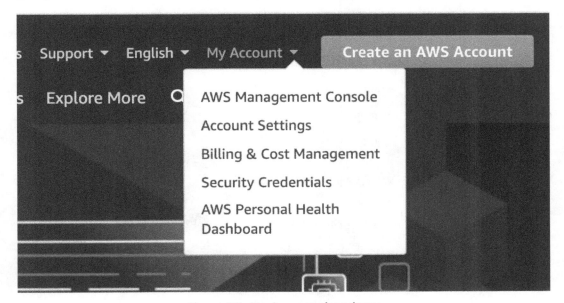

Figure 0.1: My Account dropdown

In the AWS Management Console, your Region will be displayed in the top right-hand corner. You can click on it and change the Region:

Figure 0.2: AWS Region list

One reason for changing the Region is that not all AWS services are available in all Regions. The Region table at https://aws.amazon.com/about-aws/global-infrastructure/regional-product-services/ has the current list of services available in each Region. So, if a service that you want to access is not available in your Region, you can change your Region. But be aware of the differences in the charges (if any) between Regions. Also, the artifacts that you create in one Region may not be available in another Region, for example, S3 buckets. In case you are wondering, one reason for Amazon not automatically making S3 data available across Regions is compliance and regulations. You will have to explicitly copy or recreate S3 buckets and files. While managing AWS services and Regions might look tedious at first, it is easy to get used to. As we have mentioned, there are reasons for Amazon doing things this way.

> **NOTE**
>
> Depending upon where you are, it might not be possible to access an AWS service just by changing the Region. For example, Amazon Connect is not available everywhere, and just changing the Region from the dropdown doesn't let us use Amazon Connect because of the local number assignment. In order to use Amazon Connect, we need to mention the address where Amazon Connect is available while signing up for AWS. At the time of writing this book (April 2020), Amazon Connect is available in the US, UK, Australia, Japan, Germany, and Singapore. But the good news is that Amazon is constantly expanding its services. So, by the time you read this book, Amazon Connect might be available where you are.

AWS CLI SETUP

Install the AWS CLI (version 2) as described at this URL: https://docs.aws.amazon.com/cli/latest/userguide/cli-chap-install.html. The AWS documentation describes how to install the CLI on various operating systems. To verify that installation was successful, open a command prompt and type **aws --version**.

CONFIGURATION AND CREDENTIAL FILES FOR THE AWS CLI

The AWS CLI documentation clearly describes the configuration and credential file settings. For more information, go to https://docs.aws.amazon.com/cli/latest/userguide/cli-config-files.html.

AMAZON REKOGNITION ACCOUNT

You will need to create a new Amazon Rekognition Free Tier account, using which customers can analyze up to 5,000 images for free every month for the first 12 months. To create the free account, go to https://aws.amazon.com/rekognition/.

> **NOTE**
>
> The interfaces and results might vary a little from the images shown in the chapters as Amazon periodically updates and streamlines its interfaces and retrains models.

INSTALLING PYTHON AND ANACONDA

The following section will help you to install Python and Anaconda on Windows, macOS and Linux systems.

INSTALLING PYTHON AND ANACONDA ON WINDOWS

Installing Python on Windows is done as follows:

1. Find your desired version of Anaconda on the official installation page at https://www.anaconda.com/distribution/#windows.

2. Ensure you select Python 3.7 from the download page.

3. Ensure that you install the correct architecture for your computer system; that is, either 32-bit or 64-bit. You can find out this information in the **System Properties** window of your OS.

4. After you download the installer, simply double-click the file and follow the user-friendly prompts on-screen.

INSTALLING PYTHON AND ANACONDA ON LINUX

To install Python on Linux, you have a couple of good options:

1. Open Command Prompt and verify that **Python 3** is not already installed by running **python3 --version**.

2. To install Python 3, run this:

```
sudo apt-get update
sudo apt-get install python3.7
```

3. If you encounter problems, there are numerous sources online that can help you troubleshoot the issue.

4. You can also install Python using Anaconda. Install Anaconda for Linux by downloading the installer from https://www.anaconda.com/distribution/#linux and following the instructions.

INSTALLING PYTHON AND ANACONDA ON MACOS

Similar to Linux, you have a couple of methods for installing Python on a Mac. To install Python on macOS, do the following:

1. Open the Terminal for Mac by pressing *CMD* + *Spacebar*, type **terminal** in the open search box, and hit *Enter*.

2. Install Xcode through the command line by running **xcode-select --install**.

3. The easiest way to install Python 3 is using Homebrew, which is installed through the command line by running **ruby -e "$(curl -fsSL https://raw. githubusercontent.com/Homebrew/install/master/install)"**.

4. Add Homebrew to your **$PATH** environment variable. Open your profile in the command line by running **sudo nano ~/.profile** and inserting **export PATH="/usr/local/opt/python/libexec/bin:$PATH"** at the bottom.

5. The final step is to install Python. In the command line, run **brew install python**.

6. Again, you can also install Python via the Anaconda installer, available from https://www.anaconda.com/distribution/#macos.

PROJECT JUPYTER

Project Jupyter is open source, free software that gives you the ability to run code written in Python and some other languages interactively from a special notebook, similar to a browser interface. It was born in 2014 from the **IPython** project and has since become the default choice for the entire data science workforce.

To install the Jupyter Notebook, go here: https://jupyter.org/install.

At https://jupyterlab.readthedocs.io/en/stable/getting_started/starting.html, you will find all the details you need to know to start the Jupyter Notebook server. In this book, we use the classic notebook interface.

Usually, we start a notebook from the command line with the
jupyter notebook command.

Start the notebook from the directory where you download the code files to in the
following *Installing the Code Bundle* section.

For example, in our case, we have installed the files in the following directory **/
Users/ksankar/Documents/aws_book/Artificial-Intelligence-
and-Natural-Language-Processing-with-AWS**.

In the CLI, type **cd /Users/ksankar/Documents/aws_book/Artificial-
Intelligence-and-Natural-Language-Processing-with-AWS** and then
type the **jupyter notebook** command. The Jupyter server will start and you will
see the Jupyter browser console:

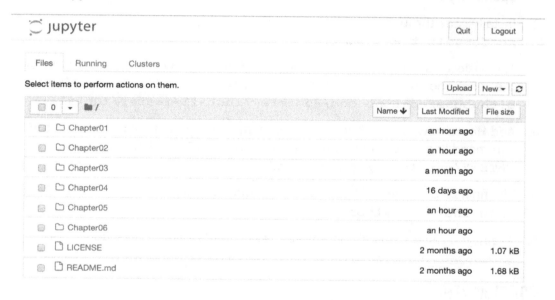

Figure 0.3: Jupyter browser console

Once you are running the Jupyter server, click **New** and choose `Python 3`. A new browser tab will open with a new and empty notebook. Rename the Jupyter file:

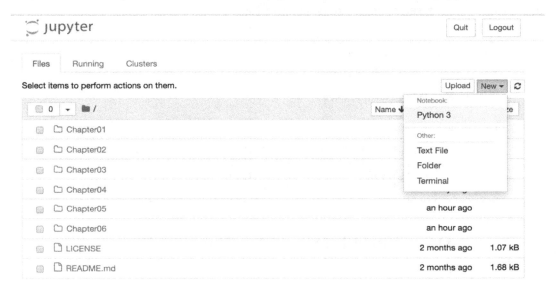

Figure 0.4: Jupyter server interface

The main building blocks of Jupyter notebooks are cells. There are two types of cells: **In** (short for input) and **Out** (short for output). You can write code, normal text, and Markdown in **In** cells, press *Shift + Enter* (or *Shift + Return*), and the code written in that particular **In** cell will be executed. The result will be shown in an **Out** cell, and you will land in a new **In** cell, ready for the next block of code. Once you get used to this interface, you will slowly discover the power and flexibility it offers.

When you start a new cell, by default, it is assumed that you will write code in it. However, if you want to write text, then you have to change the type. You can do that using the following sequence of keys: *Esc | M | Enter*:

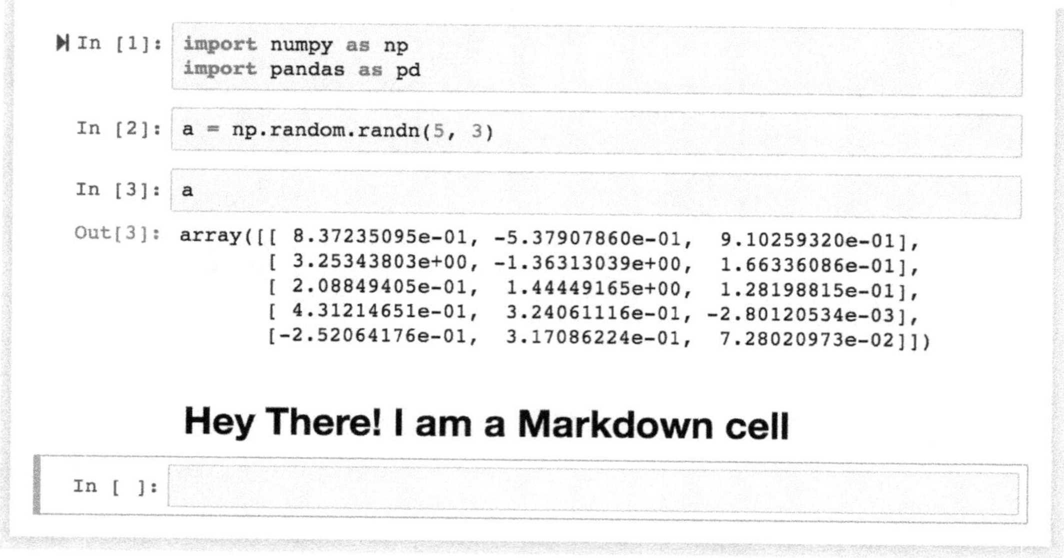

```
▶ In [1]:   import numpy as np
            import pandas as pd

  In [2]:   a = np.random.randn(5, 3)

  In [3]:   a

 Out[3]:   array([[ 8.37235095e-01, -5.37907860e-01,  9.10259320e-01],
                  [ 3.25343803e+00, -1.36313039e+00,  1.66336086e-01],
                  [ 2.08849405e-01,  1.44449165e+00,  1.28198815e-01],
                  [ 4.31214651e-01,  3.24061116e-01, -2.80120534e-03],
                  [-2.52064176e-01,  3.17086224e-01,  7.28020973e-02]])
```

Hey There! I am a Markdown cell

```
  In [ ]:
```

Figure 0.5: Jupyter Notebook

When you are done with writing some text, execute it using *Shift + Enter*. Unlike the case with code cells, the result of the compiled Markdown will be shown in the same place as the **In** cell.

To get a "cheat sheet" of all the handy key shortcuts in Jupyter, go to https://gist.github.com/kidpixo/f4318f8c8143adee5b40. With this basic introduction, we are ready to embark on an exciting and enlightening journey.

INSTALLING LIBRARIES

`pip` comes pre-installed with Anaconda. Once Anaconda is installed on your machine, all the required libraries can be installed using `pip`, for example, `pip install numpy`. Alternatively, you can install all the required libraries using `pip install -r requirements.txt`. You can find the `requirements.txt` file at https://packt.live/30ddspf.

The exercises and activities will be executed in Jupyter Notebooks. Jupyter is a Python library and can be installed in the same way as the other Python libraries – that is, with `pip install jupyter`, but fortunately, it comes pre-installed with Anaconda. To open a notebook, simply run the command `jupyter notebook` in the Terminal or Command Prompt.

ACCESSING THE CODE FILES

You can find the complete code files of this book at https://packt.live/2O67hxH.

If you have any issues or questions about installation, please email us at workshops@packt.com.

1

AN INTRODUCTION TO AWS

OVERVIEW

In this chapter, we start off with the basic concepts of **cloud computing**, **Artificial Intelligence** (**AI**), and **Machine Learning** (**ML**). These are the foundational elements that we will be working with throughout this book. The guided instructions in this chapter will equip you with the skills necessary to store and retrieve data with Amazon Simple Storage Service (S3) while you learn the core concepts of this technology. Next, you will apply your S3 knowledge by importing and exporting text data via the management console and the **Command Line Interface** (**CLI**). By the end of the chapter, you will be able to confidently work with the management console and the CLI so that you can test AI and ML services.

INTRODUCTION

We are in an era of unprecedented computing capabilities—serverless computing with autonomous functions that can scale elastically from zero to a million users and back to zero in seconds, innovative intelligent bot frameworks that can live in a contact center in the cloud that we can spin up with a small amount of configuration, and the ability to extract text from images, tables, and scanned documents such as medical records and business and tax documents.

Of course, we are talking about the cloud services available at our fingertips, specifically from Amazon. In 2004, Amazon first offered cloud computing as a service, and now (according to Forbes) the cloud market is worth over $30 billion, growing at a rate of 30-50% yearly. More and more people prefer to do their computing in the cloud.

So, what is cloud computing? It is a set of computing services of which you can use as much as you need and can afford and pay for on an *as-you-go* basis. So, enterprises switch from their own hosting to the cloud. Beyond that, you get not only a cost-efficient way of doing your computing, but you also get a wider and wider variety of these services.

While there is a huge set of cloud services offered by Amazon, in this book, we will work with **Amazon Web Services (AWS)** for **Artificial Intelligence (AI)** and **Machine Learning (ML)**. In the process, we will also use AWS Lambda for serverless computing, AWS Simple Storage Service, and AWS API Gateway for networking and content delivery.

This chapter will introduce you to the AWS interface and will teach you how to store and retrieve data with Amazon Simple Storage Service (S3). Then, you will apply your S3 knowledge by importing and exporting text data via the management console and the CLI. Lastly, you will learn how to locate and test AI and ML services.

In later chapters, you will get a chance to apply **Natural Language Processing (NLP)** techniques to analyze documents, program serverless computing, use AI/ML services for topic and theme extraction, construct your own fully capable contact center with its own telephone number, develop bots that answer calls in your own contact center, and finally, program image analysis with ML to extract text from images (such as street signs) and perform facial recognition. Overall, it is going to be an interesting journey that will end with us commanding an infrastructure of vast resources for AI and ML.

HOW IS AWS SPECIAL?

Today, there are many cloud providers, with the market share breakdown as follows: as per the Canalys analysis (https://www.canalys.com/static/press_release/2020/Canalys---Cloud-market-share-Q4-2019-and-full-year-2019.pdf), as of Q4 2019, AWS is the top vendor, owning nearly a third of the overall public cloud infrastructure market (32%), leading by a wide margin over Microsoft (18%), Google (6%), and Alibaba (5%).

These numbers vary depending on the source, and they may change in the future, but all agree that Amazon is the largest provider at the moment. One of the reasons for this is that Amazon offers a very large array of cloud services. In fact, one of their competitive advantages is exactly that: a very broad and deep cloud computing ecosystem. For example, in the area of ML, Amazon has thousands of use cases, with the professed goal of every imaginable ML service being provided on AWS. This explains our focus on doing ML on AWS.

WHAT IS ML?

ML and AI go hand in hand. ML is the art and science of predicting real-world outcomes based on knowledge of the world and its history. You build a model that allows you to predict the future. The model is based on a formula or a process that formulates this prediction. The model is trained using data.

AI is a wider area of science, which includes, together with ML, all the ways of imitating human behavior and capabilities. However, the way people use these terms vary, depending on who you ask. People also tend to use the current most popular term, mostly for search engine optimization. In this book, we will take the liberty of using these two terms interchangeably.

ML is essential to learn in today's world because it is an integral part of all industries' competitive and operational data strategies. More specifically, ML allows insights from NLP to power chatbots, ML insights are used in the financial industry; and ML applications allow efficient online recommendation engines, such as friend suggestions on Facebook, Netflix displaying movies you will probably like, and more items to consider on Amazon.

WHAT IS AI?

AI is intelligence that's demonstrated by machines. More specifically, it refers to any device that perceives its environment and takes actions that increase its chance of successfully achieving its goals. Contemporary examples are understanding human speech, competing at the highest levels of strategic games (such as Chess and Go), and autonomous cars.

AI is important because it adds intelligence to existing products. Products that are currently used will be further improved with AI capabilities; for example, Siri was added to a new generation of Apple products. Conversational chatbots can be combined with large amounts of data to improve technologies at home and in the office.

In this chapter, we will introduce you to the first few AWS services that will start you on the way to doing ML on AWS. Whenever we can, we will stick to the free tier of AWS. You get the free tier for 1 year, and it is limited in the number of computing resources you can use. Readers willing to invest a few dollars in learning with a regular AWS account will find the money well spent. Another alternative is to use packaged labs, such as **Qwiklabs**, which lets you do labs at will, with the added convenience of shutting the labs down so that you will not incur accidental charges when you leave your machines running.

WHAT IS AMAZON S3?

S3 is an online cloud object storage and retrieval service. Instead of data being associated with a server, S3 storage is server-independent and can be accessed over the internet. Data stored in S3 is managed as objects using an **Application Programming Interface** (**API**) that is accessible via the internet (HTTPS).

The benefits of using S3 are as follows:

- Amazon S3 runs on the largest global cloud infrastructure to deliver 99.99% durability.

- It provides the widest range of options to transfer data.

- It allows you to run big data analytics without moving data into a separate analytics system.

- It supports security standards and compliance certificates.

- It offers a flexible set of storage management and administration capabilities.

> **NOTE**
>
> For more information, visit https://aws.amazon.com/s3/.

WHY USE S3?

S3 is a place to store and retrieve your files. It is recommended for storing static content such as text files, images, audio files, and video files. For example, S3 can be used as a static web server if the website consists exclusively of HTML and images. The website can be connected to an FTP client to serve the static files. In addition, S3 can be used to store user-generated images and text files.

However, the two most important applications of S3 are as follows:

- To store static data from web pages or mobile apps
- To implement big data analytics

It can easily be used in conjunction with additional AWS ML and infrastructure services. For example, text documents imported to Amazon S3 can be summarized by code running in an AWS Lambda function that is analyzed using AWS Comprehend. We will cover AWS Lambda and AWS Comprehend in *Chapter 2, Analyzing Documents and Text with Natural Language Processing*, and *Chapter 3, Topic Modeling and Theme Extraction*.

THE BASICS OF WORKING ON AWS WITH S3

The first step to accessing S3 is to create an AWS free-tier account, which provides access to the AWS Management Console. The AWS Management Console is a web application that provides one method to access all AWS's powerful storage and ML/AI services.

The second step is to understand the access level. AWS defines **identity and access management (IAM)**. The same email/password is used to access IAM.

AWS FREE-TIER ACCOUNT

AWS provides a free-tier (within their individual free usage stipulations) account, and one of the included storage services is S3. Thus, you can maximize cost savings and reduce errors before making a large investment by testing services to optimize your ML and AI workflows.

AWS ACCOUNT SETUP AND NAVIGATION

Generally, you need an AWS account with Amazon. A good description of the steps is available at https://support.sou.edu/kb/articles/amazon-web-services-account-creation. The steps might vary a little bit, as Amazon might make changes to its processes.

The general steps are:

1. Create a personal account (if needed; many of you might already be Amazon customers), which might also need a security check.

2. Create an AWS account. AWS account creation also requires credit card information. But you can also use credit codes.

3. The AWS free tier offers limited capability for 1 year. The details are at https://aws.amazon.com/free/?all-free-tier.sort-by=item.additionalFields.SortRank&all-free-tier.sort-order=asc.

DOWNLOADING THE SUPPORT MATERIALS FOR THIS BOOK

In this book, you will be programming AWS APIs using Jupyter notebooks, uploading images for AI services and text files to S3, and even writing short code for Lambda functions. These files and programs are located in a GitHub repository, https://packt.live/2O67hxH. You can download the files using the **Download ZIP** button and then unzip the file:

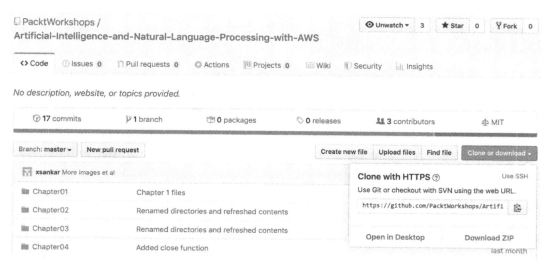

Figure 1.1: Download support files from GitHub

As an example, we have downloaded the files into the **Documents/aws-book/ The-Applied-AI-and-Natural-Language-Processing-with- AWS** directory:

Name			Date Modified	Size	Kind
▼ 📁 Chapter01			Feb 17, 2020 at 4:04 PM	1.8 MB	Folder
	▼ 📁 text_files		Jan 18, 2020 at 4:23 PM	1.8 MB	Folder
		📄 neg_sentiment__dracula.txt	Jan 18, 2020 at 4:23 PM	842 KB	Plain Text
		📄 peter_pan.txt	Jan 18, 2020 at 4:23 PM	263 KB	Plain Text
		📄 pos_sentiment__leaves_of_grass.txt	Jan 18, 2020 at 4:23 PM	738 KB	Plain Text
▼ 📁 Chapter02			Mar 17, 2020 at 5:38 PM	1.1 MB	Folder
	▶ 📁 .ipynb_checkpoints		Mar 17, 2020 at 5:38 PM	9 KB	Folder
	📄 Exercise2.01.ipynb		Jan 17, 2020 at 7:38 PM	4 KB	Document
	📄 Exercise2.02.ipynb		Jan 17, 2020 at 7:39 PM	6 KB	Document
	📄 Exercise2.03.ipynb		Jan 17, 2020 at 7:42 PM	4 KB	Document
	📄 Exercise2.04.ipynb		Mar 17, 2020 at 5:38 PM	9 KB	Document
	📄 Exercise2.05.ipynb		Jan 17, 2020 at 9:29 PM	5 KB	Document
	📄 Exercise2.06.ipynb		Jan 17, 2020 at 9:37 PM	3 KB	Document
	▶ 📁 reviews__pos		Jan 17, 2020 at 8:11 PM	2 KB	Folder
	📄 s3_trigger.py		Today at 3:23 AM	2 KB	BBEdit...cument
	📄 Sample-2016-Tax-Return.jpg		Jan 18, 2020 at 3:27 PM	1 MB	JPEG image
	📄 test_s3trigger_configured.txt		Jan 18, 2020 at 1:35 PM	114 bytes	Plain Text
▶ 📁 Chapter03			Mar 4, 2020 at 9:13 PM	4.4 MB	Folder
▼ 📁 Chapter04			Mar 14, 2020 at 2:02 PM	8 KB	Folder
	📄 lambda_function.py		Jan 20, 2020 at 3:36 PM	1 KB	BBEdit...cument
▼ 📁 Chapter05			Mar 14, 2020 at 2:02 PM	8 KB	Folder
	📄 balance.txt		Jan 24, 2020 at 7:15 PM	5 bytes	Plain Text
	📄 fetch_balance.py		Jan 24, 2020 at 9:29 PM	937 bytes	BBEdit...cument
	📄 test_event.json		Jan 18, 2020 at 4:23 PM	772 bytes	BBEdit...cument
	📄 test_response.json		Jan 18, 2020 at 4:23 PM	250 bytes	BBEdit...cument
▼ 📁 Chapter06			Mar 14, 2020 at 10:13 AM	25.2 MB	Folder
	📄 face-01-01.jpg		Mar 14, 2020 at 10:13 AM	3 MB	JPEG image
	📄 face-01-02.jpg		Mar 14, 2020 at 10:13 AM	5.2 MB	JPEG image
	📄 face-01-03.jpg		Mar 14, 2020 at 10:13 AM	3.5 MB	JPEG image
	📄 face-02-01.jpg		Mar 14, 2020 at 10:13 AM	6.3 MB	JPEG image
	📄 face-02-02.jpg		Mar 14, 2020 at 10:13 AM	5.3 MB	JPEG image
	📄 image_urls.txt		Mar 14, 2020 at 10:13 AM	266 bytes	Plain Text
	📄 Rekognition-01.jpeg		Mar 14, 2020 at 10:13 AM	128 KB	JPEG image
	📄 Rekognition-02.jpeg		Mar 14, 2020 at 10:13 AM	1.1 MB	JPEG image
	📄 Rekognition-03.jpeg		Mar 14, 2020 at 10:13 AM	122 KB	JPEG image
	📄 Rekognition-04.jpeg		Mar 14, 2020 at 10:13 AM	26 KB	JPEG image
	📄 Rekognition-05.jpeg		Mar 14, 2020 at 10:13 AM	451 KB	JPEG image

💾 Macintosh HD > 📁 Users > 👤 ksankar > 📁 Documents > 📁 aws_book > 📁 Artificial-Intelligence-and-Natural-Language-Processing-with-AWS > 📁 Chapter01

Figure 1.2: Support files from GitHub in a local directory

A WORD ABOUT JUPYTER NOTEBOOKS

Some of the programs in this book use Jupyter notebooks to run. You will recognize them by the **.ipynb** file extensions. If you haven't already used Jupyter notebooks, please follow the **Installation and setup** in the *Preface*.

IMPORTING AND EXPORTING DATA INTO S3

The way AWS handles big data is by providing the AWS Import/Export service, which allows you to transfer large amounts of data to AWS.

How it works is you mail your storage device to AWS, and AWS will transfer that data using Amazon's high-speed network. Your big data will be loaded into AWS the next business day after it arrives. Once data has been loaded, the storage device is returned to the owner. This is a more cost-efficient way of transferring huge amounts of data and is much faster than transferring it via the internet.

If the amount of data that you need to put into S3 is relatively small, you can simply upload it from your computer. Today, with the increasing capacity of broadband networks, "small" becomes bigger and bigger. Our guideline is 1 TB. Once you have more than this, you may need to think of faster ways to put the data in S3. One of them is the **AWS Import/Export Disk Service** (https://aws.amazon.com/snowball/disk/details/), where you package your data on a device provided by AWS and ship it to them. Significant amounts of data can then be loaded within a day or a few days.

HOW S3 DIFFERS FROM A FILESYSTEM

S3 is used to store almost any type of file, thus, it can get confused with a traditional filesystem because of this similarity. However, S3 differs in a few ways from a traditional filesystem. The folders in a traditional filesystem are buckets in S3; a file in a traditional filesystem is an object in S3. S3 uses objects since you can store any data type (that is, more than files) in buckets.

Another difference is how objects can be accessed. Objects stored in buckets can be accessed from a web service endpoint (such as a web browser, for example, Chrome or Firefox), so each object requires a globally unique name. The name restrictions for objects are similar to the restrictions in selecting a URL when creating a new website. You need to select a unique URL, according to the same logic that your house has a unique address.

For example, if you created a bucket (with public permission settings) named `myBucket` and then uploaded a text file named `pos_sentiment__leaves_of_grass.txt` to the bucket, the object would be accessible from a web browser via the corresponding subdomain.

CORE S3 CONCEPTS

The S3 hierarchy includes the following concepts:

- **Type of data storage**: S3 is a key-value store. You provide a unique key, and AWS stores your data as a value. You retrieve the data using the key.

- **Keys**: The key is the name assigned to an object that uniquely identifies it inside a bucket. All objects in a bucket have one key associated with them.

- **Objects**: Objects are what you store. They are not updatable: if you need to change one byte in the value, you will have to upload the entire object again.

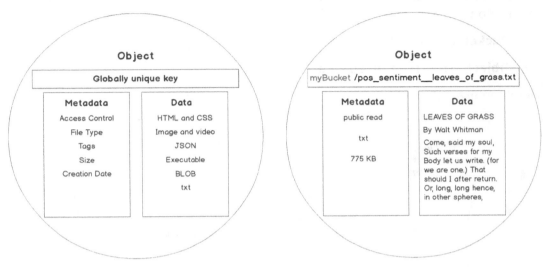

Figure 1.3: Object storage using a unique key and myBucket

- **Bucket**: Just like a folder, a bucket is a container where you store objects. Buckets are created at the root level and do not have a filesystem hierarchy. More specifically, you can have multiple buckets, but you cannot have sub-buckets within a bucket. Buckets are the containers for objects, and you can control (create, delete, and list objects in the bucket) access, view access logs, and select the geographical region where Amazon S3 will store the bucket.

- **Region**: Region refers to the geographical region, such as **us-central** or **ap-south**, where S3 stores a bucket, based on the user's preference. The region can be selected when creating a bucket. The location should be based on where the data will be accessed the most. Overall, specific region selection has the biggest impact if S3 is used to store files for a website that's exclusively accessed in a specific geographic region.

The object storage in a bucket with different forms is as follows:

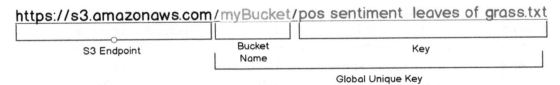

Figure 1.4: Object storage

S3 OPERATIONS

The S3 API is quite simple, and it includes the following operations for the entity in question:

- **Bucket**: Create, delete, and list keys in a bucket

- **Object**: Write, read, and delete

Here's an example:

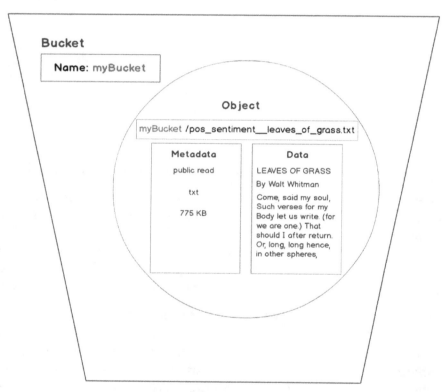

Figure 1.5: Object stored in myBucket

DATA REPLICATION

Amazon replicates data across the region in multiple servers located in Amazon's data centers. Data replication benefits include high availability and durability. More specifically, when you create a new object in S3, the data is saved in S3; however, the change needs to be replicated across the S3 regions. Overall, replication may take some time, and you might notice delays resulting from various replication mechanisms.

After deleting an object, replication can cause a lag time that allows the deleted data to display until the deletion is fully replicated. Creating an object and immediately trying to display it in the object list might be delayed as a result of a replication delay.

THE REST INTERFACE

S3's native interface is a **Representational State Transfer** (**REST**) API. It is recommended to always use HTTPS requests to perform any S3 operations. The two higher-level interfaces that we will use to interact with S3 are the AWS Management Console and the AWS CLI. Accessing objects with the API is quite simple and includes the following operations for the entity in question:

- **Bucket**: Create, delete, or list keys in a bucket

- **Object**: Write, read, or delete

EXERCISE 1.01: USING THE AWS MANAGEMENT CONSOLE TO CREATE AN S3 BUCKET

In this exercise, we will prepare a place on AWS to store data for ML. To import a file, you need to have access to the Amazon S3 console:

1. You should have already completed the account setup detailed earlier in this chapter. Go to https://aws.amazon.com/ and click **My Account** and then **AWS Management Console** to open the AWS Management Console in a new browser tab:

Figure 1.6: Accessing the AWS Management Console via the user's account

2. Click inside the search bar located under **AWS services**, as shown here:

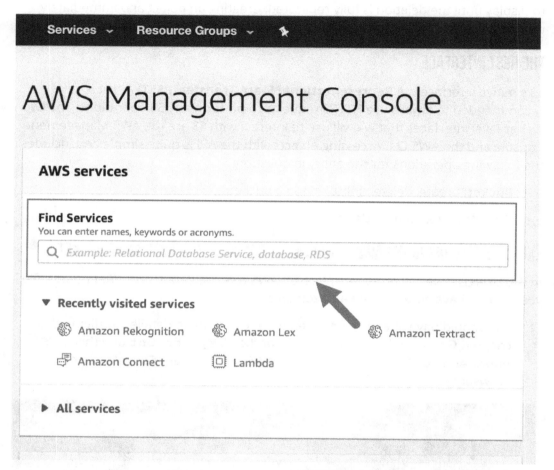

Figure 1.7: Searching AWS services

3. Type **S3** into the search bar and an auto-populated list will appear. Then, click the **S3 Scalable Storage in the Cloud** option:

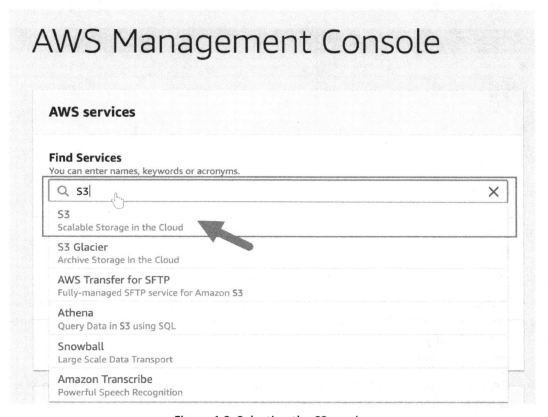

Figure 1.8: Selecting the S3 service

4. Now we need to create an S3 bucket. In the S3 dashboard, click the **Create bucket** button. If this is the first time that you are creating a bucket, your screen will look like this:

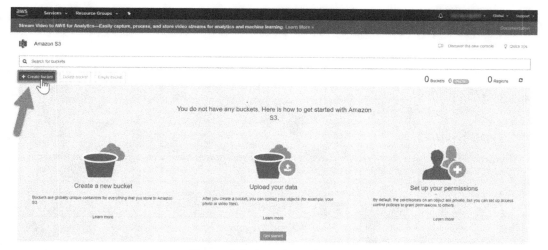

Figure 1.9: Creating a bucket

If you have already created S3 buckets, your dashboard will list all the buckets you have created. **Enter a unique bucket name**: Bucket names must be unique across S3. If you encounter a naming issue, please refer to https://docs.aws. amazon.com/AmazonS3/latest/dev/BucketRestrictions.html.

Region: If a default region is auto-populated, then keep the default location. If it is not auto populated, select a region near your current location.

5. Click the **Next** button to continue the creation of the bucket:

Figure 1.10: The Create bucket window

6. An S3 bucket provides the property options **Versioning**, **Server Access Logging**, **Tags**, **Object-Level Logging**, and **Default Encryption**; however, we will not enable them.

7. Your bucket will be displayed in the bucket list, as shown here:

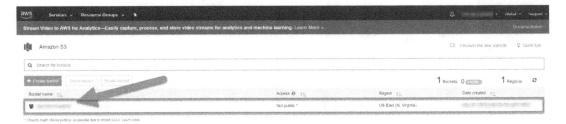

Figure 1.11: The bucket has been created

In this exercise, we have created a place for our files to be stored on the cloud. In the next exercise, we will learn the process of storing and retrieving our files from this place.

EXERCISE 1.02: IMPORTING AND EXPORTING THE FILE WITH YOUR S3 BUCKET

In this exercise, we will show you how to place your data in S3 on Amazon, and how to retrieve it from there.

Follow these steps to complete this exercise:

Importing a file:

1. Click the bucket's name to navigate to the bucket:

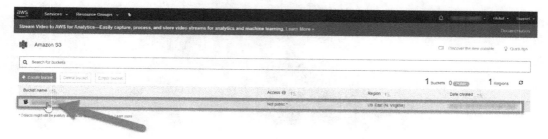

Figure 1.12: Navigate to the bucket

2. You are on the bucket's home page. Select **Upload**:

Figure 1.13: Uploading a file into the bucket

3. To select a file to upload, click **Add files**:

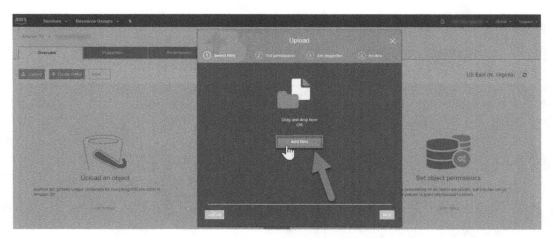

Figure 1.14: Adding a new file to the bucket

4. We will upload the **pos_sentiment__leaves_of_grass.txt** file from the https://packt.live/3e9lwfR GitHub repository. The best way is to download the repository to your local disk. Then you can select the file:

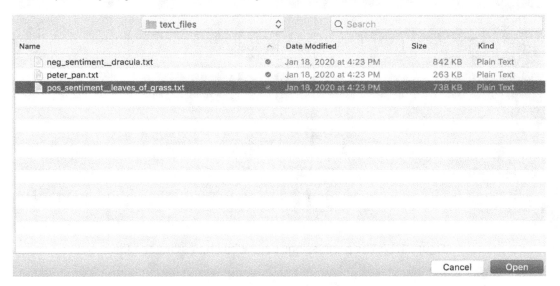

Figure 1.15: Selecting the file to upload to the S3 bucket

5. After selecting a file to upload, select **Next**:

Figure 1.16: Selecting the file to upload to the bucket

6. Click the **Next** button and leave the default options selected:

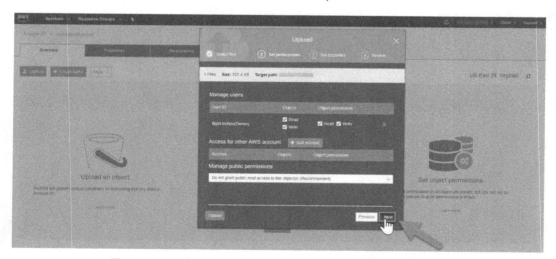

Figure 1.17: The permissions page while uploading the file

7. You can set property settings for your object, such as **Storage class**, **Encryption**, and **Metadata**. However, leave the default values as they are and then click the **Next** button:

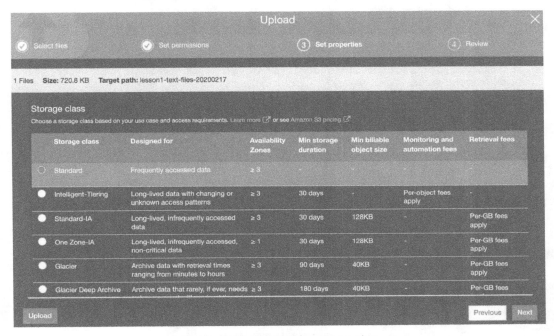

Figure 1.18: Setting the properties

8. Click the **Upload** button to upload the files:

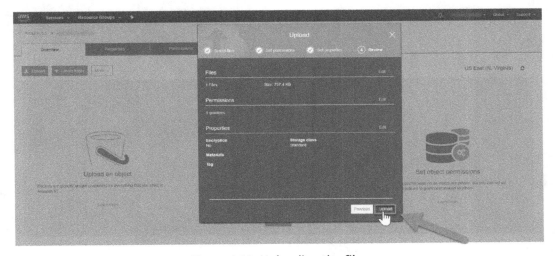

Figure 1.19: Uploading the files

9. You will be directed to your object on your bucket's home screen:

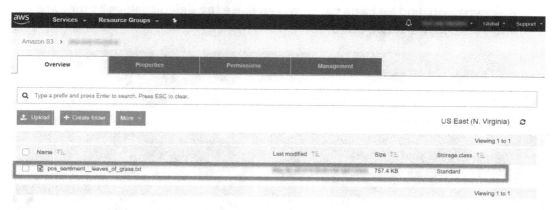

Figure 1.20: Files uploaded to the bucket

Exporting a file:

1. Select the checkbox next to the file to export (*Red Marker #1 – see the following screenshot*). This populates the file's information display screen. Click **Download** (*Red Marker #2 – see the following screenshot*) to retrieve the text file:

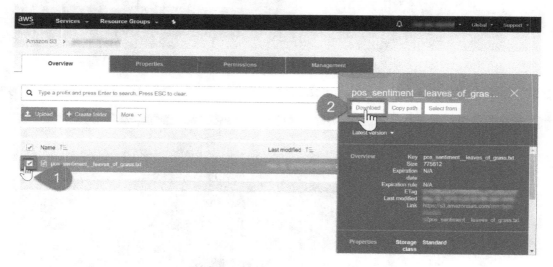

Figure 1.21: Exporting the file

The file will download, as shown in the bottom left-hand corner of the screen:

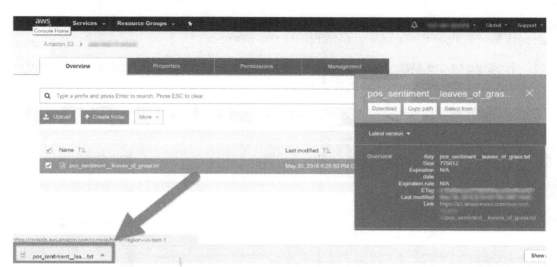

Figure 1.22: Downloading the file to export

In this exercise, you learned how to import a file to and export a file from your Amazon S3 bucket. As you can see, the process is quite easy thanks to the simple user interface.

THE AWS CLI

The CLI is an open-source tool built on the AWS SDK for Python (Boto) to perform setups, determine whether calls work as intended, verify status information, and more. The CLI provides another access tool for all AWS services, including S3. Unlike the Management Console, the CLI can be automated via scripts.

To authenticate your AWS account to the CLI, you must create a configuration file to obtain your public key and secret key. Next, you will install and then configure the AWS CLI.

EXERCISE 1.03: CONFIGURING THE CLI

In this exercise, we will configure the CLI with our AWS access key ID and AWS secret access key. Follow these steps to complete the exercise:

1. First, go to the **AWS Management Console** and then **IAM**. You might have to log in to the account. Then, click **Users**:

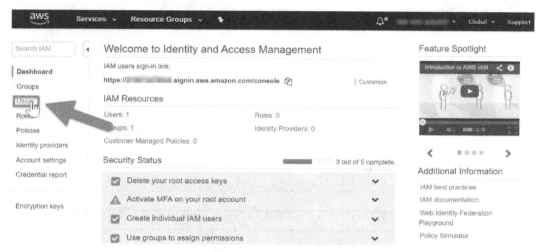

Figure 1.23: The Management Console home page with the Users option highlighted

2. In the upper-right corner of the signed-in AWS Management Console, click **My Security Credentials**:

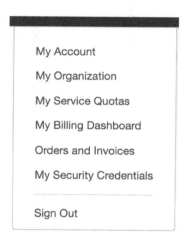

Figure 1.24: My Security Credentials

3. Next, click **Continue to Security Credentials**:

You are accessing the security credentials page for your AWS account. The account credentials provide unlimited access to your AWS resources.

To help secure your account, follow an AWS best practice by creating and using AWS Identity and Access Management (IAM) users with limited permissions.

Continue to Security Credentials   Get Started with IAM Users

☐ Don't show me this message again

Figure 1.25: Security Credentials

4. Click the **Access keys (access key ID and secret access key)** option:

Your Security Credentials

Use this page to manage the credentials for your AWS account. To manage credentials

To learn more about the types of AWS credentials and how they're used, see AWS Sec

▼ Password

> You use an email address and password to sign in to secure pages on AWS, such a
> protection, create a password that contains many characters, including numbers an
> periodically.
>
> Click here to change the password, name, or email address for your root AWS acco

▲ Multi-factor authentication (MFA)

▲ Access keys (access key ID and secret access key)

Figure 1.26: Accessing key generation

5. Then, click **Create New Access Key**:

Figure 1.27: Creating a new access key

6. Click **Download Key File** to download the key file:

Figure 1.28: Downloading the key file

The **rootkey.csv** file that contains the keys will be downloaded. You can view the details by opening the file.

> **NOTE**
>
> Store the keys in a safe location. Protect your AWS account and never share, email, or store keys in a non-secure location. An AWS representative will never request your keys, so be vigilant when it comes to potential phishing scams.

7. Open Command Prompt and type **aws configure**.

8. You will be prompted for four input variables. Enter your information, then press *Enter* after each input:

```
AWS Access Key ID
AWS Secret Access Key
```

```
Default region
Default output format (json)
```

9. The name is obtained in your console (**Oregon** is displayed here, but yours is determined by your unique location):

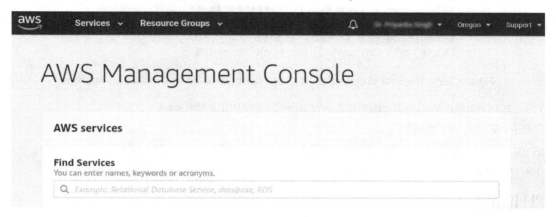

Figure 1.29: Location search

10. The codes for regions are obtained from the following **Available Regions** list:

Code	Name
us - east -1	US East (N. Virginia)
us - east - 2	US East (Ohio)
us - west -1	US West (N. California)
us - west - 2	US West (Oregon)
ca - central - 1	Canada (Central)
eu - central - 1	EU (Frankfurt)
eu - west -1	EU (Ireland)
eu - west - 2	EU (London)
eu - west - 3	EU (Paris)
ap - northeast - 1	Asia Pacific (Tokyo)
ap - northeast - 2	Asia Pacific (Seoul)
ap - northeast - 3	Asia Pacific (Osaka-Local)
ap - southeast - 1	Asia Pacific (Singapore)
ap - southeast - 2	Asia Pacific (Sydney)
ap - south - 1	Asia Pacific (Mumbai)
sa - east - 1	South America (São Paulo)

Figure 1.30: List of available regions

11. The command Prompt's final input variable will look as follows. Then, press *Enter*:

```
(base) USS-Defiant-2:aws_book ksankar$ aws configure
AWS Access Key ID [****************IIBQ]:
AWS Secret Access Key [****************TDRU]:
Default region name [us-west-2]:
Default output format [json]:
(base) USS-Defiant-2:aws_book ksankar$
```

Figure 1.31: The last step in the AWS CLI configuration in Command Prompt

You can change the configuration anytime by entering the **aws configure** command.

In this exercise, you configured the security credentials for your AWS account. We will use these credentials to access the AWS APIs in the rest of the book.

CLI USAGE

When using a command, specify at least one path argument. The two-path arguments are **LocalPath** and **S3Uri**:

- **LocalPath**: This represents the path of a local file or directory, which can be written as an absolute or relative path.

- **S3Uri**: This represents the location of an S3 object, prefix, or bucket. The command form is **s3://myBucketName/myKey**. The path argument must begin with **s3://** to indicate that the path argument refers to an S3 object.

The overall command structure is **aws s3 <Command> [<Arg> …]**. The following table shows the different commands with a description and an example:

Commands	Description	Example usage
mb	Creates a bucket.	aws s3 mb s3://mybucket
cp	Copies a local file to an S3 bucket.	aws s3 cp myNewFile.txt s3://mybucket
cp	Copies an s3 object to a local file.	aws s3 cp s3://mybucket/myNewFile.txt myNewFile2.txt
ls	Lists the contents of an S3 bucket.	aws s3 ls
rm	Deletes an S3 object.	aws s3 rm s3://mybucket/myNewFile.txt
rb	Deletes an empty S3 bucket. Note: A bucket must be completely empty of objects before it can be deleted.	aws s3 rb s3://mybucket

Figure 1.32: Command list

RECURSION AND PARAMETERS

Importing files one at a time is time-consuming, especially if you have many files in a folder that need to be imported. A simple solution is to use a recursive procedure. A recursive procedure is one that can call itself and saves you, the user, from entering the same import command for each file.

Performing a recursive CLI command requires passing a parameter to the API. This sounds complicated, but it is incredibly easy. First, a parameter is simply a name or option that is passed to a program to affect the operation of the receiving program. In our case, the parameter is **recursive**, and the entire command to perform the recursive command is as follows:

```
aws s3 cp s3://myBucket . --recursive
```

With this command, all the S3 objects in the bucket are copied to the specified directory:

Parameter	Description	Example usage
-recursive	If used with the cp command, all S3 objects in the bucket are copied to the specified directory.	aws s3 cp s3//mybucket. -recursive

Figure 1.33: Parameter list

ACTIVITY 1.01: PUTTING THE DATA INTO S3 WITH THE CLI

Let's start with a note about the terminology used in this activity. Putting data into S3 can also be called *uploading*. Getting it from there is called *downloading*. Sometimes, it is also called importing and exporting. Please do not confuse this with AWS Import/Export, which is a specific AWS service for sending a large amount of data to AWS or getting it back from AWS.

In this activity, we will be using the CLI to create a bucket in S3 and import a second text file. Suppose that you are creating a chatbot. You have identified text documents that contain content that will allow your chatbot to interact with customers more effectively. Before the text documents can be parsed, they need to be uploaded to an S3 bucket. Once they are in S3, further analysis will be possible. To ensure that this has happened correctly, you will need to install Python, set up the Amazon CLI tools, and have a user authenticated with the CLI:

1. Configure the CLI and verify that it can successfully connect to your AWS environment.

2. Create a new S3 bucket.

3. Import your text file into the bucket.

4. Export the file from the bucket and verify the exported objects.

> **NOTE**
>
> The solution for this activity can be found on page 276.

USING THE AWS CONSOLE TO IDENTIFY ML SERVICES

The AWS Console provides a web-based interface to navigate, discover, and utilize AWS services for AI and ML. In this topic, we will explore two ways to use the Console to search ML services. Also, we will test an ML API with text data retrieved from a website.

EXERCISE 1.04: NAVIGATING THE AWS MANAGEMENT CONSOLE

In this exercise, we will navigate the AWS Management Console to locate ML services. Starting from the console, https://console.aws.amazon.com/console/, and only using console search features, let's navigate to the Amazon Lex (https://console.aws.amazon.com/lex/) service information page:

1. Click https://console.aws.amazon.com/console/ to navigate to the AWS Console. You might have to log in to your AWS account. Then, click **Services**:

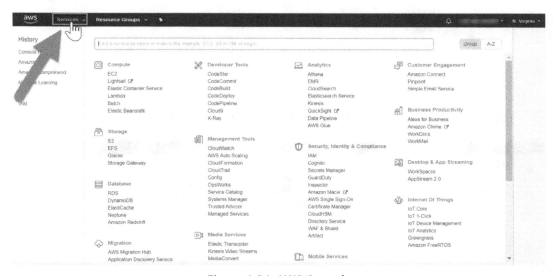

Figure 1.34: AWS Console

2. Scroll down the page to view all the ML services. Then, click **Amazon Lex**. If Lex is not available at your location, you may consider switching to a different one.

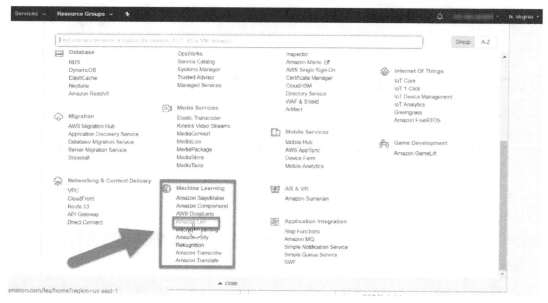

Figure 1.35: Options for ML

3. You will be redirected to the **Amazon Lex** home screen:

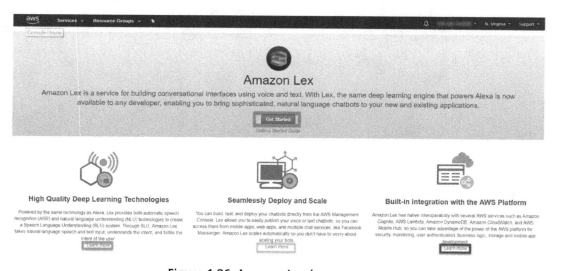

Figure 1.36: Amazon Lex home screen

You will get a chance to work with Amazon Lex in *Chapter 5, Using Speech with the Chatbot*. For now, you can click the different **Learn More** links to get to know Lex's features a bit better. If you're itching to try it out right away, you may click **Get Started**.

Locating new AWS services is an essential skill for discovering more tools to provide solutions for your data projects. Now, let's test the API features of Amazon Comprehend.

EXERCISE 1.05: TESTING THE AMAZON COMPREHEND API FEATURES

Now that you have mastered S3, let's do a quick exercise that extends beyond storing a file and prepares you for the rest of the chapters. In this exercise, we will display text analysis output by using a partial text file input in the API explorer. Exploring an API is a skill that saves development time by making sure that the output is in the desired format for your project. Here, we will test the AWS Comprehend text analysis features.

> **NOTE**
>
> You will work with Comprehend in more detail in *Chapter 4, Conversational Artificial Intelligence*. We will also introduce the various AWS AI services and how to work with them. Here, we are doing an exercise to get you familiar with interacting with AWS in multiple ways.

Here is the user story: suppose that you are creating a chatbot. Before taking any steps, we first need to understand the business goal or statements or objectives. Then we need to select the relevant AWS services. For example, if our business goal is related to storage, we will go for the storage domain.

You have identified a business topic and the corresponding text documents with content that will allow the chatbot to make your business successful. Your next step is to identify/verify an AWS service to parse the text document for sentiment, language, key phrases, and entities. Amazon's AI services include AWS Comprehend, which does this very well.

Before investing time in writing a complete program, you need to test the AWS service's features via the AWS Management Console's interface. To ensure that this happens correctly, you will need to search the web for an article (written in English or Spanish) that contains the subject matter that you're interested in. You are aware that exploring APIs is a skill that can save development time by ensuring that the output is in the desired format for your project.

Now that we have the user story, let's carry out this task:

Similarly, to *Exercise 1.01, Using the AWS Management Console to Create an S3 Bucket*, you should already have done the account setup as detailed earlier in this chapter.

1. Go to https://aws.amazon.com/ and click **My Account** and then **AWS Management Console** to open the AWS Management Console in a new browser tab:

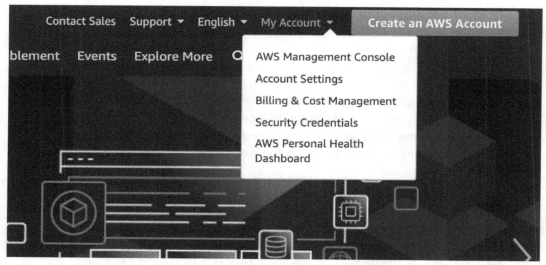

Figure 1.37: Accessing the AWS Management Console via the user's account

2. Click inside the search bar (under **Find Services**) in the AWS Management Console to search for **Amazon Comprehend** and you will be directed to the **Amazon Comprehend Console** screen as shown below:

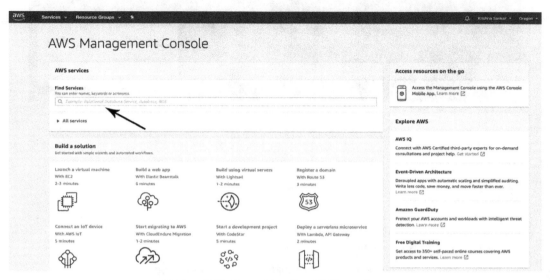

Figure 1.38: Searching for AWS services

3. Type in **amazon comp**. As you type, Amazon will autocomplete and show the services that match the name typed in the search box:

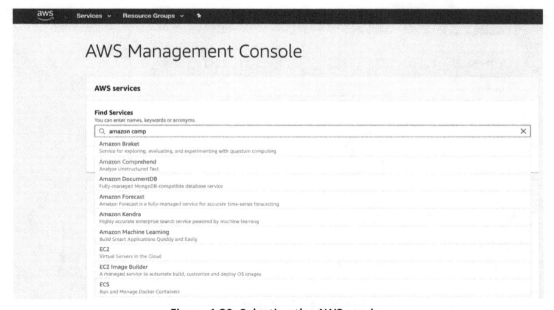

Figure 1.39: Selecting the AWS service

4. You will see the **Amazon Comprehend** landing page:

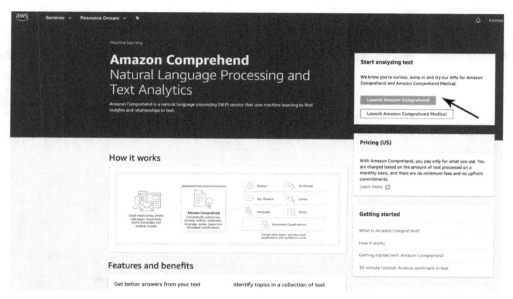

Figure 1.40: The Amazon Comprehend page

5. Click **Launch Amazon Comprehend** and you will be directed to the **Real-time analysis** page. You can either use their built-in model or you can provide a custom one. We will use their built-in model:

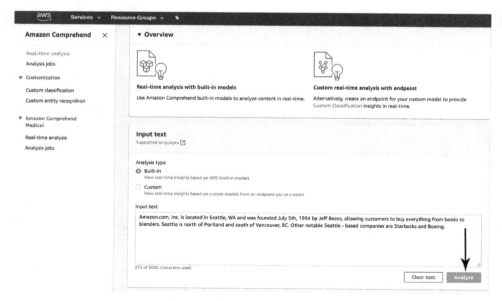

Figure 1.41: Real-time analysis

You can input text and click **Analyze**. Let's copy a poem by Walt Whitman from http://www.gutenberg.org/cache/epub/1322/pg1322.txt and analyze it. Navigate to **Topic modeling and Documentation**. There is a GUI for exploring the API, and the right side provides real-time output for text input.

6. Click **Clear text** to clear all default services. Navigate to open the following URL in a new tab: http://www.gutenberg.org/cache/epub/1322/pg1322.txt.

7. Copy the first poem and paste it in the **Input text** box:

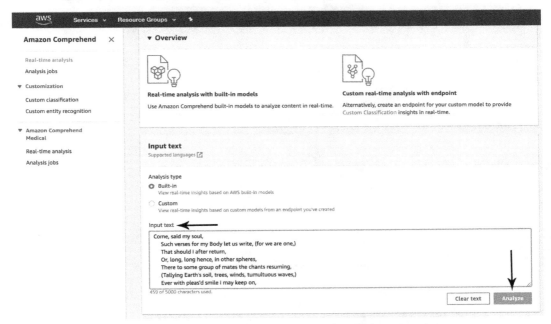

Figure 1.42: Amazon Comprehend real-time analysis screen

8. Click **Analyze** to see the output:

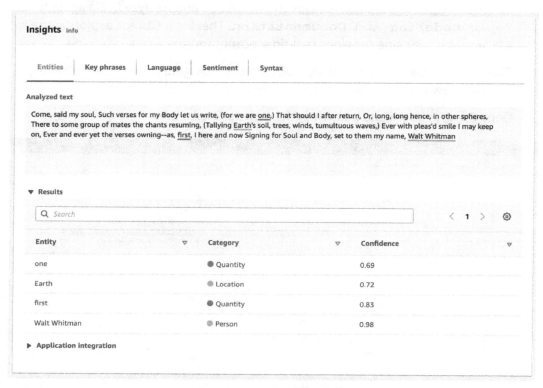

Figure 1.43: Analyzing the output

9. Review the **Entities**, **Key phrases**, and **Language** tabs and click the **Sentiment** tab to view the sentiment analysis:

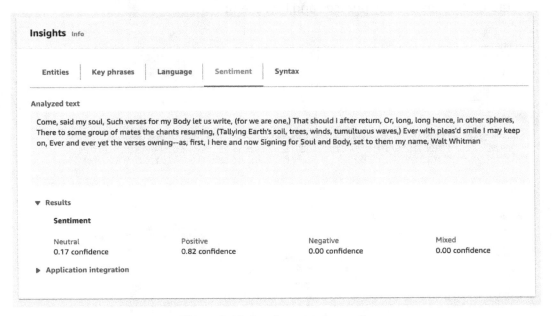

Figure 1.44: Sentiment tab results

10. You can try other tabs. The language will show English with 99% confidence, and the **Syntax** tab is interesting and has lots of information. The **Key phrases** tab underlines the key phrases and lists them:

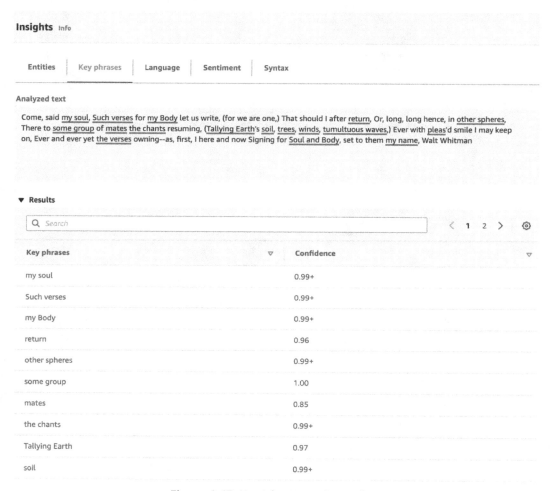

Figure 1.45: Key phrases tab results

Try some other text – maybe movie comments from IMDb or comments from Amazon product reviews – and see how Amazon Comprehend handles sentiment. A cool thing to try would be sarcasm or even comments that change their polarity at the last minute, for example, "The book is really good, but the movie is dreadful" or "The screenplay and direction were done by people who couldn't fathom what was good about the novel," for interesting results.

THE UTILITY OF THE AWS CONSOLE INTERFACE TO AI SERVICES

The Comprehend console interface is very useful for testing ideas. As you will see in later chapters, we can use a similar interface to Amazon Textract to see if we can extract tables and other information from forms such as tax returns, company statements such as profit and loss or balance sheets, medical forms, and so forth.

While we need programming and development to develop a robotic process automation application, the console interface helps us to quickly test our business hypotheses. For example, maybe you want to automate a loan processing pipeline in which you are manually entering information from different documents. To see if any AWS AI services would fit the need, you can scan all the relevant documents and test them with the AWS Textract console. Later, in *Chapter 5, Computer Vision and Image Processing*, you will work with scanned documents and Amazon Textract.

You can also check how accurately the AWS built-in models can extract the required information. Maybe you will need custom models, maybe the documents are not easily understandable by a machine, but you can find them earlier and plan accordingly. Maybe your application involves medical record handling, which might require more sophisticated custom models. In fact, you can upload a custom model and test it in the console as well.

SUMMARY

In this chapter, we started with understanding the basics of cloud computing, AWS, ML, and AI. We then explored S3, created buckets, and exported and imported data to and from S3. At the same time, we explored the AWS command line and its uses. Finally, we worked with the console interface of AWS Comprehend as an example of testing various ideas that relate to analyzing texts and documents.

In the next chapter, you will learn more about AWS AI services, serverless computing, and how to analyze text documents using **natural language processing (NLP)**. Researching new AWS services is essential for discovering additional solutions to solve many machine learning problems that you are working on. Additionally, as you saw, AWS has multiple ways of interacting with its services to help test business ideas, evaluate AI/ML models, and do quick prototyping.

2

ANALYZING DOCUMENTS AND TEXT WITH NATURAL LANGUAGE PROCESSING

OVERVIEW

This chapter describes the use of Amazon Comprehend to summarize text documents and create Lambda functions to analyze the texts. You will learn how to develop services by applying the serverless computing paradigm, and use Amazon Comprehend to examine texts to determine their primary language. You will extract information such as entities (people or places), key phrases (noun phrases that are indicative of the content), emotional sentiments, and topics from a set of documents.

By the end of this chapter, you will able to set up a Lambda function to process and analyze imported text using Comprehend and extract structured information from scanned paper documents using Amazon Textract.

INTRODUCTION

Since 2005, when Amazon formally launched its **Elastic Compute Cloud (EC2)** web service, cloud computing has grown from a developer service to mission-critical infrastructure. The spectrum of applications is broad—most highly scalable consumer platforms such as Netflix are based on AWS, and so are many pharmaceuticals and genomics, as well as organizations such as the BBC and The Weather Channel, BMW, and Canon. As of January 2020, there are about 143 distinct AWS services spanning 25 categories, from compute and storage to quantum technologies, robotics, and machine learning. In this book, we will cover a few of them, as shown in the following diagram:

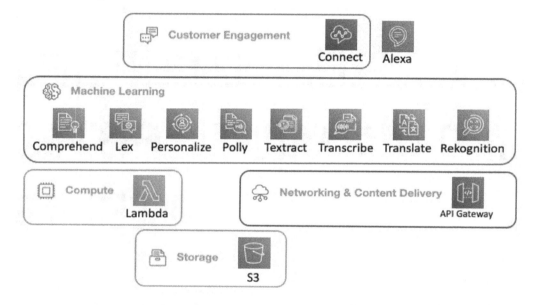

Figure 2.1: Amazon AI services covered

S3 is the versatile object store that we use to store the inputs to our AI services as well as the outputs from those services. You have been working with S3 since *Chapter 1, An Introduction to AWS*.

Lambda is the glue service that makes serverless computing possible. You will use Lambda later in this chapter to analyze text using Comprehend.

API Gateway is a delivery service that can enable you to create microservices that can be accessed by various clients, such as web, mobile, and server applications, via internet protocols such as HTTP, WebSocket, and REST. API Gateway gives you the ability to expose your microservices in a secure and scalable way. In the age of microservices and the "API-first" approach, the greatest challenge is the creation, publishing, monitoring, and maintenance of API endpoints. Almost all AWS services are APIs and use the API Gateway infrastructure.

Amazon's machine learning services, the main focus of our book, are a set of 16 services as of January 2020. They are also called AI services, and currently, the terms are interchangeable. Let's take a quick look at the ones we are interested in.

Comprehend, the topic of this chapter, is a very versatile text analytics service. It performs a variety of tasks—keyphrase extraction, sentiment analysis (positive, negative, neutral, or mixed), syntax analysis, entity recognition, medical **Named Entity Recognition** (**NER**), language detection, and topic modeling. You will see this in action later in this chapter.

Lex is a platform for building conversational AI, bots, or intelligent assistants. Conversational AI capabilities such as **automatic speech recognition** (**ASR**) and **natural language understanding** (**NLU**) are built into the Lex framework. Lex provides a very intuitive object model consisting of bots, utterances, slots, and sessions, as well as integration with Amazon Lambda, thus enabling you to develop interesting, intelligent bots in a serverless environment. We will see more of Lex in *Chapter 4, Conversational Artificial Intelligence*.

Personalize is a very useful service that allows you to personalize your bots. For example, incorporating personalized recommendations/content delivery, personalized searching based on previous interactions, or even personalized notifications and marketing based on user behavior! While we will not be using Amazon Personalize in this book, we wanted to bring your attention to services closely related to the ones covered in this book. That way, you can add extremely rich features as you expand the power of your bots and NLP services.

Polly is a text-to-speech service using **neural text-to-speech** (**NTTS**) technologies. It is very flexible and powerful, offering two styles: a newscaster reading style and a normal conversational style. The voice need not be monotone—Amazon Polly supports **Speech Synthesis Markup Language** (**SSML**), which enables you to adjust the speaking style, volume, speech rate, pitch, phrasing, emphasis, intonation, and other characteristics.

Textract, as the name implies, extracts text from documents. It is an **optical character recognition** (**OCR**) solution that is suitable for process automation. It can extract key-value pairs or tables from documents such as tax forms, legal documents, medical forms, bank forms, patent registration, and so forth.

Transcribe is a speech-to-text **Automatic Speech Recognition** (**ASR**) service and is very versatile; for example, it can recognize multiple speakers and you can filter out words. It is very useful in medical transcription, for time-stamped subtitle generation, and for transcribing customer interactions.

Translate is another very useful service that's able to translate more than 50 languages in a scalable, real-time fashion.

Rekognition, of course, is a visual analysis and image detection service capable of a variety of tasks, such as facial recognition, video analysis, object detection, and recognizing text in images. *Chapter 6, Computer Vision and Image Processing* is dedicated to Amazon Rekognition.

Unlike the AI services we have looked at so far in this chapter, **Amazon Connect** is a very feature-rich contact center application. It consists of an omnichannel cloud contact center with high-quality audio, web/mobile secure chat, and a web-based contact control panel. The Contact Lens for Amazon Connect is a set of Contact center analytics services that adds capabilities such as full-text search and sentiment analysis, with forthcoming features such as theme detection and custom vocabulary. The integration with Amazon Lex for chatbots is an interesting capability where we can leverage the flexibility of Lex to create intelligent and useful bots.

Amazon Alexa, of course, is a platform for a conversational interface as well as a set of hardware devices such as smart speakers that leverage the Alexa service to become smart assistants.

The reason for including customer engagement platforms such as Connect and Alexa is to show the wider possibilities of the work we are doing in this book. While we will not be directly showing how to develop bots for an Amazon Connect or Amazon Alexa-based bot **voice user interface** (**VUI**), we want to open your mind to the possibility of an omnichannel customer experience across different integration points—web, mobile, smart speakers, and so forth.

As you can see, the services cover a wide variety of layers, from the storage and infrastructure layer to the AI services layer, and finally extending to the UX.

SERVERLESS COMPUTING

Serverless computing is a relatively new architecture that takes a different spin on the cloud application architecture. Let's start with a traditional on-premise server-based architecture.

Usually, a traditional application architecture starts with a set of computer hardware, a host operating system, virtualization, containers, and an application stack consisting of libraries and frameworks tied together by networking and storage. On top of all this, we write business logic. In essence, to maintain a business capability, we have to maintain the server hardware, operating system patches, updates, library updates, and so forth. We also have to worry about scalability, fault tolerance, and security at the least.

With cloud computing, the application architecture is free of computer hardware as well as having elasticity. We still have to maintain the OS, libraries, patches, and so on. This where serverless computing comes in—in the words of Amazon, serverless computing "shifts more of your operational responsibilities to AWS."

Serverless computing improves upon cloud computing, eliminating infrastructure management, starting from provisioning to scaling up and down, depending on the load, as well as the patching and maintenance of the whole runtime stack. As Amazon depicts it, serverless computing definitely "reduces cost and increases agility and innovation" as well as enabling automated high availability, if designed properly.

An O'Reilly report defines serverless computing as "an architectural approach to software solutions that relies on small independent functions running on transient servers in an elastic runtime environment." So, there are servers—serverless is not the right term, but in some sense, the servers are transparent, managed by Amazon during the execution of a Lambda function, which is usually in milliseconds.

AMAZON LAMBDA AND FUNCTION AS A SERVICE

Essentially, serverless computing is enabled by functions, more precisely, **Function as a Service (FaaS)**. Amazon Lambda is the prime example of an enabling platform for serverless computing.

You write the business logic as a set of Lambda functions that are event-driven, stateless, fault-tolerant, and autoscaling. A Lambda function has an upstream side and a downstream side—it responds to upstream events; the runtime processor executes the embedded code and the results are sent to downstream destinations. The upstream events could be generated by something put into a queue or something that is dropped into an S3 bucket or a **Simple Notification Service (SNS)** message. And the downstream can be S3 buckets, queues, DynamoDB, and so forth. The runtime supports multiple languages, such as Python, Go, Java, Ruby, Node.js, and .NET.

A Lambda function is much more granular than a microservice—you can think of it as a nano service. It is charged on a 100 ms basis and will time out after 15 minutes. The payload size is 6 MB. That gives you an estimate of the size of a Lambda function. Also, as you have noticed, there are no charges when a Lambda function is idling – that means we can scale down to zero. And you can implement data parallelism easily—trigger a Lambda function for each row of data. As one Lambda function can trigger another Lambda function, you can even do task parallelism. Of course, all of this requires careful architecture, but it's worth the effort.

Amazon's serverless platform covers compute, storage, networking, orchestration, API proxy, analytics, and developer tooling. We will look at some of these components—Lambda for compute, S3 for storage, API Gateway for networking.

SERVERLESS COMPUTING AS AN APPROACH

Industry analysts and technologists consider serverless computing as an approach and a set of principles. Amazon Lambda is not serverless computing but an enabler of the approach. The serverless computing architecture does reduce what you have to build—some of the traditional code that we write now manifests as a function chaining pipeline, the configuration of events, triggers, and attributes of Lambda functions. The essential business logic does need to be written, and that will reside inside the Lambda functions. As a result, there is a very well-defined separation between the platform and the business code, and that is the value of serverless computing.

AMAZON COMPREHEND

Amazon Comprehend is a text analytics service. It has a broad spectrum of capabilities. Amazon Comprehend can extract key phrases and entities. It can do language detection and topic modeling. It can also perform sentiment analysis as well as syntax analysis. Amazon Comprehend is multilingual. Some of the applications of Amazon Comprehend include:

- Understanding the main themes and topics of various unstructured text items such as support tickets, social media posts, customer feedback, customer complaints, and business documents such as contracts and medical records.

- Knowledge management by categorizing business documents such as internal procedures, white papers, notes and descriptions, media posts, and emails.

- Brand monitoring—effectively responding to social media posts, reviews, and other user-generated content from various channels. Respond faster by prioritizing the content as well as routing the content to the appropriate person or process. To prioritize and respond faster, businesses need to analyze the content for language, topics, and the entities mentioned in the media – all of which are capabilities of Amazon Comprehend.

- One important capability of Comprehend is the fact that underneath the hood, it improves models by monitoring errors and training AI models with new and improved data.

- Also, you can fine-tune models with your domain-specific data, thus increasing the accuracy to fit your application while leveraging the general capability of the AI models.

- One interesting application of Comprehend is to extract information from business documents such as contract numbers, terms of contracts, various codes, and even the dosage of medication

An interesting end-to-end use case is to use Amazon Comprehend to analyze a collection of text documents and organize the articles by topic, identify the most frequently mentioned features, and group articles by subject matter, to enable personalized recommendations for website visitors.

Figure 2.2: Amazon Comprehend search flow

Amazon Comprehend Medical is a feature-rich service for analyzing patient health records, doctor's notes, and reports from clinical trials as well as links to medical ontologies. It can even figure out medication dosages, test results, and treatment information that can be used for analysis by healthcare professionals:

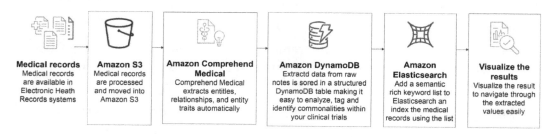

Medical records
Medical records are available in Electronic Heath Records systems

Amazon S3
Medical records are processed and moved into Amazon S3

Amazon Comprehend Medical
Comprehend Medical extracts entities, relationships, and entity traits automatically

Amazon DynamoDB
Extractd data from raw notes is sored in a structured DynamoDB table making it easy to enalyze, tag and identify commonalities within your clinical trials

Amazon Elasticsearch
Add a semantic rich keyword list to Elasticsearch an index the medical records using the list

Visualize the results
Visualize the result to navigate through the extracted values easily

Figure 2.3: Amazon Comprehend Medical flow

The Amazon Comprehend service continually learns from new data from Amazon product descriptions and consumer reviews, and thus, it perpetually improves its ability to understand a variety of topics from government, health, media, education, advertising, and so on.

In *Chapter 1, An Introduction to AWS,* you learned how to use Amazon Comprehend to extract insights by using **Natural Language Processing (NLP)** from the contents of documents. In this chapter, we will dig deeper and you will learn how to use the Amazon Comprehend API to produce insights by recognizing the language, entities, key phrases, sentiments, and topics in a document. This will allow you to understand deep learning-based NLP to build more complex applications, which we will cover further.

In the second part of this chapter, you will learn about AWS Lambda, and how to integrate this service with Amazon Comprehend. You will also integrate a database to provide the foundation to build scalable NLP processing applications.

WHAT IS AN NLP SERVICE?

Amazon Comprehend is an NLP service. The overall goal of an NLP service is to make machines understand our spoken and written language. Virtual assistants, such as Alexa or Siri, use NLP to produce insights from input data. The input data is structured by a language, which has a unique grammar, syntax, and vocabulary. Thus, processing text data requires identifying the language first and applying subsequent rules to identify the document's information. NLP's general task is to capture this information as a numeral representation. This general task is split into specific tasks, such as identifying languages, entities, key phrases, emotional sentiments, and topics.

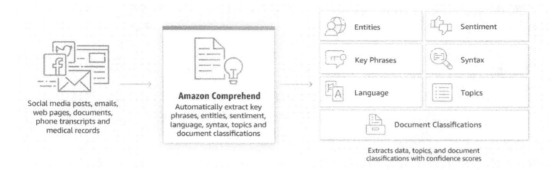

Figure 2.4: Amazon Comprehend data flow

As we discussed earlier, Amazon Comprehend uses pre-trained models to perform document analysis tasks. This is very good because it enables a business to develop capabilities without going through an exhaustive AI model training effort. And Amazon keeps up with the latest developments in ML and AI, constantly retraining the models—so the models get better without any work from users. Also, there are capabilities for fine-tuning the models by training them with your domain-specific content.

USING AMAZON COMPREHEND TO INSPECT TEXT AND DETERMINE THE PRIMARY LANGUAGE

Amazon Comprehend is used for searching and examining texts and then gathering insights from a variety of topics (health, media, telecom, education, government, and so on) and languages in the text data format. Thus, the first step to analyze text data and utilize more complex features (such as topic, entity, and sentiment analysis) is to determine the dominant language. Determining the dominant language ensures the accuracy of more in-depth analysis. To examine the text in order to determine the primary language, there are two operations (**DetectDominantLanguage** and **BatchDetectDominantLanguage**).

Both operations expect the text in the UTF-8 format with a length of at least 20 characters and a maximum of 5,000 bytes. If you are sending a list, it should not contain more than 25 items.

The response includes what language was identified using a two-letter code. The following table shows the language codes for different languages:

> **NOTE**
>
> Check out https://docs.aws.amazon.com/comprehend/latest/dg/how-languages.html for an updated list of the supported languages.

Code	Language	Code	Language	Code	Language
af	Afrikaans	hy	Armenian	ps	Pushto
am	Amharic	ilo	Iloko	qu	Quechua
ar	Arabic	id	Indonesian	ro	Romanian
as	Assamese	is	Icelandic	ru	Russian
az	Azerbaijani	it	Italian	sa	Sanskrit
ba	Bashkir	jv	Javanese	si	Sinhala
be	Belarusian	ja	Japanese	sk	Slovak
bn	Bengali	kn	Kannada	sl	Slovenian
bs	Bosnian	ka	Georgian	sd	Sindhi
bg	Bulgarian	kk	Kazakh	so	Somali
ca	Catalan	km	Central Khmer	es	Spanish
ceb	Cebuano	ky	Kirghiz	sq	Albanian
cs	Czech	ko	Korean	sr	Serbian
cv	Chuvash	ku	Kurdish	su	Sundanese
cy	Welsh	la	Latin	sw	Swahili
da	Danish	lv	Latvian	sv	Swedish
de	German	lt	Lithuanian	ta	Tamil
el	Greek	lb	Luxembourgish	tt	Tatar
en	English	ml	Malayalam	te	Telugu
eo	Esperanto	mr	Marathi	tg	Tajik
et	Estonian	mk	Macedonian	tl	Tagalog
eu	Basque	mg	Malagasy	th	Thai
fa	Persian	mn	Mongolian	tk	Turkmen
fi	Finnish	ms	Malay	tr	Turkish
fr	French	my	Burmese	ug	Uighur
gd	Scottish Gaelic	ne	Nepali	uk	Ukrainian
ga	Irish	new	Newari	ur	Urdu
gl	Galician	nl	Dutch	uz	Uzbek
gu	Gujarati	no	Norwegian	vi	Vietnamese
ht	Haitian	or	Oriya	yi	Yiddish
he	Hebrew	pa	Punjabi	yo	Yoruba
hi	Hindi	pl	Polish	zh	Chinese (Simplified)
hr	Croatian	pt	Portuguese	zh-TW	Chinese (Traditional)
hu	Hungarian				

Figure 2.5: Amazon Comprehend's supported languages

There are three ways to invoke dominant language detection. The result is the code for the dominant language in the content and a confidence score determined by the Comprehend algorithms:

- **DetectDominantLanguage** will return the dominant language in a single document.

- **BatchDetectDominantLanguage** works on a set of documents and will return a list of the dominant language in each of the documents.

- While both of the preceding APIs work in synchronous mode, that is, you send the content to the API and it will return the results, **StartDominantLanguageDetectionJob** works on a collection of jobs asynchronously. This API is well suited to large jobs that take more time.

```json
{
    "Languages": [
        {
            "LanguageCode": "en",
            "Score": 09793212413787842
        }
    ]
}
```

Figure 2.6: Dominant language score confidence output

EXERCISE 2.01: DETECTING THE DOMINANT LANGUAGE IN A TEXT DOCUMENT USING THE COMMAND-LINE INTERFACE

In this exercise, you will learn how to detect the dominant language in a text using Comprehend's **DetectDominantLanguage** function. The following steps describe how to detect the dominant language:

> **NOTE**
>
> The source code for the Jupyter notebook is available via GitHub in the repository at https://packt.live/2O4cw0V.
>
> The files for this chapter are located in the **Chapter02** folder in the GitHub repository https://packt.live/31TIzbU. As we mentioned in *Chapter 1, An Introduction to AWS*, you should have downloaded the GitHub files into a local subdirectory.
>
> As an example, we have downloaded the files in the **Documents/ aws-book/The-Applied-AI-and-Natural-Language- Processing-with-AWS** directory.

1. Open a new Jupyter Notebook.

> **NOTE**
>
> For configuration instructions, refer the section titled *Pre checkup* on GitHub: https://packt.live/2O4cw0V.

2. Before we begin, the **boto3** library must be installed. On a fresh Jupyter Notebook cell, type in the following command to install it:

```
!pip install boto3
```

3. Now, let's go ahead and import Boto3. Boto3 is nothing but the AWS SDK for Python. (https://boto3.amazonaws.com/v1/documentation/api/latest/index.html):

```
import boto3
```

4. Then, import the JSON module to serialize the JSON (https://docs.python.org/3.6/library/json.html):

```
import json
```

5. Instantiate a new Comprehend client:

```
comprehend = boto3.client(service_name='comprehend')
```

6. Next, we assign English and Spanish strings to be analyzed by Comprehend:

```
english_string = 'Machine Learning is fascinating.'
spanish_string = 'El aprendizaje automático es fascinante.'
```

7. Next, we print a string to indicate the respective variable that our script is about to execute:

```
print('Calling DetectDominantLanguage')
print('english_string result:')
```

8. Lastly, call Comprehend's **detect_dominant_language** method with the **english_string** and **spanish_string** variables (https://docs.aws.amazon. com/comprehend/latest/dg/API_DetectDominantLanguage.html).

   json.dumps() writes the JSON data to a Python string in the terminal:

```
print('\n English string result:')
print(json.dumps(comprehend.detect_dominant_language\
                (Text = english_string), sort_keys=True, \
                indent=4))
print('\n spanish_string result:')
print(json.dumps(comprehend.detect_dominant_language\
                (Text = spanish_string), sort_keys=True, \
                indent=4))
print('End of DetectDominantLanguage\n')
```

> **NOTE**
>
> The code snippet shown above uses a backslash (\ ) to split the logic across multiple lines. When the code is executed, Python will ignore the backslash, and treat the code on the next line as a direct continuation of the current line.

9. Save the notebook.

10. Press *Shift + Enter* to run the two notebook cells. Executing the cells will produce the following output (see the following screenshot):

```
Calling DetectDominantLanguage
english_string result:
{
    "Languages": [
        {
            "LanguageCode": "en",
            "Score": 0.993855357170105
        }
    ],
    "ResponseMetadata": {
        "HTTPHeaders": {
            "content-length": "63",
            "content-type": "application/x-amz-json-1.1",
            "date": "Sat, 18 Jan 2020 03:04:17 GMT",
            "x-amzn-requestid": "05fbb292-5f10-42dd-8a3e-1e47aabb9bac"
        },
        "HTTPStatusCode": 200,
        "RequestId": "05fbb292-5f10-42dd-8a3e-1e47aabb9bac",
        "RetryAttempts": 0
    }
}

spanish_string result:
{
    "Languages": [
        {
            "LanguageCode": "es",
            "Score": 0.9917230010032654
        }
    ],
    "ResponseMetadata": {
        "HTTPHeaders": {
            "content-length": "64",
            "content-type": "application/x-amz-json-1.1",
            "date": "Sat, 18 Jan 2020 03:04:17 GMT",
            "x-amzn-requestid": "a270a7ac-4f2e-4c84-8d74-0f77d4869328"
        },
        "HTTPStatusCode": 200,
        "RequestId": "a270a7ac-4f2e-4c84-8d74-0f77d4869328",
        "RetryAttempts": 0
    }
}
End of DetectDominantLanguage
```

Figure 2.7: Detecting the dominant language output – English and Spanish

As expected, the **english_text** string is identified as English (with the **en** language code) with a ~0.99 confidence score.

Also as expected, the **spanish_text** string is identified as Spanish (with the **es** language code) with a ~0.99 confidence score.

EXERCISE 2.02: DETECTING THE DOMINANT LANGUAGE IN MULTIPLE DOCUMENTS BY USING THE CLI

In this exercise, you will learn how to use Comprehend's **DetectDominantLanguage** operation for multiple documents. The following steps describe how to detect the dominant language:

> **NOTE**
>
> The *Pre checkup instructions* and the source code for this exercise are available via GitHub in the repository at https://packt.live/2Z8Vbu4.

1. Open a new Jupyter Notebook.

2. On a fresh empty cell, import the AWS SDK for Python (boto3:https://boto3.amazonaws.com/v1/documentation/api/latest/index.html):

```
import boto3
```

3. Then, import the JSON module to serialize the JSON (https://docs.python.org/3.6/library/json.html):

```
import json
```

4. Instantiate a new Comprehend client:

```
comprehend = boto3.client(service_name='comprehend')
```

5. Next, assign a list of English and Spanish strings to be analyzed by Comprehend:

```
english_string_list = \
['Machine Learning is fascinating.', \
 'Studying Artificial Intelligence is my passion.']
spanish_string_list = \
['El aprendizaje automático es fascinante.', \
 'Estudiar Inteligencia Artificial es mi pasión.']
```

6. Lastly, we call Comprehend's **batch_detect_dominant_language** method with the **english_string_list** and **spanish_string_list** variables (https://docs.aws.amazon.com/comprehend/latest/dg/API_DetectDominantLanguage.html). Then, **json.dumps()** writes the JSON data to a Python string to the terminal:

```
print('Calling BatchDetectDominantLanguage')

print('english_string_list results:')
print(json.dumps(comprehend.batch_detect_dominant_language\
            (TextList=english_string_list), \
            sort_keys=True, indent=4))

print('\nspanish_string_list results:')
print(json.dumps(comprehend.batch_detect_dominant_language\
            (TextList=spanish_string_list), \
            sort_keys=True, indent=4))
print('End of BatchDetectDominantLanguage\n')
```

7. Save the notebook.

8. Press *Shift + Enter* to run the two notebook cells. Executing the cells will produce the following output (see the following partial screenshot—the output is too long to fit; you can see the full output in the notebook):

```
Calling BatchDetectDominantLanguage
english_string_list results:
{
    "ErrorList": [],
    "ResponseMetadata": {
        "HTTPHeaders": {
            "content-length": "180",
            "content-type": "application/x-amz-json-1.1",
            "date": "Wed, 26 Feb 2020 18:24:44 GMT",
            "x-amzn-requestid": "07562e42-020d-4e62-a01b-0d0806f43baf"
        },
        "HTTPStatusCode": 200,
        "RequestId": "07562e42-020d-4e62-a01b-0d0806f43baf",
        "RetryAttempts": 0
    },
    "ResultList": [
        {
            "Index": 0,
            "Languages": [
                {
                    "LanguageCode": "en",
                    "Score": 0.993855357170105
                }
            ]
        },
        {
            "Index": 1,
            "Languages": [
                {
                    "LanguageCode": "en",
                    "Score": 0.9923509955406189
                }
```

Figure 2.8: Detecting the dominant language (multiple documents) output—English

The important concepts to remember are that Comprehend has the ability to detect different languages and can take text input as a single string or in a batch format as a list of strings.

In this topic, we reviewed how Comprehend's **DetectDominantLanguage** method is structured, and how to pass in both strings and a list of strings. Next, we will extract entities, phrases, and sentiments from a set of documents.

EXTRACTING INFORMATION FROM A SET OF DOCUMENTS

At a business level, knowing if and why a customer is angry or happy when they contact a virtual assistant is extremely important, to retain the customer. At an NLP level, this requires more information to be extracted and a more complex algorithm. The additional information to extract and quantify is **entities**, **key phrases**, **emotional sentiment**, and **topics**.

DETECTING NAMED ENTITIES—AWS SDK FOR PYTHON (BOTO3)

An entity is a broader concept—it is something that has an identity of its own. An entity can be a person or a place, a company name or an organization; it can also be a number (say quantity, price, number of days) or a date, a title, a policy number, or a medical code. For example, in the text "Martin lives at 27 Broadway St.", **Martin** might be detected as a **PERSON**, while **27 Broadway St** might be detected as a **LOCATION**.

Entities also have a score to indicate the confidence level that the entity type was detected correctly. The following table shows a complete list of entity types and descriptions:

Type	Description
COMMERCIAL_ITEM	A branded device, product, merchandise, and so on
DATE	A full date (for example, 10/22/2018), day (Wednesday), month (June), or time (10:30 a.m.)
EVENT	An event, such as a celebration, ceremony, holiday, and so on
LOCATION	A specific location, such as a state, city, pond, apartment, and so on
ORGANIZATION	Large organizations, such as an institution, government, assembly, company, religion, sports team, and so on
OTHER	Entities that don't fit into any of the other entity categories
PERSON	Individuals, customers, groups of people, nicknames, fictional characters
QUANTITY	A quantified amount, such as currency, percentages, numbers, bytes, and so on
TITLE	An official name given to any creation or creative work, such as painting, article, play, and so on

Figure 2.9: AWS Comprehend entity types and descriptions

There are three ways to invoke the detection of entities:

- **DetectEntities** will return the entities in a single document.

- **BatchDetectEntities** works on a set of documents and will return a list of the entities in each of the documents.

- While both the preceding APIs work in synchronous mode, that is, you send the content to the API and it will return the results, **StartEntitiesDetectionJob** works on a collection of jobs asynchronously. This API is well suited to large jobs that take more time.

DETECTENTITIES – INPUT AND OUTPUT

DetectEntities takes a **LanguageCode** and a string of text as an input and then provides the following information about each entity within the input text: **BeginOffset**, **EndOffset**, **Score**, **Text**, and **Type**. The following table shows a complete list of AWS Comprehend **DetectEntities**, types, and descriptions:

Type	Description	Type	
BeginOffset	A character offset in the input text that shows where the entity begins (the first character is at position 0). The offset returns the position of each UTF-8 code point in the string.	Integer	No
EndOffset	A character offset in the input text that shows where the entity ends. The offset returns the position of each UTF-8 code point in the string. A code point is the abstract character from a particular graphical representation.	Integer	No
Score	The level of confidence that Amazon Comprehend has in the accuracy of the detection.	Float	No
Text	The text of the entity.	String	No
Type	The entity's type. (For example: PERSON, LOCATION, ORGANIZATION, COMMERCIAL_ITEM, EVENT, DATE, QUANTITY, TITLE, or OTHER).	String	No

Figure 2.10: AWS Comprehend entity types and descriptions

EXERCISE 2.03: DETERMINING THE NAMED ENTITIES IN A DOCUMENT (THE DETECTENTITIES METHOD)

In this exercise, we will determine the named entities in a document. For this, we will use Amazon Comprehend's **DetectEntities** operation. The following are the steps for detecting named entities:

> **NOTE**
>
> The *Pre checkup instructions* and the source code for this exercise are available via GitHub in the repository at https://packt.live/2ADssUI.

1. Open a new Jupyter Notebook.

2. Import the AWS SDK for Python (boto3: https://boto3.amazonaws.com/v1/documentation/api/latest/index.html) by using the following command:

```
import boto3
```

3. Now, import the **JSON** module to serialize **JSON** from https://docs.python.org/3.6/library/json.html by using the following command:

```
import json
```

4. Now, instantiate a new Comprehend client:

```
comprehend = boto3.client(service_name='comprehend')
```

5. Now, after instantiating a new Comprehend client, provide the **English** text to analyze:

```
english_string = "I study Machine Learning in "\
                 "Seattle on Thursday."
print('Calling DetectEntities')
```

6. Now, **json.dumps()** writes JSON data to a Python string:

```
print(json.dumps(comprehend.detect_entities\
                (Text = english_string, LanguageCode='en'), \
                sort_keys=True, indent=4))
print('End of DetectEntities\n')
```

7. Press *Shift + Enter* to run the two notebook cells. The output of the preceding code is shown in the following screenshot:

```
Calling DetectEntities
{
    "Entities": [
        {
            "BeginOffset": 28,
            "EndOffset": 35,
            "Score": 0.999705970287323,
            "Text": "Seattle",
            "Type": "LOCATION"
        },
        {
            "BeginOffset": 39,
            "EndOffset": 47,
            "Score": 0.999932050704956,
            "Text": "Thursday",
            "Type": "DATE"
        }
    ],
    "ResponseMetadata": {
        "HTTPHeaders": {
            "content-length": "201",
            "content-type": "application/x-amz-json-1.1",
            "date": "Wed, 01 Apr 2020 15:31:22 GMT",
            "x-amzn-requestid": "8d6b7472-c300-48c4-a7ec-ced728741f77"
        },
        "HTTPStatusCode": 200,
        "RequestId": "8d6b7472-c300-48c4-a7ec-ced728741f77",
        "RetryAttempts": 0
    }
}
End of DetectEntities
```

Figure 2.11: AWS Comprehend DetectEntities output

The confidence scores were both ~0.99, as the inputs were simple examples. As expected, **Seattle** was detected as a **LOCATION**, and **Thursday** was detected as a **DATE**:

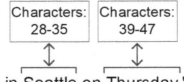

Figure 2.12: AWS Comprehend BeginOffset and EndOffset review

EXERCISE 2.04: DETECTING ENTITIES IN A SET OF DOCUMENTS (TEXT FILES)

In this exercise, we will determine the named entities in multiple documents. For this, we will use Amazon Comprehend's **DetectEntities** operation. The following are the steps for detecting the named entities from a set of documents:

> **NOTE**
>
> The *Pre checkup instructions* and the source code for this exercise are available via GitHub in the repository at https://packt.live/31UCuMs.

1. Open a new Jupyter Notebook.

2. Import the AWS SDK for Python (boto3: https://boto3.amazonaws.com/v1/documentation/api/latest/index.html) by using the following command:

```
import boto3
```

3. Now, import the **JSON** module to serialize **JSON** from https://docs.python.org/3.6/library/json.html by using the following command:

```
import json
```

4. We also need to do some file operations to iterate through the documents. Import the **glob** module to find text files ending **.txt** from https://docs.python.org/3.6/library/glob.html by using the following command:

```
import glob
```

5. We also need the **os** library. Import the **os** module from https://docs.python.org/3.6/library/os.html by using the following command:

```
import os
```

6. Now, instantiate a new Comprehend client:

```
comprehend = boto3.client(service_name='comprehend')
```

Let's get a list of all the documents (assumes in Jupyter notebook you navigated to **Chapter02/Exercise02.04/** directory and the opened the notebook **Exercise2.04.ipynb**):

```
data_dir = '../reviews_pos/*.txt'
# Works for Linux, OSX. Change to \\ for windows
file_list = glob.glob(data_dir)
```

> **NOTE**
>
> The **#** symbol in the code snippet above denotes a code comment. Comments are added into code to help explain specific bits of logic. In this exercise, we are assuming the **.txt** files are stored in the **review_pos** directory. Depending on where you have downloaded and stored the **.txt** files on your system, the highlighted path must be modified in the code.

7. Now, we can iterate through the documents and detect the entities in the documents. We will be calling **detect_entities** on each of the documents. As before, we will also use **json.dumps()** to write the JSON data to a Python string:

```
for file in file_list:
  with open(file, 'r', encoding="utf-8") as f:
    file_as_str = f.read()
    # python string formatting to print the text file name
    print('Calling detect_entities_from_documents.py on file: %s' \
          % file[-15:])
    # json.dumps() writes JSON data to a Python string
    print(json.dumps(comprehend.detect_entities\
                (Text = file_as_str, LanguageCode='en'), \
                sort_keys=True, indent=4))
    print('End of detect_entities\n')
```

8. Press *Shift + Enter* to run the two notebook cells. The output of the preceding code is shown in the following screenshot. It is a long output—we are showing the output for one file. You will see the entities listed for all the files in the `/reviews__pos/*.txt` subdirectory:

```
Calling detect_entities_from_documents.py on file: cv471_16858.txt
{
    "Entities": [
        {
            "BeginOffset": 27,
            "EndOffset": 32,
            "Score": 0.9988731741905212,
            "Text": "1500s",
            "Type": "DATE"
        },
        {
            "BeginOffset": 35,
            "EndOffset": 42,
            "Score": 0.9942895174026489,
            "Text": "england",
            "Type": "LOCATION"
        },
        {
            "BeginOffset": 45,
            "EndOffset": 54,
            "Score": 0.9999986886978149,
            "Text": "elizabeth",
            "Type": "PERSON"
        },
        {
            "BeginOffset": 173,
            "EndOffset": 181,
            "Score": 0.6192143559455872,
            "Text": "catholic",
            "Type": "ORGANIZATION"
        },
        {
            "BeginOffset": 360,
            "EndOffset": 368,
            "Score": 0.4906325340270996,
            "Text": "catholic",
            "Type": "ORGANIZATION"
        },
        {
            "BeginOffset": 394,
            "EndOffset": 403,
            "Score": 0.9999994039535522,
            "Text": "elizabeth",
            "Type": "PERSON"
        },
```

Figure 2.13: DetectEntities output

In this exercise, we extended entity detection to a set of documents, calling Amazon Comprehend's **DetectEntities** recursively.

DETECTING KEY PHRASES

A key phrase for AWS is analogous to a noun phrase, which represents an actual thing. In English, when we put together different words that represent one concrete idea, we call it a noun phrase.

For example, **A fast machine** is a noun phrase because it consists of **A**, the article; **fast**, an adjective; and **machine**, which is a noun. AWS looks for appropriate word combinations and gives scores that indicate the confidence that a string is a noun phrase.

EXERCISE 2.05: DETECTING KEY PHRASES

In this exercise, we will detect key phrases. To do so, we will use Amazon Comprehend's **DetectKeyPhrase** operation. The following are the steps for detecting key phrases:

> **NOTE**
>
> The *Pre checkup instructions* and the source code for this exercise are available via GitHub in the repository at https://packt.live/2Z75cl4.

1. Import the AWS SDK for Python (boto3: http://boto3.readthedocs.io/en/latest/) by using the following command:

```
import boto3
```

2. Now, import the JSON module to serialize the JSON from https://docs.python.org/3.6/library/json.html by using the following command:

```
import json
```

3. Now, instantiate a new Comprehend client by using the following code:

```
comprehend = boto3.client(service_name='comprehend')
```

4. Now, provide the **English** text to analyze using the following code:

```
english_string = 'robert redfords a river runs through '\
                 'is not a film i watch often. it is a '\
                 'masterpiece, one of the better films of '\
                 'recent years. The acting and direction is '\
                 'top-notch never sappy , always touching.'
print('Calling DetectKeyPhrases')
# json.dumps() writes JSON data to a Python string
print(json.dumps(comprehend.detect_key_phrases\
    (Text = english_string, LanguageCode='en'), \
    sort_keys=True, indent=4))
print('End of DetectKeyPhrases\n')
```

5. Run the code by executing the cells with *Shift + Enter*. You will see the following output:

```
Calling DetectKeyPhrases
{
    "KeyPhrases": [
        {
            "BeginOffset": 0,
            "EndOffset": 6,
            "Score": 0.8170492053031921,
            "Text": "robert"
        },
        {
            "BeginOffset": 16,
            "EndOffset": 23,
            "Score": 0.9999998807907104,
            "Text": "a river"
        },
        {
            "BeginOffset": 44,
            "EndOffset": 52,
            "Score": 0.9881498217582703,
            "Text": "a film i"
        },
        {
            "BeginOffset": 76,
            "EndOffset": 89,
            "Score": 0.9999999403953552,
            "Text": "a masterpiece"
        },
        {
            "BeginOffset": 98,
            "EndOffset": 114,
            "Score": 0.9999999403953552,
            "Text": "the better films"
        },
        {
            "BeginOffset": 118,
            "EndOffset": 130,
            "Score": 0.9999999403953552,
            "Text": "recent years"
        },
    ,
```

Figure 2.14: AWS Comprehend DetectKeyPhrase output

DETECTING SENTIMENTS

Amazon Comprehend has the capability to detect sentiments, usually used for social media posts, blog posts, reviews, emails, and other user-generated content. Amazon Comprehend can determine the four shades of sentiment polarity: positive, negative, neutral, and mixed. Mixed sentiment is interesting as it can differentiate between different aspects; for example, a user might like your website but not be thrilled about the price of a product.

EXERCISE 2.06: CONDUCTING SENTIMENT ANALYSIS

In this exercise, we will carry out sentiment analysis. To do so, we will use Amazon Comprehend's **DetectSentiment** operation. The following are the steps for detecting sentiment:

> **NOTE**
>
> The *Pre checkup instructions* and the source code for this exercise are available via GitHub in the repository at https://packt.live/3ebVNU1.

1. Open a new Jupyter Notebook.

2. Import the **AWS SDK** for Python (boto3) from http://boto3.readthedocs.io/en/latest/ by using the following command:

```
import boto3
```

3. Now, import the **JSON** module to serialize JSON from https://docs.python.org/3.6/library/json.html by using the following command:

```
import json
```

4. Now, instantiate a new Comprehend client, using the following code:

```
comprehend = boto3.client(service_name='comprehend')
```

5. Then, provide a text string to analyze, using the following code:

```
english_string = 'Today is my birthday, I am so happy.'
print('Calling DetectSentiment')
# json.dumps() #writes JSON data to a Python string
print('english_string results:')
print(json.dumps(comprehend.detect_sentiment\
     (Text = english_string, LanguageCode='en'), \
     sort_keys=True, indent=4))
print('End of DetectSentiment\n')
```

6. Run the code by executing the cells with *Shift + Enter*. The output is as follows:

```
Calling DetectSentiment
english_string results:
{
    "ResponseMetadata": {
        "HTTPHeaders": {
            "content-length": "166",
            "content-type": "application/x-amz-json-1.1",
            "date": "Sat, 18 Jan 2020 05:35:24 GMT",
            "x-amzn-requestid": "d98486ca-6707-4dd8-82b7-afd269e5f86d"
        },
        "HTTPStatusCode": 200,
        "RequestId": "d98486ca-6707-4dd8-82b7-afd269e5f86d",
        "RetryAttempts": 0
    },
    "Sentiment": "POSITIVE",
    "SentimentScore": {
        "Mixed": 3.509177759042359e-06,
        "Negative": 6.833979568909854e-05,
        "Neutral": 0.0013381546596065164,
        "Positive": 0.9985899329185486
    }
}
End of DetectSentiment
```

Figure 2.15: AWS Comprehend—DetectSentiment output

In this exercise, we saw how easy it is to perform sentiment analysis using AWS Comprehend. **DetectSentiment** correctly predicted the sentiment of the statement *Today is my birthday, I am so happy* as positive.

SETTING UP A LAMBDA FUNCTION AND ANALYZING IMPORTED TEXT USING COMPREHEND

We have used Amazon Comprehend to do various NLP tasks, such as detecting entities and key phrases and carrying out sentiment analysis.

INTEGRATING COMPREHEND AND AWS LAMBDA FOR RESPONSIVE NLP

In this topic, we will be integrating AWS Lambda functions with Comprehend, which provides a more powerful, scalable infrastructure. You can use AWS Lambda to run your code in response to events, such as changes to data in an Amazon S3 bucket.

Executing code in response to events provides a real-world solution for developing scalable software architecture. Overall, this increases our data pipeline and provides the ability to handle more complex big data volumes and NLP operations.

WHAT IS AWS LAMBDA?

AWS Lambda is a compute service that runs code without provisioning or managing servers. AWS Lambda executes code only when needed, and scales automatically. AWS Lambda runs your code on a high-availability compute infrastructure, which performs the administration of the compute service. More specifically, AWS Lambda performs the following: server and operating system maintenance, capacity provisioning and automatic scaling, code monitoring, and logging.

Overall, the goal of AWS Lambda is to make short, simple, modular code segments that you can tie together into a larger processing infrastructure.

WHAT DOES AWS LAMBDA DO?

Lambda allows users to run small segments of code (Java, Node, or Python) to complete a specific task. These specific tasks can be storing and then executing changes to your AWS setup, or responding to events in S3 (we will explore the latter later in this topic). Before Lambda, you would typically need a separate EC2 server to run your entire code; however, Lambda allows small segments of code to run without the need for EC2.

LAMBDA FUNCTION ANATOMY

AWS Lambda provides two options for implementing Python code. First, you can upload a complete Python code file. Second, you can use the Lambda function editor entirely inline, which means that you can enter and modify the code directly, without having to upload any files to AWS. The code that you enter will be executed when the Lambda function is invoked. The second option will allow for easier testing, so we will use it.

Let's examine the structure of a Lambda function:

- When you create a function (for example, **s3_trigger**), AWS creates a folder named the same, with a Python file named **Lambda_function.py** within the folder. This file contains a stub for the **Lambda_handler** function, which is the entry point of our Lambda function. The entry point takes two parameters as arguments: The **event** argument and the **context** argument.

- The **event** argument provides the value of the payload, which is sent to the function from the **calling** process. It typically takes the form of a Python **dict** type, although it could also be one of **list**, **str**, **int**, **float**, or **NoneType**.

- The **context** argument is of the type **LambdaContext** and contains runtime information. You will be using this parameter for an exercise in a later section. The return value of the function can be any type that is JSON-serializable. This value gets returned to the calling application, after serializing.

We will incorporate Lambda, S3, and Amazon Comprehend, to automatically perform document analysis when a text document is uploaded to S3. The architecture of a Lambda function is as follows:

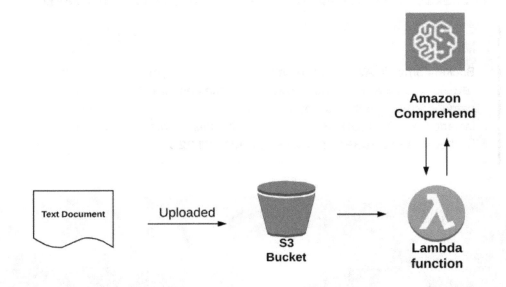

Figure 2.16: Architecture diagram

EXERCISE 2.07: SETTING UP A LAMBDA FUNCTION FOR S3

In this exercise, we will integrate the following AWS services: S3, Lambda, and Amazon Comprehend. To perform this exercise, the architecture should be recollected. Upload a file (**`test_s3trigger_configured.txt`**) to S3 and view the results of Comprehend's analysis. The following are the steps for setting up a Lambda function:

Creating the S3 bucket

1. You should have an AWS account and have completed the exercises and activities in *Chapter 1, An Introduction to AWS*.

2. First, navigate to the Amazon S3 service, https://console.aws.amazon.com/s3/, and click **`Create bucket`**:

Figure 2.17: S3 Bucket creation for the Lambda trigger

For **Bucket name**, type **aws-ml-s3-trigger**, and then click **Create**:

> **NOTE**
>
> Bucket names in AWS have to be unique, otherwise you will get an error **"Bucket name already exists"**. One easy way to get a unique name is to append the bucket name with today's date plus the time, for instance, YYYYMMDDHHMM. While writing this chapter, I created the bucket **aws-ml-s3-trigger-202001181023** .

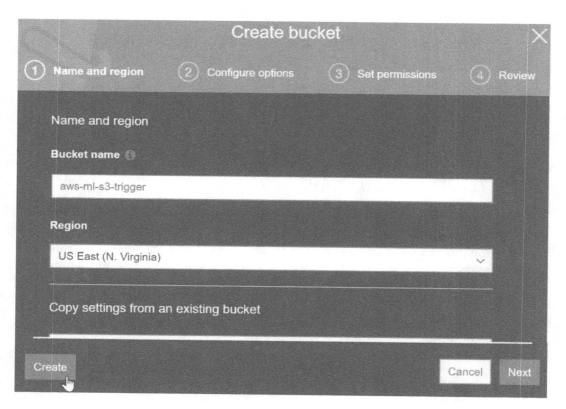

Figure 2.18: Creating an S3 bucket

3. Your bucket will be created, and you will be redirected to the bucket list in the **S3 buckets** screen as shown:

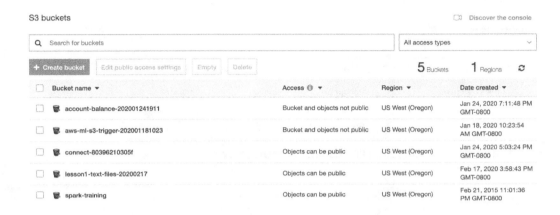

Figure 2.19: S3 Bucket list screen

4. Next, navigate to Amazon Lambda, under **Services**, and click **Lambda** under **Compute**:

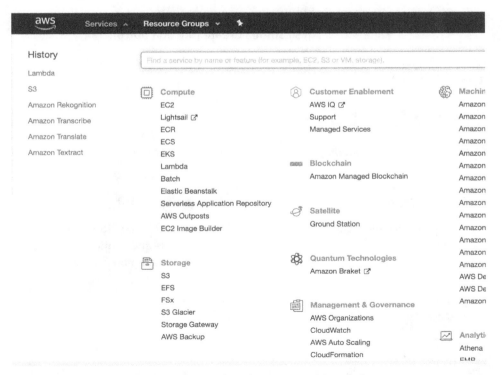

Figure 2.20: Services | Compute | Lambda

5. You will see the Lambda console, as shown here:

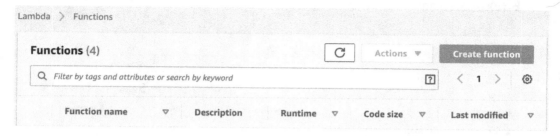

Figure 2.21: Lambda console

6. In the Lambda console, click **Create function**:

Figure 2.22: AWS Lambda Create function button

7. Choose **Author from scratch** from the options. For **Name**, type **s3_trigger**:

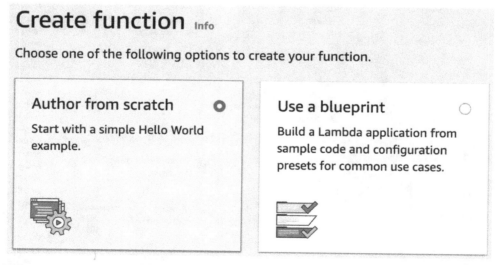

Figure 2.23: AWS Lambda—Creating a function with the Author from scratch option

8. For the runtime options, choose **Python 3.6** from the list:

Figure 2.24: AWS Lambda—Python 3.6 selection

9. Click **Choose or create an execution role** and choose **Create new role from AWS policy template(s)** and enter the name **s3TriggerRole** in the **Role name** field:

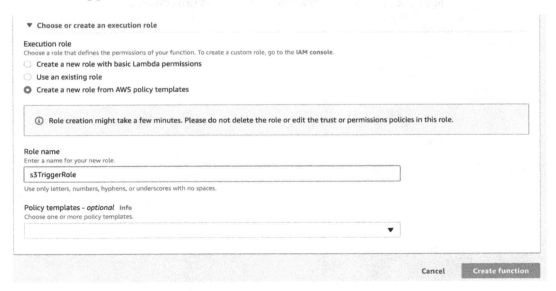

Figure 2.25: AWS Lambda Create Role template

10. Click the dropdown in **Policy templates** and select **Amazon S3 object read-only permissions**. You will see AWS Lambda Policy template dropdown box, as shown here:

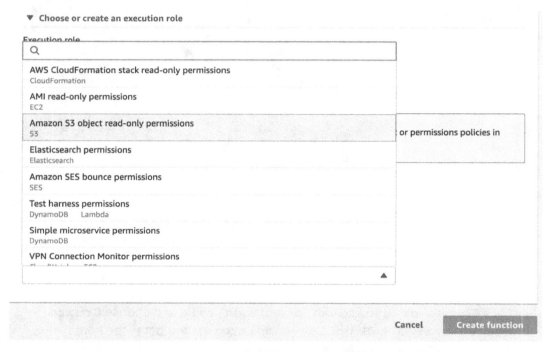

Figure 2.26: AWS Lambda Policy templates dropdown box

11. Then, click the **Create function** button to create the Lambda function in AWS. The final AWS Lambda Create function screen looks as follows:

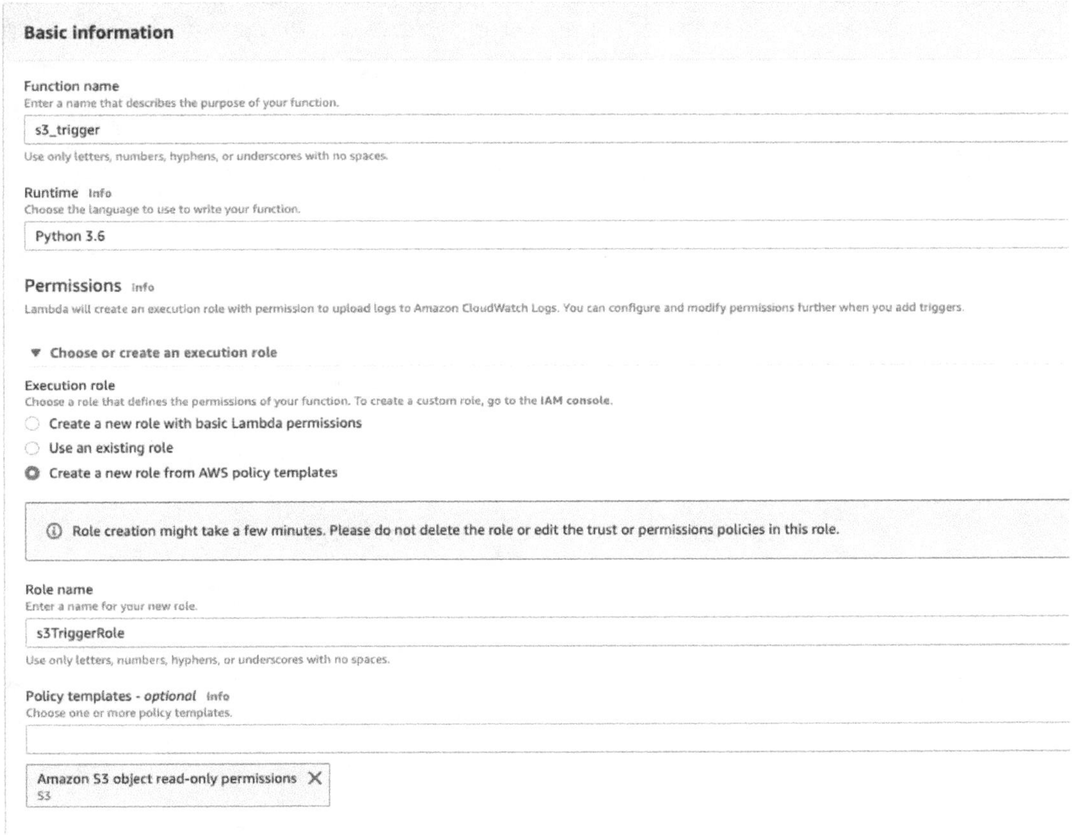

Basic information

Function name
Enter a name that describes the purpose of your function.

s3_trigger

Use only letters, numbers, hyphens, or underscores with no spaces.

Runtime Info
Choose the language to use to write your function.

Python 3.6

Permissions Info

Lambda will create an execution role with permission to upload logs to Amazon CloudWatch Logs. You can configure and modify permissions further when you add triggers.

▼ Choose or create an execution role

Execution role
Choose a role that defines the permissions of your function. To create a custom role, go to the IAM console.

○ Create a new role with basic Lambda permissions

○ Use an existing role

● Create a new role from AWS policy templates

ⓘ Role creation might take a few minutes. Please do not delete the role or edit the trust or permissions policies in this role.

Role name
Enter a name for your new role.

s3TriggerRole

Use only letters, numbers, hyphens, or underscores with no spaces.

Policy templates - *optional* Info
Choose one or more policy templates.

Amazon S3 object read-only permissions ✕
S3

Figure 2.27: AWS Lambda—Create a function screen

12. You will see the Lambda function designer. There is lot of information displayed. Let's focus on the essentials for this exercise:

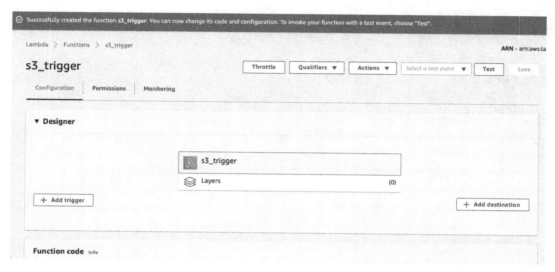

Figure 2.28: AWS Lambda—function designer

13. Click **Add trigger**, and from the drop-down menu, select **S3**:

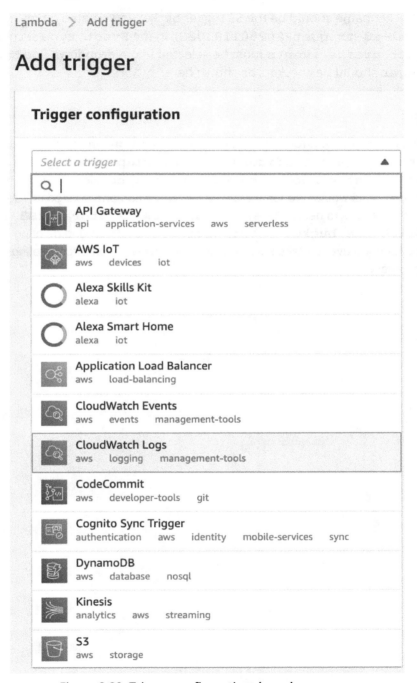

Figure 2.29: Trigger configuration drop-down menu

14. Take a quick look at the options and select **Add**:

The bucket name should be the S3 trigger bucket you created (in my case, it was `aws-ml-s3-trigger-202001181023`); in the **Event type** section, **All object create events** must be selected in the dropdown and **Enable Trigger** should be checked, as shown here:

> **NOTE**
>
> You might get the error "**An error occurred when creating the trigger: Configurations overlap. Configurations on the same bucket cannot share a common event type.**" This would happen if you created a function and deleted it. The easiest way is to delete the event via **Services | Storage/S3 | Click the bucket | Properties | Events** and deleting the Lambda event. Make sure you click the **Save** button after deleting the event.

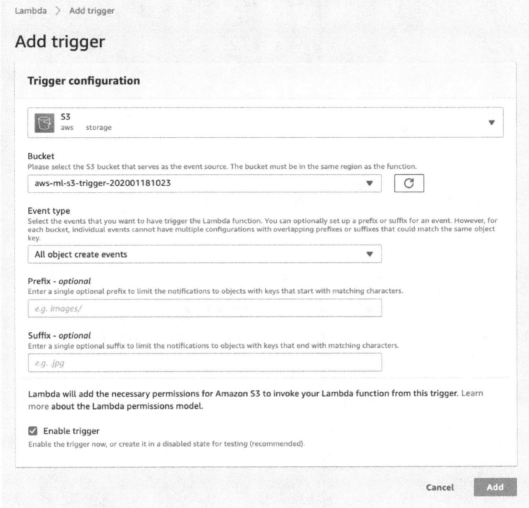

Figure 2.30: Amazon S3 Trigger configuration

You will see S3 on the Lambda **Designer** screen:

Figure 2.31: Lambda function designer with S3

15. Again, choose **Add trigger** and choose **CloudWatch/Events/
    EventBridge**:

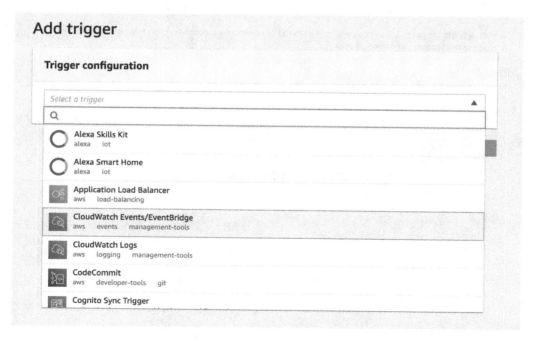

Figure 2.32: Adding the trigger configuration

16. Then click the box next to **Rule**:

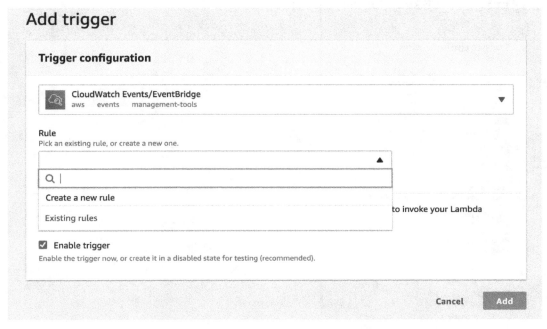

Figure 2.33: Add trigger – creating a new rule

17. Select **Create a new rule**. The following screen will be displayed. Type **s3_
trigger_CWRule** for the rule name.

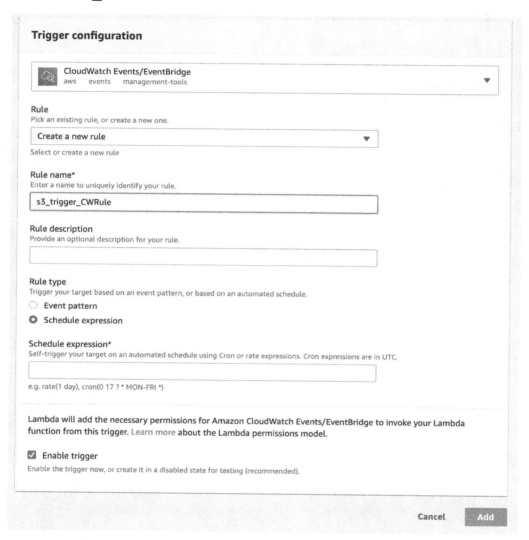

Figure 2.34: Add Trigger—New Rule Configuration

18. Choose **Event pattern** in **Rule type**. Then select **Simple Storage Service (S3)** from the dropdown and **All events** and click **Add**:

Rule name*
Enter a name to uniquely identify your rule.

```
s3_trigger_CWRule
```

Rule description
Provide an optional description for your rule.

Rule type
Auto Scaling
EC2
Health
Relational Database Service (RDS)
✓ Simple Storage Service (S3)
Step Functions

Figure 2.35: Adding an S3 rule type

19. Let's explore the interface a bit more so that you can get comfortable navigating through different pages. Click **Functions** in the top-left corner:

Lambda > Functions > s3_trigger

s3_trigger

Figure 2.36: Top navigation bar to navigate back to functions

20. Click **s3_trigger** to go back to the function you are working on:

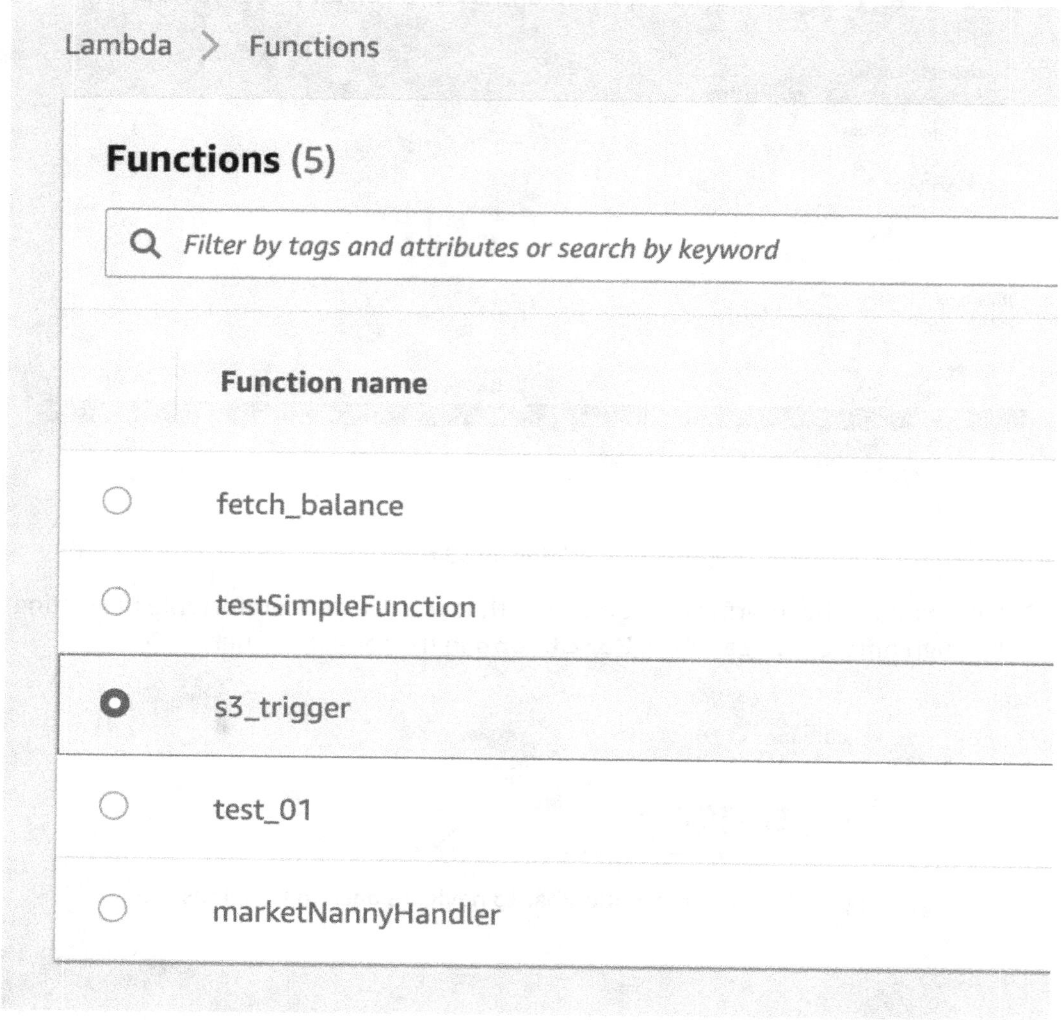

Lambda > Functions

Functions (5)

Q *Filter by tags and attributes or search by keyword*

	Function name
○	fetch_balance
○	testSimpleFunction
●	s3_trigger
○	test_01
○	marketNannyHandler

Figure 2.37: Selecting the lambda function to work on

21. Next, scroll down the screen to the **Function code** section. The default code will be the same as, or similar to, the following:

Figure 2.38: AWS Lambda—the default lambda_function screen

Here, we can enter and edit our code entirely within the **lambda_function** screen (as long as **Code entry type** is set to **Edit code inline**, which is the default value in the drop-down menu).

> **NOTE**
>
> For this step, you may either follow along and type in the code or obtain it from the source code folder at https://packt.live/2O6WsLW.

22. First, we import the **AWS SDK** for Python (boto3: http://boto3.readthedocs.io/en/latest/):

```
import boto3
```

23. Then, import the JSON module to serialize the JSON (https://docs.python.org/3.6/library/json.html):

```
import json
```

24. Next, create a function that takes two parameters—**event** and **context**:

```
def Lambda_handler(event, context):
```

25. Next, create the **s3** client object:

```
s3 = boto3.client("s3")
```

26. Add an **if** event to check whether an event occurs.

27. Next, replace **<input Bucket name>** with the bucket you created (**aws-ml-s3-trigger-202001181023**, in are example):

```
bucket = "<input Bucket name>"
```

28. Next, access the first index of the **Records** event to obtain the text file object:

```
text_file_obj = event["Records"][0]
```

29. Next, assign the **filename** text to a variable and print the filename:

```
filename = str(text_file_obj['s3']['object']['key'])
print("filename: ", filename)
```

30. Next, create the file object by getting the bucket and key:

```
file_obj = s3.get_object(Bucket = Bucket, Key = filename)
```

31. Assign the text to the **body_str_obj** variable:

```
body_str_obj = str(file_obj['Body'].read())
```

32. Create the **comprehend** variable:

```
comprehend = boto3.client(service_name="comprehend")
```

33. The next three lines of code call the respective Comprehend functions to detect the sentiment, entities, and key phrases from the text document. Then, the output is printed to the console:

```
sentiment_response = comprehend.detect_sentiment\
                    (Text = body_str_obj, \
                    LanguageCode = "en")
print(«sentiment_response: \n», sentiment_response)
entity_response = comprehend.detect_entities\
                    (Text = body_str_obj, LanguageCode = "en")
print("\n\nentity_response: \n", entity_response)
key_phases_response = comprehend.detect_key_phrases\
                    (Text = body_str_obj, \
                    LanguageCode = "en")
print("\n\nkey_phases_response: \n", key_phases_response)
```

34. The final statement returns the **'Hello from Lambda'** string, like so:

```
return {
        'statusCode' :200,
        'body' : json.dumps('Hello from Lambda')
    }
```

35. Now, click the **Save** button:

```
    lambda_function ×

1   import boto3
2   import json
3
4   def lambda_handler(event, context):
5       # create a s3 object
6       s3 = boto3.client("s3")
7
8       # check if an event is True
9       if event:
10          # enter the specific bucket name to the 'bucket' variable
11          bucket = "aws-ml-s3-trigger-202001181023"
12
13          # event - AWS Lambda uses this parameter to pass in event data to the handler.
14          # This parameter is usually of the Python dict type. It can also be list, str, int, float, or NoneType type
15          text_file_obj = event["Records"][0]
16          # assign the uploaded text file name to the 'filename' variable
17          filename = str(text_file_obj['s3']['object']['key'])
18
19          # print the filename
20          print("filename: ", filename)
21
22          # create the file object
23          file_obj = s3.get_object(Bucket = bucket, Key = filename)
24
25          # access the file_obj's body. Invoke the read() function and convert to a str object.
26          # assign to the variable 'body_str_obj'
27          body_str_obj = str(file_obj['Body'].read())
28
29          # create a comprehend object
30          comprehend = boto3.client(service_name="comprehend")
31
32          # call detect_sentiment()
33          sentiment_response = comprehend.detect_sentiment(Text = body_str_obj, LanguageCode = "en")
34          print("sentiment_response: \n", sentiment_response)
35
36          # call detect_entities()
37          entity_response = comprehend.detect_entities(Text = body_str_obj, LanguageCode = "en")
38          print("\n\nentity_response: \n", entity_response)
39
40          # call detect_key_phrases()
41          key_phases_response = comprehend.detect_key_phrases(Text = body_str_obj, LanguageCode = "en")
42          print("\n\nkey_phases_response: \n", key_phases_response)
43
44          return {
45              'statusCode' :200,
46              'body' : json.dumps('Hello from Lambda')
47          }
48
```

Figure 2.39: AWS Lambda – save screen

From this exercise, the **s3_trigger** function has access to S3, but not Amazon Comprehend. We need to attach a policy to the **s3_trigger** function to allow it to access Amazon Comprehend to execute the text analysis functions (**detect_sentiment**, **detect_entities**, and **detect_key_phrases**).

EXERCISE 2.08: ASSIGNING POLICIES TO S3_TRIGGER TO ACCESS COMPREHEND

In this exercise, we will attach the policies to the **S3_trigger** function to allow it to access Comprehend. The steps for completion for assigning the policies are as follows:

1. In the Amazon Management Console, click **Services** at the top left:

Figure 2.40: AWS Services from the AWS Management Console

2. Navigate to the **Identity and Access Management** dashboard in the **Security, Identity, & Compliance** section. You can also type **IAM** and select it from the dropdown:

Figure 2.41: IAM dashboard

3. Now, once you get to the IAM dashboard, click **Roles**:

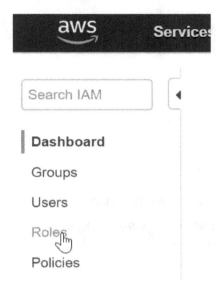

Figure 2.42: Left-hand side of the IAM dashboard

4. Now, the screen will be populated with the role list. Click **s3TriggerRole** in the role list:

Figure 2.43: Role list—selecting s3TriggerRole

5. The **s3TriggerRole** option will be enabled. Then, click **Attach policies**:

Figure 2.44: Permissions tab for s3TriggerRole

6. Type **Comprehend** to filter the policies. Then, click the checkbox next to **ComprehendFullAccess**:

Figure 2.45: ComprehendFullAccess policy selection

7. Once you have selected the checkbox, click **Attach policy** (located in the lower right-hand corner of the screen):

Figure 2.46: Attaching the selected policies

8. You will be redirected to the **s3TriggerRole** screen, and you will receive the following message:

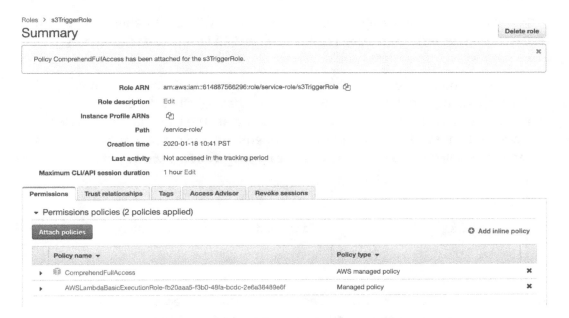

Roles > s3TriggerRole
Summary
Delete role

Policy ComprehendFullAccess has been attached for the s3TriggerRole.

Role ARN	arn:aws:iam::614887566296:role/service-role/s3TriggerRole
Role description	Edit
Instance Profile ARNs	
Path	/service-role/
Creation time	2020-01-18 10:41 PST
Last activity	Not accessed in the tracking period
Maximum CLI/API session duration	1 hour Edit

Permissions | Trust relationships | Tags | Access Advisor | Revoke sessions

▼ Permissions policies (2 policies applied)

Attach policies   ⊕ Add inline policy

Policy name ▼	Policy type ▼	
ComprehendFullAccess	AWS managed policy	✖
AWSLambdaBasicExecutionRole-fb20aaa5-f3b0-48fa-bcdc-2e6a38489e6f	Managed policy	✖

Figure 2.47: Successfully attached policies message

With that, we have successfully attached the policies to the **S3_trigger** function thus allowing it to access Comprehend.

ACTIVITY 2.01: INTEGRATING LAMBDA WITH AMAZON COMPREHEND TO PERFORM TEXT ANALYSIS

In this activity, we will integrate the Lambda functions with Comprehend to perform text analysis (**detect_sentiment**, **detect_entities**, and **detect_key_phrases**) when a document is uploaded to S3.

Suppose that you are creating a chatbot. You have identified a business topic and the corresponding text documents, with content that will allow the chatbot to make your business successful. Your next step is to integrate the Lambda functions with Comprehend, for sentiment, key phrases, and entities. To ensure that this happens correctly, you will need to have **test_s3trigger_configured.txt**.

> **NOTE**
>
> The **test_s3trigger_configured.txt** file can be found on GitHub at link https://packt.live/3gAxqku.

Before you execute **s3_trigger**, consider the output, based on the following aspects of the text: sentiment (positive, negative, or neutral), entities (quantity, person, place, and so on), and key phrases:

1. First, navigate to the **S3_trigger** Lambda function.

2. Add **test_s3trigger_configured.txt** to the S3 bucket, to verify the Lambda **S3_trigger** function.

3. Now, upload the file into the bucket and monitor the file.

4. Next, click **View logs** in **CloudWatch** by using the log stream.

5. Now, expand the output in a text format.

   The following will be the output:

   Sentiment_response -> Classified as 60.0% likely to be positive

   Sentiment_response:

```
{'Sentiment': 'POSITIVE',
'SentimentScore':{'Positive': 0.6005121469497681,
                  'Negative': 0.029164031147956848,
                  'Neutral': 0.3588017225265503,
                  'Mixed': 0.01152205839753151},
```

`entity_response` -> Classified as 70.5% likely to be a quantity

`entity_response`:

```
{Entities':[{'Score':0.7053232192993164,
            'Type': 'QUANTITY','Text': '3 trigger',
            'BeginOffset': 35, 'EndOffset': 44}],
```

`key_phases_response` -> Classified as 89.9% likely "a test file" and 98.5% likely "the s3 trigger" are the key phrases:

`key_phases_response`:

```
{'KeyPhrases': [{'Score': 0.8986637592315674,
              'Text': 'a test file',
              'BeginOffset': 8, 'EndOffset': 19},
            {'Score': 0.9852105975151062,
              'Text': 'the s3 trigger', 'BeginOffset': 30,
              'EndOffset': 44}],
```

> **NOTE**
>
> The solution for this activity can be found on page 279.

AMAZON TEXTRACT

Another interesting NLP Amazon service is Textract. Essentially, Textract can extract information from documents, usually business documents such as tax forms, legal documents, medical forms, bank forms, patent registrations, and so forth. It is an **optical character recognition (OCR)** solution for scanning structured documents, suitable for **robotic process automation** (**RPA**). Textract is a relatively new service—previewed in November 2018 and generally available in May 2019.

The advantage of Textract is that it understands documents and can extract tables and/or key-value pairs suitable for downstream processing. A lot of business processes, such as health insurance processing, tax preparation, loan application processing, monitoring and evaluation of existing loans, compliance evaluation, and engineering evaluations take in these documents, usually processing them manually to extract information and then start digital processes. Using Amazon Textract, the manual intake of various documents can be automated, resulting in a faster turnaround when approving loans, accelerated processing of health claims, or approving an engineering design quickly, thus achieving good business value.

EXERCISE 2.09: EXTRACTING TAX INFORMATION USING AMAZON TEXTRACT

In this exercise, you will take a page of a sample tax return document from documentcloud.org (https://www.documentcloud.org/documents/3462212-Sample-2016-Tax-Return.html) and see how much information Textract can extract:

> **NOTE**
>
> The sample document (page 1 of US Tax form 1040) is available at
> https://packt.live/2O5e1Mn.

1. For this exercise, we will use the Textract interface directly. This is very useful to try out and to see how a document is amenable to OCR.

2. First, go to the Textract dashboard by selecting **Services | Machine Learning | Amazon Textract**. There are lots of interesting details on that page. Take the time to read through the materials:

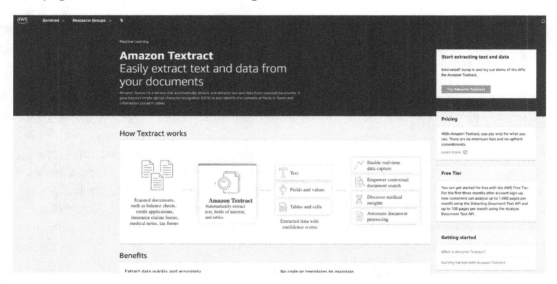

Figure 2.48: Amazon Textract dashboard

3. Click **Try Amazon Textract**. A very simple utilitarian page appears:

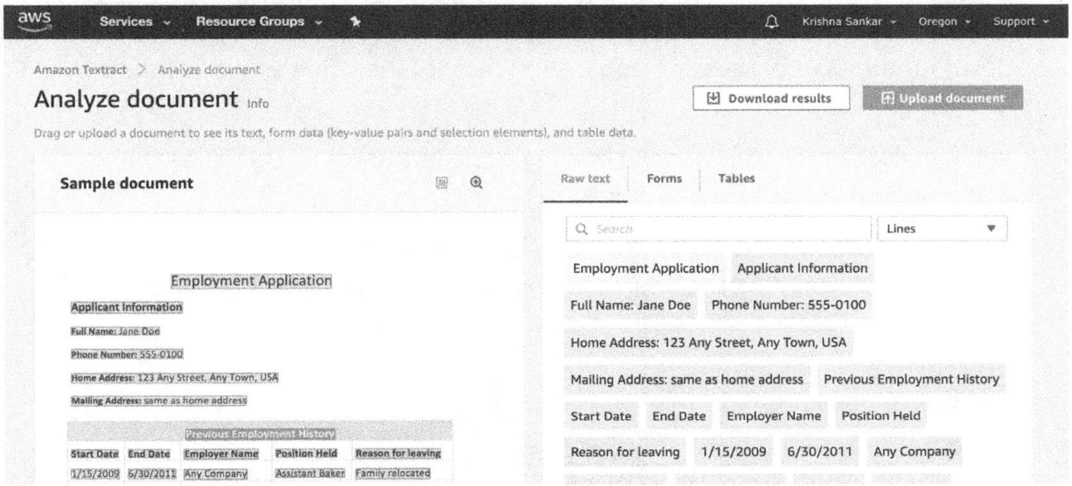

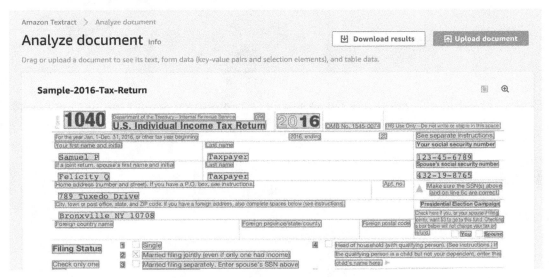

Figure 2.49: Amazon Textract Analyze document

4. Click **Upload document** and upload the **Sample-2016-Tax-Return.jpeg** file. The service thinks for a minute and shows very informative tabs and the information it has extracted:

Figure 2.50: Amazon Textract Analyze document screen with the sample tax form

The raw text is interesting, but we are looking for more value for our automation pipeline.

5. Click the **Forms** tab and you will see a very interesting page—it can get the value as well as the key. For example, line 7 is extracted as **7 Wages, salaries, tips, etc. Attach Form(s) W-2 7** and a value of **93,500**. Now, a downstream loan processing application can get the value as well as the context and act on it.

You can click other fields on the image on the left-hand side and see the extracted entry on the right-hand side.

You can download the results as JSON, CSV, table, and text formats. As expected, **keyvalues.csv** has the line 7 we saw earlier as the key and **93,500** as the value:

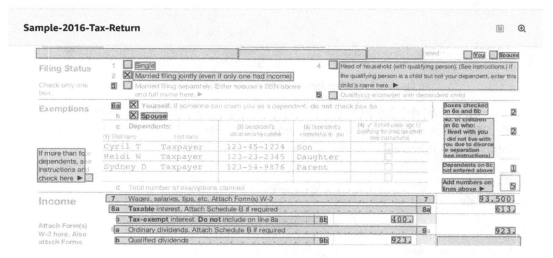

Figure 2.51: Amazon Textract Analyze document screen with the sample tax document form

6. You can see the extracted fields in a table format (with the keys as the caption and the value in the grey box under the captions) as shown below:

Figure 2.52: Amazon Textract Analyze document screen with the sample tax document Forms tab showing the key value

7. The **Tables** tab is also interesting. Textract was able to extract two tables—the top and the bottom portion—but was not able to extract the middle one:

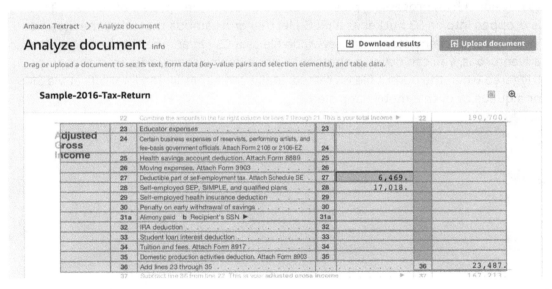

Figure 2.53: Amazon Textract Analyze document screen with the sample tax form showing Tables (form)

8. You can see the extracted fields in a table format by clicking the **Tables** tab:

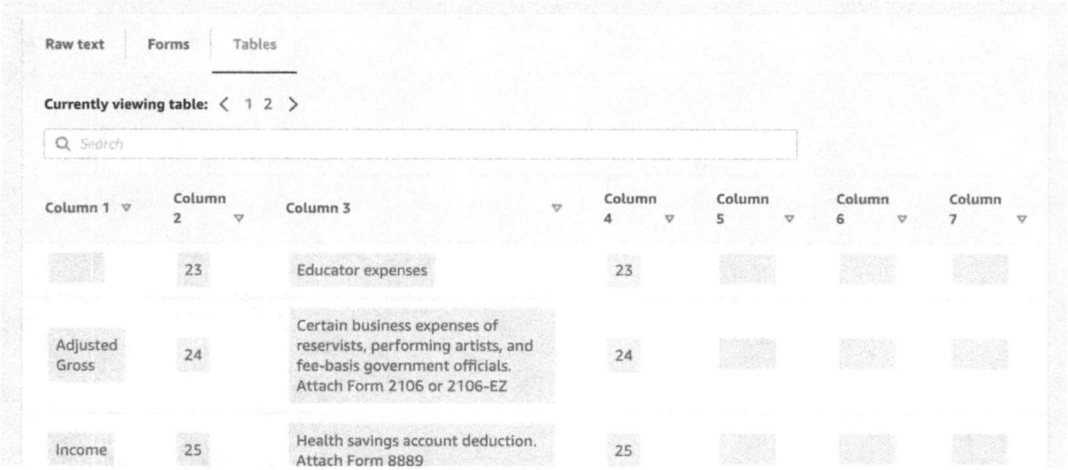

Column 1	Column 2	Column 3		Column 4	Column 5	Column 6	Column 7
	23	Educator expenses		23			
Adjusted Gross	24	Certain business expenses of reservists, performing artists, and fee-basis government officials. Attach Form 2106 or 2106-EZ		24			
Income	25	Health savings account deduction. Attach Form 8889		25			

Figure 2.54: Amazon Textract Analyze document screen
with the sample tax form showing Tables (extracted)

Now that you have a feel for what Textract can do, another useful exercise would be to develop a loan processing pipeline using Lambda. When page 1 of US Tax 1040 is dropped into an S3 bucket as a JPEG file, trigger a Lambda that takes the file and invokes Textract and stores the key-value file as a CSV in another bucket. If you feel adventurous, you can develop another Lambda downstream of Textract that gets triggered when the output file is created, and it can either alert a loan officer via SMS or a queue or even a mobile app alert.

SUMMARY

In this chapter, we started with high-level concepts around Amazon AI services and serverless computing. On a conceptual level, you learned about serverless computing as well as the various AI services available on the AWS platform.

Overall, the culmination of these independent functions provides the foundation for building complex machine learning-based NLP applications (for example, Siri, Alexa, and so on). Knowing how and why the individual functions operate will allow you to build your own AWS-based NLP applications.

Then, we dived into the details of Amazon Comprehend—how Comprehend's `DetectDominantLanguage` method is structured, and how to pass in both strings and a list of strings. You learned how to extract entities, sentiments, key phrases, and topics, which provide the data for complex NLP. This allows Amazon Comprehend to become more efficient by automating text analysis upon a text document that's been uploaded to S3.

You also learned how to use Amazon Textract to extract structured information (tables and key-value pairs) out of scanned documents as a prelude to process automation.

In the next chapter, we will explore topic modeling and perform theme extraction.

3

TOPIC MODELING AND THEME EXTRACTION

OVERVIEW

This chapter describes the use of Topic Modeling to understand common themes in a document set by analyzing documents using Amazon Comprehend. You will learn the fundamentals of the algorithm used for Topic Modeling, **Latent Dirichlet Allocation** (**LDA**). Learning LDA will allow you to apply Topic Modeling to a multitude of unique business cases. You will then perform Topic Modeling on two documents with a known topic structure. By the end of this chapter, you will be able to extract and analyze common themes through Topic Modeling with Amazon Comprehend and describe the basics of Topic Modeling analysis. You will also be able to perform Topic Modeling on a set of documents and analyze the results.

INTRODUCTION

Topic Modeling is an important capability for business systems to make sense of unstructured information, ranging from support tickets to customer feedback and complaints, to business documents. Topic Modeling helps process automation to route customer feedback and mail; it enables a business to categorize and then effectively respond to social media posts, reviews, and other user-generated content from the various channels. It enables businesses to respond faster to critical items by understanding the topics and themes on incoming omnichannel interactions as well as responding most effectively by routing the materials to the most appropriate teams. Another two areas where Topic Modeling helps are knowledge management and brand monitoring.

TOPIC MODELING WITH LATENT DIRICHLET ALLOCATION (LDA)

The subjects or **common themes** of a set of documents can be determined with Amazon Comprehend. For example, you have a movie review website with two message boards, and you want to determine which message board is discussing two newly released movies (one about sport and the other about a political topic). You can provide the message board text data to Amazon Comprehend to discover the most prominent topics discussed on each message board.

The machine learning algorithm that Amazon Comprehend uses to perform Topic Modeling is called **Latent Dirichlet Allocation** (**LDA**). LDA is a learning-based model that's used to determine the most important topics in a collection of documents.

How LDA works is that it considers every document to be a combination of topics, and each word in the document is associated with one of these topics.

For example, if the first paragraph of a document consists of words such as **eat**, **chicken**, **restaurant**, and **cook**, then you conclude that the topic can be generalized to **Food**. Similarly, if the second paragraph of a document contains words such as **ticket**, **train**, **kilometer**, and **vacation**, then you can conclude that the topic is **Travel**.

BASIC LDA EXAMPLE

LDA has lots of math behind it—concepts such as **Expectation Maximization**, Gibs sampling, priors, and a probability distribution over a "bag of words". If you want to understand the mathematical underpinnings, a good start is the Amazon documentation on SageMaker (https://docs.aws.amazon.com/sagemaker/latest/dg/lda-how-it-works.html). Let's look at LDA more pragmatically and understand it empirically through an example.

Say you have one document with six sentences, and you want to infer two common topics.

The sentences are as follows:

- They loved each other greatly.

- Most people experience love without noticing that there is anything remarkable about it.

- It was partly the war; the revolution did the rest.

- The war was an artificial break in life, as if life could be put off for a time. What nonsense!

- I said life, but I mean life as you see it in a great picture, transformed by genius, creatively enriched.

- Only now have people decided to experience it not in books and pictures, but in themselves, not as an abstraction, but in practice.

When you feed these sentences into an LDA algorithm, specifying the number of topics as two, it will discover the following:

Sentence-Topics

Sentence 1: Topic 0

Sentence 2: Topic 0

Sentence 3: Topic 1

Sentence 4: Topic 1

Sentence 5: Topic 0

Sentence 6: Topic 0

Topic terms

Topic 0: life 12%, people 8%, experience 8%, love 5%, and so forth

Topic 1: 62% revolution, 23% war, and the rest 15%

Of course, knowing that the sentences are from the book *Dr. Zhivago* by the famous Russian author *Boris Pasternak*, the topics war and life/love seem reasonable.

While this example is a simplistic depiction of a complex algorithm, it gives you an idea. As discussed in this chapter, in various business situations, an indication of what a document or an e-mail or a social media post is about is very valuable for downstream systems—and the ability to perform that classification automatically is priceless.

WHY USE LDA?

LDA is useful when you want to group a set of documents based on common topics, without thinking about the documents themselves. LDA can create subjects from inferring the general topics by analyzing the words in the documents. This is usually utilized in suggestion frameworks, report arrangement, and record synopsis. In conclusion, LDA has many uses. For example, you have 30,000 user emails and want to determine the most common topics to provide group-specific recommended content based on the most prevalent topics. Manually reading, or even outsourcing the manual reading, of 30,000 emails would take an excessive investment in terms of time and money, and the accuracy would be difficult to confirm. However, Amazon Comprehend can seamlessly provide the most common topics in 30,000 emails in a few steps with incredible accuracy. First, convert the emails to text files, upload them to an S3 bucket, and then imitate a Topic Modeling job with Amazon Comprehend. The output is two CSV files with the corresponding topics and terms.

AMAZON COMPREHEND—TOPIC MODELING GUIDELINES

The most accurate results are obtained if you provide Comprehend with the largest possible corpus. More specifically:

- You should use no fewer than 1,000 records in every subject.

- Each document ought to be something like three sentences in length.

- If a document comprises, for the most part, numeric information, you should expel it from the corpus.

Currently, Topic Modeling is limited to two document languages: **English** and **Spanish**.

A Topic Modeling job allows two format types for input data (refer to the following *Figure 3.1*). This allows users to process both collections of large documents (for example, newspaper articles or scientific journals), and short documents (for example, tweets or social media posts).

Input Format Options:

Format	Description
One document per file	Each file contains one input document. This is best for collections of large documents.
One document per line	The input is a single file. Each line in the file is considered a document. This is best for short documents, such as social media postings.

Figure 3.1: AWS Comprehend—Topic Modeling input format options

Output Format Options:

Files	Description
topic-terms.csv	List of topics in the collection. For each topic, the list includes, by default, the top terms by topic according to their weight.
doc-topics.csv	Lists the documents associated with a topic and the proportion of the document that is concerned with the topic. If you specified ONE_DOC_PER_FILE, the document is identified by the file name.

Figure 3.2: AWS Comprehend—Topic Modeling output files description

After Amazon Comprehend processes your document collection, the modeling outputs two CSV files: **topic-terms.csv** (see *Figure 3.2*) and **doc-topics.csv**.

The `topic-terms.csv` file provides a list of topics in the document collection with the terms, respective topics, and their weights. For example, if you gave Amazon Comprehend two hypothetical documents, **learning to garden** and **investment strategies**, it might return the following to describe the two topics in the collection:

Topic	Term	Weight
0	learn	0.22
0	garden	0.21
0	soil	0.1
0	dig	0.09
0	shovel	0.08
0	season	0.07
0	grow	0.06
0	sun	0.01
0	seeds	0.009
0	growth	0.0008
1	money	0.28
1	stock	0.19
1	returns	0.1
1	risk	0.07
1	hedge	0.06
1	algorithmic	0.05
1	strategy	0.03
1	loss	0.01
1	software	0.009
1	profit	0.008

Figure 3.3: Sample Topic Modeling output (topic-terms.csv) for two documents' input

The **doc-topics.csv** file provides a list of the documents provided for the Topic Modeling job, and the respective topics and their proportions in each document. Given two hypothetical documents, **learning_to_garden.txt** and **investment_strategies.txt,** you can expect the following output:

Docname	Topic	Proportion
learning_to_garden.txt	0	1
investment_strategies.txt	1	1

Figure 3.4: Sample Topic Modeling output (doc-topics.csv) for two documents' input

EXERCISE 3.01: USING AMAZON COMPREHEND TO PERFORM TOPIC MODELING ON TWO DOCUMENTS WITH KNOWN TOPICS

In this exercise, we will use two documents (**Romeo and Juliet** and **War of the Worlds**) to better understand LDA. We will use Amazon Comprehend to discover the main topics in the two documents. Before proceeding to the exercise, just look at an overview of the data pipeline architecture. The text files are stored in S3, and then we direct Comprehend to look for the files in the input bucket. Comprehend analyzes the documents and puts the results back in S3 in the output bucket:

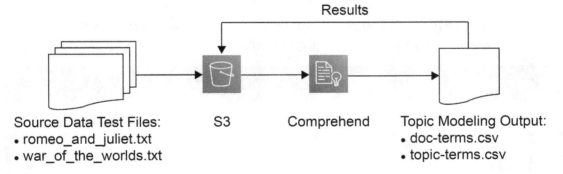

Figure 3.5: Data pipeline architecture overview

Complete the Topic Modeling of a known topic structure:

1. First, you need to get to the S3 console. Please refer to *Chapter 1, An Introduction to AWS*, for account setup instructions. Go to https://aws.amazon.com/ and click **My Account** followed by **AWS Management Console**. Click **Services**, and then search or select **S3** in a new browser tab. You will see the S3 console as shown in the following screenshot:

Figure 3.6: Amazon S3 console

2. We need an input and output S3 bucket. Let's create both. Now, click the **Create bucket** button to create a bucket:

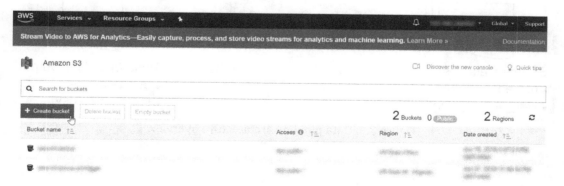

Figure 3.7: Creating a bucket

3. For the bucket name, enter a unique name that describes the function. Here, the name **aws-ml-input-for-topic-modeling** is used. Click the **Create** button:

> **NOTE**
>
> The bucket names in AWS have to be unique. So, you might get an error saying, "Bucket name already exists." One easy way to get a unique name is to append the bucket name with today's date (plus time, if required); say, YYYYMMDDHHMM. While writing this chapter, we created a bucket, **aws-ml-input-for-topic-modeling-20200301**.
>
> Clicking **Create** in the following window uses all the default settings for properties and permissions, while clicking **Next** allows you to adjust these settings according to your needs.

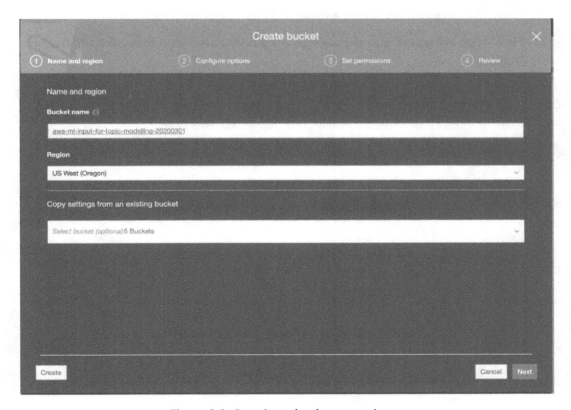

Figure 3.8: Creating a bucket name input

4. Click **Next**, then **Next** again to go to **Configure options**, click **Next** once more to go to **Set permissions**, and finally click on **Create Bucket** in the **Review** tab:

5. Now, click the bucket and then the **Create folder** button to create a folder:

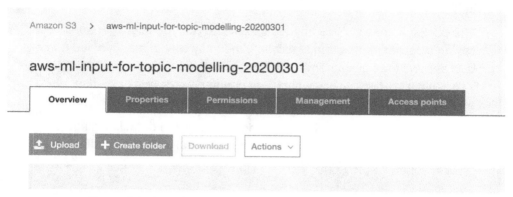

Figure 3.9: Creating a folder in S3 for Topic modeling input

6. Now, type in **known_structure** as the folder name, and then click the **Save** button:

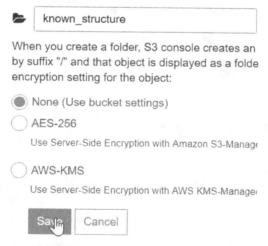

Figure 3.10: Saving the known_structure folder name

7. After clicking the **Save** button, your folder will be generated. Now, click the **known_structure** folder:

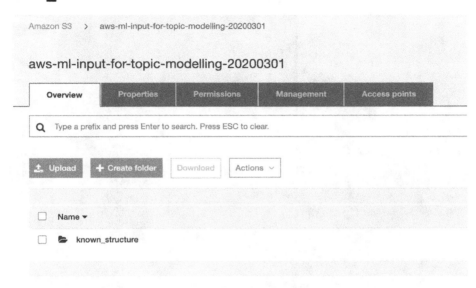

Figure 3.11: The input bucket screen

8. Now, click the **Upload** button:

Figure 3.12: The Upload button

9. Now, you will be prompted to add files to the folder. Click **Add files**, or drag the files onto the screen:

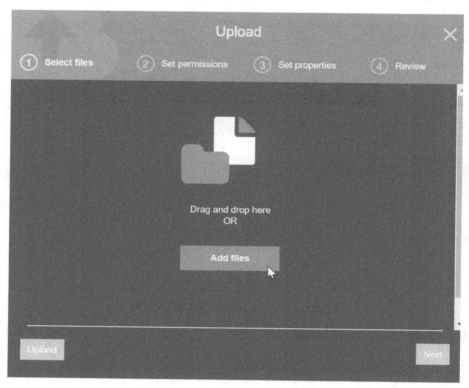

Figure 3.13: The Add files button

10. The files for this chapter are located in the **Chapter03** folder in the GitHub repository at https://packt.live/3eba6rM. As we mentioned in *Chapter 1, An Introduction to AWS*, you should have downloaded the GitHub files to a local subdirectory.

By way of an example, we have downloaded the files to the **Documents/ aws-book/The-Applied-AI-and-Natural-Language-Processing- with-AWS** directory. Navigate to **Upload** and select the following two text files from your local disk. As you may have guessed, the files for this exercise are located in the **Exercise3.01** subdirectory:

Once the files have been selected, click on the **Open** button to upload the files:

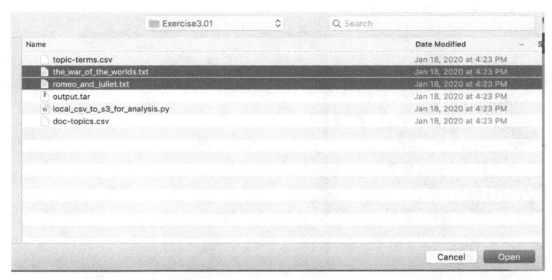

Figure 3.14: Selecting files to upload from the local directory

The following figure shows the uploading of text files:

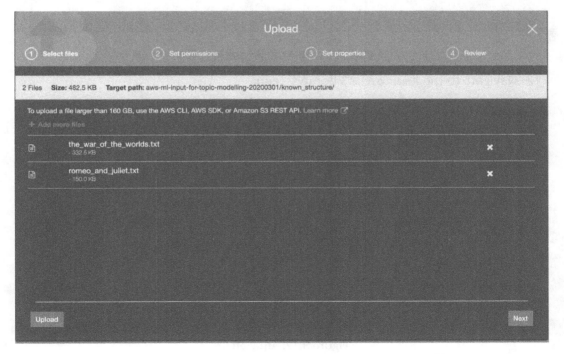

Figure 3.15: Uploading for the two known_structure text files

11. Click **Next** in the `Set permissions` and `Set Properties` tabs. Select **Upload** in the **Review** tab:

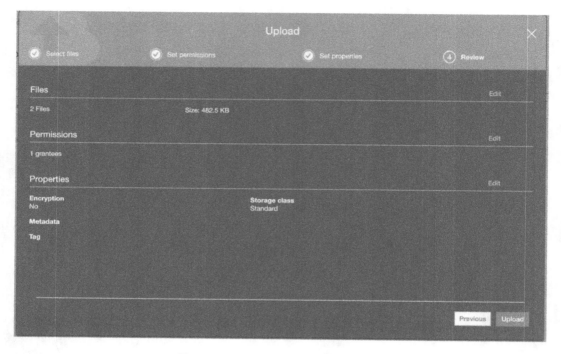

Figure 3.16: Amazon S3 upload files

12. Navigate to the **Amazon S3** home screen:

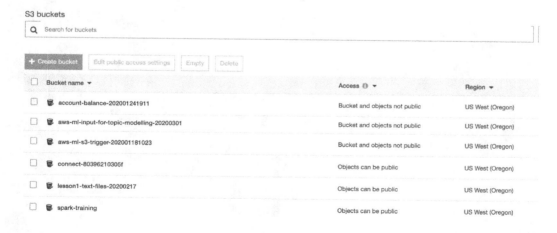

Figure 3.17: Amazon S3

13. Next, create an output S3 bucket. Use the same S3 bucket creation process. To do so, click the **Create bucket** button:

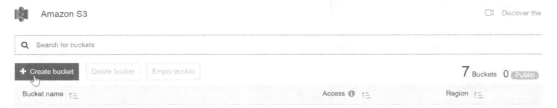

Figure 3.18: Creating a bucket

14. Now, name the bucket and then click the **Create** button:

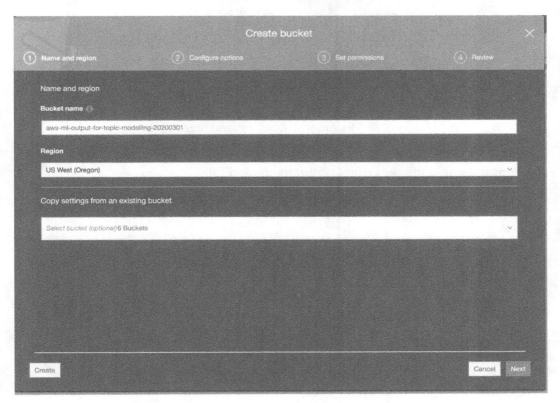

Figure 3.19: Creating bucket output for Topic Modeling

15. Click **Next** under `Configure Options`, **Next** under `Set permissions`, and `Create Bucket` in the **Review** window.

    Now you have two buckets, one for input with two text files, and an empty output bucket. Let's now proceed to Amazon Comprehend.

16. Navigate to Amazon Comprehend: https://console.aws.amazon.com/comprehend/. If you are presented with the following screen, click **Launch Amazon Comprehend**:

Figure 3.20: The Amazon Comprehend home screen

17. Now, click the first `Analysis jobs` option in the left-hand side toolbar (**not** the one under Amazon Comprehend Medical):

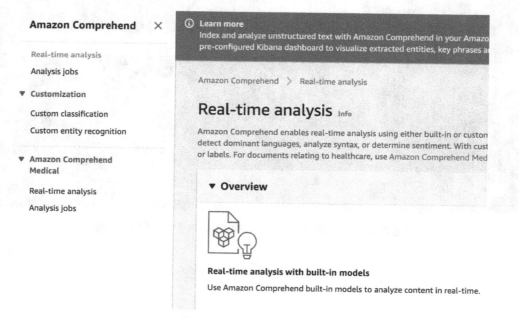

Figure 3.21: The Amazon Comprehend organization screen

18. Now, click the **Create job** button:

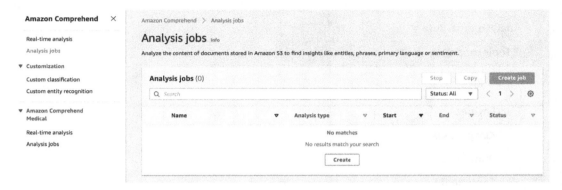

Figure 3.22: The Amazon Comprehend Create job button

19. Enter **known_structure_topic_modeling_job** in the **Name** field:

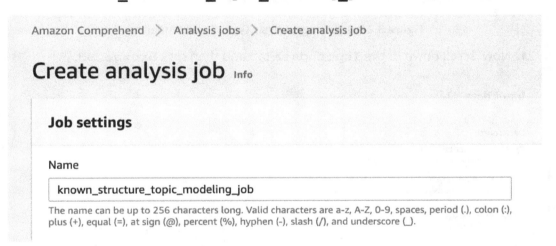

Figure 3.23: Name of the Topic Modeling job

20. Select **Topic Modeling** in the **Analysis type** drop-down box:

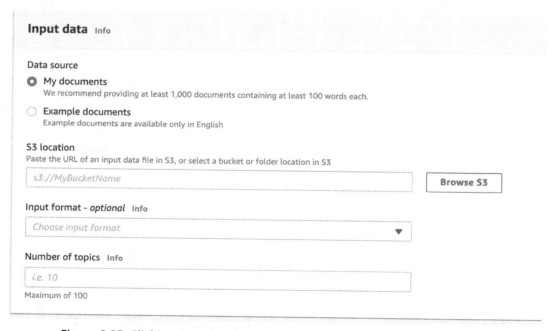

We recommend providing at least 1,000 documents containing at least 100 words each.

Figure 3.24: Selecting analysis type (Topic Modeling)

21. Now, scroll down to the **Input data** tab and then click **Browse S3**:

Input data Info

Data source

◉ My documents
We recommend providing at least 1,000 documents containing at least 100 words each.

○ Example documents
Example documents are available only in English

S3 location
Paste the URL of an input data file in S3, or select a bucket or folder location in S3

s3://MyBucketName   Browse S3

Input format - *optional* Info

Choose input format ▾

Number of topics Info

i.e. 10

Maximum of 100

Figure 3.25: Clicking Search to locate the Topic Modeling input data source

22. The list of S3 buckets will be displayed:

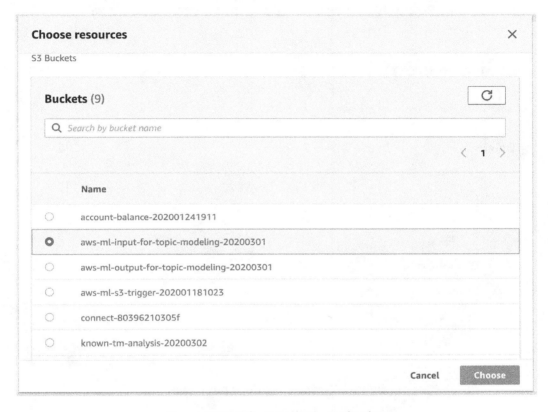

Figure 3.26: Selecting the input bucket

23. Select the input bucket (in my case, it is **aws-ml-input-for-topic-modeling-20200301**) and click on the bucket. Then, the folder will be displayed:

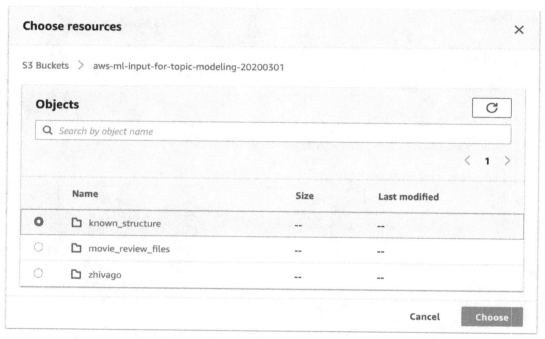

Figure 3.27: Selecting the input folder

24. Click the radio button next to **known_structure** and then click the **Choose** button, which will direct you to the following screen:

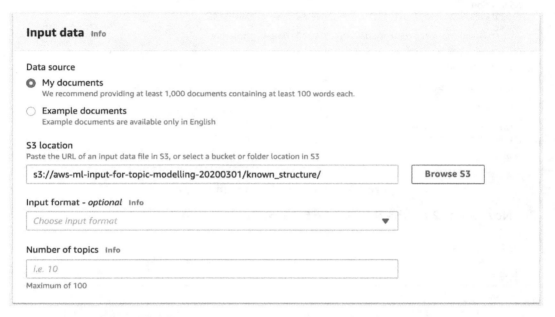

Figure 3.28: The Input data section with the S3 location filled in

25. Now, from the drop-down menu, select **One document per file**:

S3 location
Paste the URL of an input data file in S3, or select a bucket or folder location in S3

s3://aws-ml-input-for-topic-modelling-20200301/known_structure/   Browse S3

Input format - *optional* Info

One document per file	▲
One document per file	
One document per line	
2	

Maximum of 100

Figure 3.29: Selecting One document per file

26. Now, enter **2** for the **Number of Topics** you need to have:

Number of topics Info

2

Maximum of 100

Figure 3.30: Entering 2 for the number of topics to perform Topic Modeling

27. Next, click **Browse S3** in the **Output data** tab:

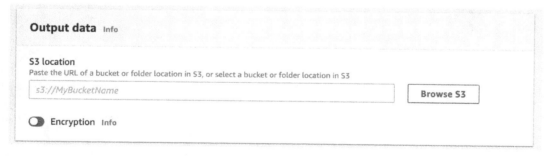

Output data Info

S3 location
Paste the URL of a bucket or folder location in S3, or select a bucket or folder location in S3

s3://MyBucketName   Browse S3

⬤ Encryption Info

Figure 3.31: Output data tab and the Browse S3 button for the Topic Modeling S3 output location

28. Select the output bucket (in our case, it is **aws-ml-output-for-topic-modeling-20200301)** and then click **Choose**:

Figure 3.32: Selecting the output S3 bucket

29. Make sure that the **Output data** tab looks similar to the following screenshot:

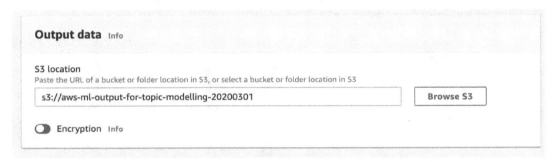

Figure 3.33: Output data tab with the output bucket name

30. Scroll down to the **Access permissions** tab, and then select the option **Create an IAM role**:

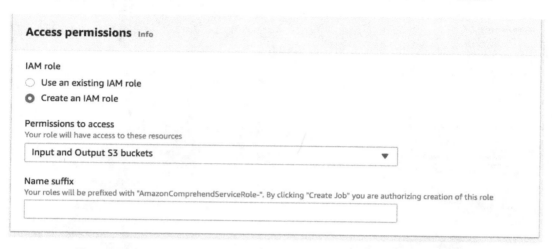

Figure 3.34: Selecting Create an IAM role and providing permission to Input and Output S3 buckets

Check to make sure that **Input and Output S3 buckets** is listed under **Permissions to access**:

31. Enter **myTopicModelingRole** in the **Name suffix** field and then click the **Create job** button:

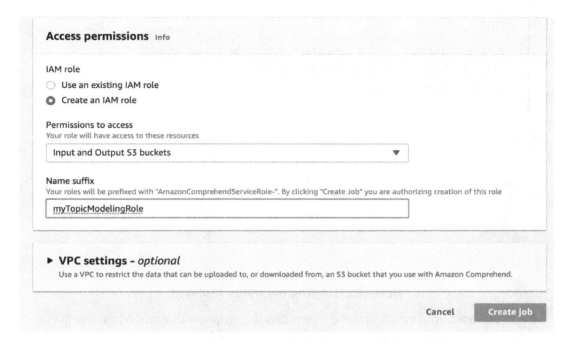

Figure 3.35: Clicking the Create job button

32. Creating the job may take a few minutes and you might see a message "Propagating IAM role, please remain on the page." Once the creation is complete, you will be redirected to the Comprehend home screen as follows:

Figure 3.36: The Comprehend home screen

> **NOTE**
>
> Bear in mind that clicking **Create job** starts the job as well. There is no separate "start a job" button. Also, if you want to redo the job, you will have to use the **Copy** button.

33. While the job is being processed, the status displayed will be **In Progress**:

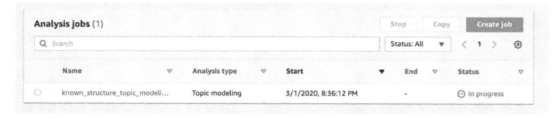

Figure 3.37: In progress status displayed

34. On our account, it took around 4 minutes to complete the job. When the status changes to **Completed**, click the Topic Modeling job name:

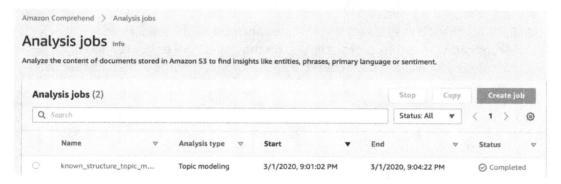

Figure 3.38: Completed status displayed

35. Now, scroll down to the **Output** section:

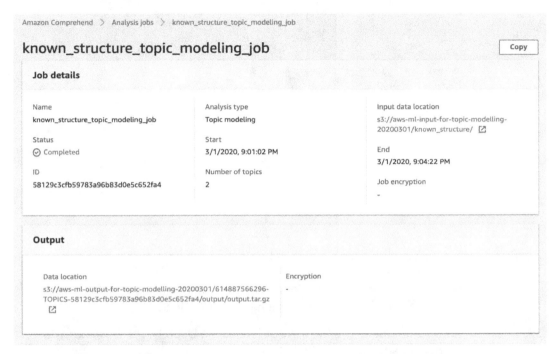

Figure 3.39: Topic Modeling output display home screen

36. Click the hyperlink under **Data location**:

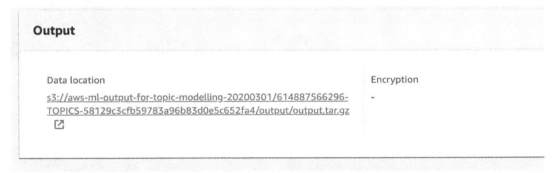

Figure 3.40: Topic Modeling data output hyperlinked location

This will take you directly to the S3 bucket:

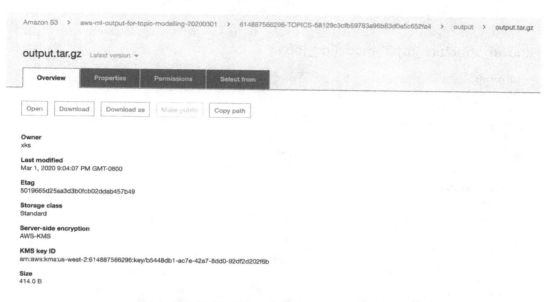

Figure 3.41: Topic Modeling output file in S3

37. Click **Download** and save the file in your local disk. Usually, the **Downloads** folder is an ideal location:

Figure 3.42: Topic Modeling downloading the output file to the local disk

38. Extract **output.tar.gz** and usually, it will show up in a directory output:

Figure 3.43: Output files from Topic Modeling

39. Now examine the two files: **topic-terms.xlsx** and **doc-topics.xlsx**:

> **NOTE**
>
> Your **topic-terms.csv** and **doc-topics.csv** results should
> be the same as the following results. If your results are NOT the same,
> use the output files for the remainder of the chapter, which are located
> at *Chapter03/Exercise3.01/topic-terms.csv* https://packt.live/3iHlH5y and
> *Chapter03/Exercise3.01/doc-topics.csv* https://packt.live/2ZMTaTw.

The following is the output generated. As we had indicated that we want to have topics, Comprehend has segregated the relevant words into two groups/topics as well as the weights. It doesn't know what the topics are, but has inferred the similarity of the words to one of the two topics:

topic	term	weight
0	martian	0.01230843
0	people	0.00799511
0	house	0.0059477
0	black	0.0059392
0	time	0.00585474
0	road	0.00563831
0	thing	0.00539951
0	stand	0.00523221
0	pit	0.0048801
0	brother	0.00448389
1	thou	0.44513163
1	thy	0.13558617
1	rom	0.13241126
1	nurse	0.09137733
1	love	0.09092529
1	you	0.05385929
1	romeo	0.05070904

topic-terms ╋

Figure 3.44: topic-terms.csv result

The **doc-topics.csv** shows the affinity of the documents to the topics. In this case, it is very deterministic, but if we have more topics, the proportion will show the strength of the topics in each of the documents:

docname	topic	proportion
romeo_and_juliet.txt	1	1
the_war_of_the_worlds.txt	0	1

doc-topics   +

Figure 3.45: doc-topics.csv results

In this exercise, we used Amazon Comprehend to infer topics embedded in a set of documents. While this is easier to do with two documents; Amazon Comprehend is very effective when we have hundreds of documents with multiple documents and we want to perform process automation.

EXERCISE 3.02: PERFORMING KNOWN STRUCTURE ANALYSIS PROGRAMMATICALLY

While it is easy to look at one or two outputs, when we want to scale and analyze hundreds of documents with different topics, we need to use Comprehend programmatically. That is what we will do in this exercise.

In this exercise, we will programmatically upload the CSV files (**doc-topics.csv** and **Topic-terms.csv**) to S3, merge the CSV files on the Topic column, and print the output to the console. The following are the steps for performing known structure analysis:

> **NOTE**
>
> For this step, you will be using Jupyter Notebook. You may either follow along with the exercise and type in the code or obtain it from the source code folder, **local_csv_to_s3_for_analysis.ipynb**, and paste it into the editor. The source code is available on GitHub in the following repository: https://packt.live/2BOqjWT. As explained in *Chapter 1, An Introduction to AWS*, you should have downloaded the repository to your local disk.

1. First, we will import **boto3** using the following command:

```
import boto3
```

2. Next, we will import **pandas** using the following command:

```
import pandas as pd
```

3. Now, we will create the S3 client object using the following command:

```
# Setup a region
region = 'us-west-2'
# Create an S3 client
s3 = boto3.client('s3',region_name = region)
```

4. Next, we will create a variable with a unique bucket name. Here, the selected bucket name is **known-tm-analysis**, but you will need to create a unique name:

```
# Creates a variable with the bucket name
#'<insert a unique bucket name>'
bucket_name = 'known-tm-analysis-20200302'
```

5. Next, create a new bucket:

```
# Create a location Constraint
location = {'LocationConstraint': region}
# Creates a new bucket
s3.create_bucket(Bucket=bucket_name,\
           CreateBucketConfiguration=location)
```

6. Create a list of the CSV filenames to import:

```
filenames_list = ['doc-topics.csv', 'topic-terms.csv']
```

> **NOTE**
>
> Ensure that the two CSV files (highlighted) in the aforementioned step are stored in the same location where you're running the Jupyter Notebook code. An alternative is to specify the exact path as it exists on your local system.

7. Now, iterate on each file to upload to S3 using the following line of code:

```
for filename in filenames_list:
    s3.upload_file(filename, bucket_name, filename)
```

> **NOTE**
>
> Do not execute *steps 7* and *8* yet. We will show the code for the entire **for** block in *step 9*.

8. Next, check whether the filename is **doc-topics.csv**: and get the **doc-topics.csv** file object and assign it to the **obj** variable.

```
if filename == 'doc-topics.csv':
    obj = s3.get_object(Bucket=bucket_name, Key=filename)
```

9. Next, read the **csv** object and assign it to the **doc_topics** variable. You can see the entire code block, including steps *7* and *8* below:

```
for filename in filenames_list:
    # Uploads each CSV to the created bucket
    s3.upload_file(filename, bucket_name, filename)
    # checks if the filename is 'doc-topics.csv'
    if filename == 'doc-topics.csv':
        # gets the 'doc-topics.csv' file as an object
        obj = s3.get_object(Bucket=bucket_name, Key=filename)
        # reads the csv and assigns to doc_topics
        doc_topics = pd.read_csv(obj['Body'])
    else:
        obj = s3.get_object(Bucket=bucket_name, Key=filename)
        topic_terms = pd.read_csv(obj['Body'])
```

10. Now, merge the files on the Topic column to obtain the most common terms per document using the following command:

```
merged_df = pd.merge(doc_topics, topic_terms, on='topic')
# print the merged_df to the console
print(merged_df)
```

11. Next, execute the notebook cells using the *Shift + Enter* keys:

12. The console output is a merged DataFrame that provides the docnames with their respective terms and the term's weights (refer to the following):

```
# Create a location Constraint
location = {'LocationConstraint': region}
# Creates a new bucket
s3.create_bucket(Bucket=bucket_name,CreateBucketConfiguration=location)
```

```
[5]: {'ResponseMetadata': {'RequestId': '0A449359650B9B28',
  'HostId': 'FidcK1B8Tn0814WLh3BLwHTc+mLXVdcdsuHJc2N18XKsfVRWun9iVjC2F+Af/RRZqP+QeHczn/s=',
  'HTTPStatusCode': 200,
  'HTTPHeaders': {'x-amz-id-2': 'FidcK1B8Tn0814WLh3BLwHTc+mLXVdcdsuHJc2N18XKsfVRWun9iVjC2F+Af/RRZqP+QeHczn/s
=',
   'x-amz-request-id': '0A449359650B9B28',
   'date': 'Mon, 02 Mar 2020 20:07:45 GMT',
   'location': 'http://known-tm-analysis-20200302.s3.amazonaws.com/',
   'content-length': '0',
   'server': 'AmazonS3'},
  'RetryAttempts': 0},
 'Location': 'http://known-tm-analysis-20200302.s3.amazonaws.com/'}
```

Figure 3.46: Output from the s3.create_bucket call

```
# print the merged_df to the console
print(merged_df)
```

	docname	topic	proportion	term	weight
0	romeo_and_juliet.txt	1	1.0	thou	0.445132
1	romeo_and_juliet.txt	1	1.0	thy	0.135586
2	romeo_and_juliet.txt	1	1.0	rom	0.132411
3	romeo_and_juliet.txt	1	1.0	nurse	0.091377
4	romeo_and_juliet.txt	1	1.0	love	0.090925
5	romeo_and_juliet.txt	1	1.0	you	0.053859
6	romeo_and_juliet.txt	1	1.0	romeo	0.050709
7	the_war_of_the_worlds.txt	0	1.0	martian	0.012308
8	the_war_of_the_worlds.txt	0	1.0	people	0.007995
9	the_war_of_the_worlds.txt	0	1.0	house	0.005948
10	the_war_of_the_worlds.txt	0	1.0	black	0.005939
11	the_war_of_the_worlds.txt	0	1.0	time	0.005855
12	the_war_of_the_worlds.txt	0	1.0	road	0.005638
13	the_war_of_the_worlds.txt	0	1.0	thing	0.005400
14	the_war_of_the_worlds.txt	0	1.0	stand	0.005232
15	the_war_of_the_worlds.txt	0	1.0	pit	0.004880
16	the_war_of_the_worlds.txt	0	1.0	brother	0.004484

Figure 3.47: known_structure Topic Modeling merged results

13. To verify the CSV files, navigate to S3 (reload the page if the new bucket does not appear), and the new bucket will have been created in S3. Click on the bucket to verify a successful import:

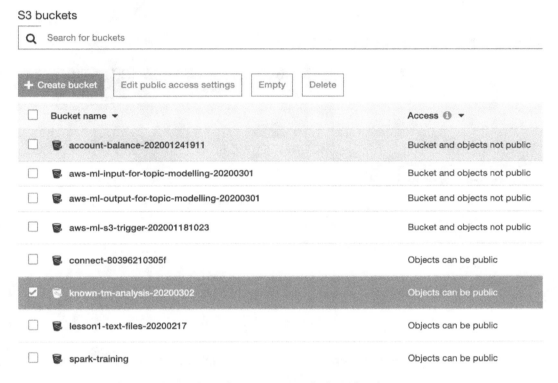

Figure 3.48: known-tm-analysis S3 bucket

There will be two CSV files in the bucket – **doc-topics.csv** and **topic-terms.csv**:

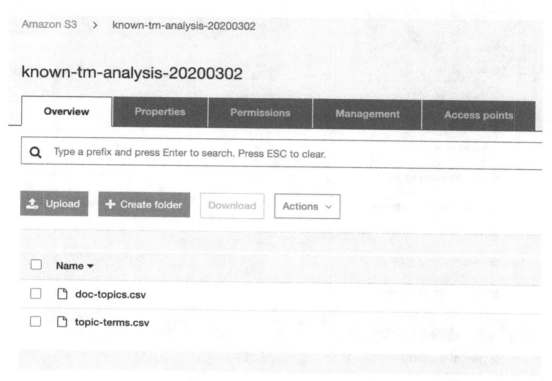

Figure 3.49: Topic Modeling results uploaded to S3

In this exercise, we learned how to use Comprehend programmatically. We programmatically uploaded two CSV files to S3, merged them on a column, and printed the output to the console.

ACTIVITY 3.01: PERFORMING TOPIC MODELING ON A SET OF DOCUMENTS WITH UNKNOWN TOPICS

In this activity, we will perform Topic Modeling on a set of documents with unknown topics. Suppose your employer wants you to build a data pipeline to analyze negative movie reviews that are in individual text files with a unique ID filename. Thus, you need to perform Topic Modeling to determine which files represent the respective topics. Overall, negative reviews represent a loss to the company, so they are prioritizing negative reviews over positive reviews. The company's end goal is to incorporate the data into a feedback chatbot application. To ensure that this happens correctly, you need a file that contains negative comments. The expected outcome for this activity will be the Topic Modeling results from the negative movie review files.

Performing Topic Modeling:

1. Navigate to the following link (or to your local directory where you have downloaded the GitHub files) to obtain the text data file that contains negative review comments: https://packt.live/38Nw4jT.

2. Create a bucket for Topic Modeling with a unique name.

3. Create a folder for Topic Modeling.

4. Import the dependencies of the Python library, such as **os** and **boto3**.

5. Mention your unique bucket name.

6. Gather all of the working directories of the local path and make them into text files.

7. Create a list for all of the text files.

8. Iterate the files and upload them to S3.

9. Create a job in Organization using Amazon Comprehend.

10. As per requirements, choose the input data. This may be **My document** or **Example document**.

11. Choose the file from the data source.

12. Apply the input format.

13. Provide the number of topics to perform the modeling.

14. Choose an IAM role and create a job.

15. Download the output file and extract the file.

16. The generated output will include the two CSV files.

Analysis of Unknown Topics:

17. Import dependences of the Python library, such as **boto3** and **pandas**.

18. Create an S3 client.

19. Create a new bucket with a unique name.

20. Create a list of CSV filenames to import.

21. Check the filename and assign it to the **obj** variable.

22. Read the **obj** variable.

23. Merge the files on the Topic column.

24. Print the merged files to the console.

This is a long activity. Yet, you were able to manage 1,000 files, upload them to S3, perform Topic Modeling using Amazon Comprehend, and then merge the results into a table that had more than 40,000 rows. In real-world situations, you will be handling thousands of documents, not just one or two. That is the reason we did this activity using Jupyter Notebook and Python.

However, this is only the first step in a multi-step automation process — an important and essential step of inferencing on the unstructured documents. While Comprehend analyzed the documents and gave us a list of topics, it is still our job to figure out what to do with them.

> **NOTE**
>
> The solution for this activity can be found on page 291.

SUMMARY

In this chapter, we learned about analyzing Topic Modeling results from AWS Comprehend. You are now able to incorporate S3 to store data and use it to perform analysis. Also, we learned how to analyze documents where we know the topics before performing Topic Modeling, as well as documents where the topic is unknown. We know that the latter requires additional analysis to determine the relevant topics.

We did not build the downstream systems that analyze the topic lists and then route the document appropriately. For example, you might have a mapping of the topics to a SharePoint folder for knowledge management or a workflow to route the files via email to appropriate persons depending on the topics detected. While the broader topic of **Robotic Process Automation** (**RPA**) is beyond the scope of this book, you have learned how to use Amazon Comprehend to implement the Topic and Theme detection steps for process automation.

Another application of what you learned in this chapter is document clustering for knowledge management. In this case, we would restrict the number of topics to 10 and then segregate the documents based on their major topics. For example, if these documents were news articles, this process would divide the articles into 10 subjects, which are easier to handle in downstream systems such as a new recommendation engine.

As you can see, Topic Modeling can be applied in a variety of applications and systems. Now you have the skills required to perform Topic Modeling using Amazon Comprehend.

In the next chapter, we will dive into the concept of chatbots and their use of natural language processing.

4

CONVERSATIONAL ARTIFICIAL INTELLIGENCE

OVERVIEW

This chapter teaches you how to design a chatbot using Amazon Lex. You will start by learning the basics of **Conversational Artificial Intelligence** and some of the best practices that go behind using that technology to design custom chatbots. Then, you will use Amazon Lex to create a custom chatbot that gets the latest stock market quotes by recognizing the intent in text. By the end of this chapter, you would be well-versed with the basics of chatbots, and the process that goes into designing them. Using this knowledge, you will be able to create your own chatbots to solve a variety of business challenges.

INTRODUCTION TO CONVERSATIONAL AI

Like the other chapters in this book, this chapter spans the conceptual aspects as well as pragmatic hands-on building – this time, the domain is Conversational AI. From many reports, it's stated that the conversational AI market will grow more than 30% per year and that the majority of customers, as well as employees, will be interacting with digital assistants.

The challenge in creating responsive, intelligent, and interactive bots is that, for machines, conversation is very hard to achieve. Let's look at the top three reasons why this is the case:

- Conversation conveys only the essential information – most of the information that's derived from a conversation is not even in the conversation. That is because humans have common sense, reasoning, shared context, knowledge, and assumptions at hand. We also overload a conversation with meanings derived from tonality, facial expressions, and even non-verbal communication, that is, via body language. These factors make conversations hard to comprehend, even though fewer words are exchanged. So, a conversational AI that looks at only the words that are exchanged probably misses 90% of the embedded information.

- It is not just a bunch of computer algorithms – the computer theoretic view is only part of a conversation exchange. We also need to incorporate linguistics, conversation implicature, and other domains. Again, this is a very hard task for computers – they can do neural networks very well, but grammar, not so much.

- Consumers are spoiled by extremely good conversation interactions. While the conversation domain is very complex, products such as Alexa, Siri, and Google Assistant are achieving huge progress in conversational AI. This adds a degree of high expectation for a business that is developing interactions based on conversational AI. Even for the most mundane tasks oriented around conversational interactions, consumers expect the sophistication of Alexa, Siri, or Google Assistant. So, your conversational systems have to cross that barrier.

This brings us nicely to the start of this chapter: Amazon Lex uses the same technology as Alexa and the Amazon Contact Center uses Amazon Connect, which means that we get to deploy their best practices. In fact, Amazon Connect was developed in order to meet the strict requirements of their customer service departments. So, we are in luck – we can leverage the state-of-the art interactions that our customers are used to in their daily lives.

INTERACTION TYPES

When we talk about conversational AI, there are two main types – task-oriented and open-ended conversation. As the name implies, task-oriented conversations function to fulfill a task (for example, query balances in an account, order an item, check the weather, check the price of a stock, and find out how many vacation days are remaining). Open-ended general conversations are broader as they cover various topics – this could be the weather, movies, financial well-being, investing, and so on. In this chapter, we will focus on task-oriented conversations.

OMNICHANNEL

Another point to keep in mind is the omnichannel aspect of conversations – conversations can be had via a chatbot with a text interface or via a **voice UI** (**VUI**); they can jump from one to the other, and with the new concept of Visual IVR, they might even be concurrent. That is why we will cover chatbots and then voice in this chapter. Multimodality is an important part of conversational AI.

In short, in this chapter, you will learn how to build a chatbot using **Amazon Lex**. We will also cover the design of conversational AIs. We will then dive into Amazon Connect and explore adding voice to our bots. First, we'll talk about how to design a chatbot. Then, we will dive into exploring the Amazon Lex service by creating a sample chatbot.

WHAT IS A CHATBOT?

A chatbot is a specific instance of a task-oriented conversational AI – the goal is to be able to hold a conversation with the user to the extent required in order to resolve customer queries, perform a task that the customer requests, or suggest a way to move forward from them.

As in normal conversation, the means by which we interact with the bot can be written text or speech. Often, the chatbots are integrated with messaging platforms, such as Slack, Facebook, Kik, and WeChat. This can also be integrated with a custom web or mobile interface.

It is easier, of course, to integrate within an existing messaging platform, since the user is likely to be familiar with the interface. Moreover, these platforms provide support to the chatbot developers with infrastructure and development tools.

Some examples of chatbots include systems for ordering products, reporting, internal communication, and scheduling.

WHAT IS NATURAL LANGUAGE UNDERSTANDING?

NLP is the general term for a set of technologies that deal with natural language. **Natural Language Understanding** (**NLU**) is a focused subset of NLP that deals with actual conversational input.

NLU can handle unstructured inputs and convert them into a structured, machine-understandable form. Words that the user enters are transformed into intents and entities, or slots. The NLU chatbot is further able to infer intents and slots from user input, which may be similar to – but not the same as – the examples it has been trained with.

CORE CONCEPTS IN A NUTSHELL

Before we can get started with building chatbots, you will need to understand some concepts first. Let's take a look at the technical meaning of the term *chatbot* and the names of the pieces that make up a chatbot and work together to deliver a conversational experience to the user.

CHATBOT

A chatbot, also known as a `bot` or artificial conversation entity, is a piece of software that can converse using natural language with the user. The goal is for the user to believe that they can interact freely and naturally with the bot, almost as if speaking with another person.

UTTERANCES

Things that the user says to the bot are called **utterances**. The bot regards the utterances from the user as input and is able to parse them into machine-recognizable formats. Some examples of utterances are as follows:

- I'd like to see the dentist.

- Can you tell me what the weather is like today?

INTENT

An **intent** is something that a user wants to do, based on the content of their utterances. An intent can be a single step (for example, get a balance) or a multi-step process (for example, booking a trip that includes booking tickets, booking a hotel, booking transportation, and so on). The bot infers the intent from the user's utterances as well as the context and supports them based on its internal set of business rules or application flow, with the result of either a change in its internal state or an action being performed. These also typically result in a response being provided to the user as feedback or information.

So, from the preceding utterance examples, a bot may infer intents such as the following:

- I'd like to see the dentist => SeeDentist.
- Can you tell me what the weather is like today? => GetWeather.

Inferring intent is a large part of what NLU platforms such as Lex do behind the scenes. A number of training examples, in the form of sentences that the user might provide, are fed to the platform, and a probabilistic model is built from these examples. This means that, in practice, the platform should be able to infer the correct intent from input, which is similar to, but not necessarily a part of, the examples that the system was trained on.

PROMPTS

When the bot requires more information from the user or is unclear about an intent, it can ask the user follow-up questions, in order to collect more data. These are called **prompts**. Prompts typically fill in slot values that are required, although your application logic may attempt to fill in values that are optional as well if you desire.

SLOT

A slot is a piece of information, or parameter, that is associated with an intent. Information can be provided within the initial user request, and Lex will be able to parse out the information and correctly assign it to the corresponding slot correctly. If this information is not provided as a part of the request, then the bot should be able to prompt the user for the information separately. Slots may be optional or required.

The type of information represented by a **slot** is known as the **slot type**. There are a number of built-in slot types within Lex that represent common types of information, such as a city or state. The following are a few examples of common slot types that are incorporated into Lex:

Slot Type	Description	Samples
AMAZON Actor	Names of actors and actresses	Tim Roth, Amy Adams
AMAZON Airline	Names of a variety of airlines	Air France, British Airways
AMAZON Animal	Names of many different animals	Blister beetle, opossum
AMAZON Artist	Full names of artists	Michael Jackson, Paul McCartney
AMAZON Color	Names of colors	Light brown, lemon

Figure 4.1: Table of slot types built into Lex

Of course, this is just a very limited subset of examples. There are many more built-in types, as well as different types for different languages.

> **NOTE**
>
> You can refer to the following link to get a full list of built-in intents and slots: https://docs.aws.amazon.com/lex/latest/dg/howitworks-builtins.html.

Most of the built-in intents and slots are documented as part of the Alexa Skills Kit documentation, with some differences for Lex, which are documented at the preceding link. Make sure to keep the link bookmarked and refer to the page regularly, since Amazon keeps updating the service and things may change.

If the type of information that you would like your bot to handle is not represented by one of these built-in types, you can define your own, along with the actual values that the slot is allowed to take.

FULFILLMENT

Note that the bot will not be able to proceed to the next step until it fills in all of the required slot values. Naturally, this does not apply to slot values that are optional.

When all of the required slots for an intent have been filled, the slot is then ready for fulfillment. At this stage, the bot is ready to execute the business logic that's required to fulfill the intent. Business logic may be any of the following actions:

- Changes in the internal state

- Running code internally

- Calling an internal or external service to get information from it

- Calling an internal or external service to post information to it

The fulfillment action can be performed with or without some feedback to the user, but as a matter of best practice, it is always better to err on the side of more feedback to the user, rather than less.

BEST PRACTICES FOR DESIGNING CONVERSATIONAL AI

Before we dive into some of the best practices, we will go over two quick points. We are only covering the most important ones and there are excellent materials and books available for a more in-depth study. Second, you will encounter situations where these tips might need to be ignored – this may include delivery pressures and resource constraints, but they may just be wrong due to advances in technologies. However, we need to be aware of the potential technical debt that can be created and document them somewhere for future reference. A few best practices are as follows:

1. When thinking about bots, think **Search**, not a single question-answer session. This requires a little thought — the bot should want to understand what the user wants and participate in an iterative collaborative interaction to facilitate what the user is looking for. For example, a user might ask "How much money do I have?" and you can resolve this to the balance in the checking account and returning an answer. However, the user might be looking to invest based on a stock tip or may be contemplating a large purchase. So, a follow-up question such as "Does this make sense? What are you thinking of?" might be a good strategy. The quintessential example is the question "What is the nearest restaurant?". For this, you can give a clinically correct answer based on distance, but the restaurant might be closed. So, volunteering more information such as "The nearest restaurant is x minutes away, but it is closed now. Are you looking for an open restaurant to go to now?" might be a good response.

2. Conversation is a continuum from simple commands and notifications to deep nested conversations, as shown in the following diagram:

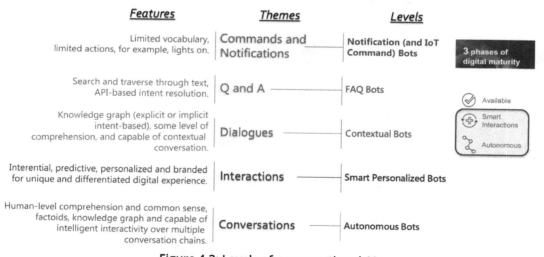

Figure 4.2: Levels of conversational AI

At the current maturity of technologies, we are at level 3 – Dialogues via Contextual Bots, which is at its very initial stages. Understanding these levels and positioning your bot service in the continuum is very important for estimating what is possible as well as the effort required, especially when it comes to the expectations of users.

3. Think of conversational AI – chatbots or voice assistants or a combination of the two, as interactions of **Available, Smart, and Autonomous.**

4. A bot (chatbot, voice, or even the Visual IVR) is an experience. This means that you need to develop a minimum lovable product — it shouldn't be too ambitious and complex with lots of features; also, it shouldn't be too narrow such that it doesn't serve a good purpose completely. Keep the steps small and show value while ensuring that they do what they need to do.

5. There is a misconception that bots do not have **visual branding**. The conversational UX, as a "transparent" user experience, still provides a good amount of visual aspects that impact the branding of your bot.

6. **Monitor, adapt and improve** — the utterance monitoring log is your friend. Use analytics extensively to ask questions about the user's learning curve — How long does it take for the user to understand the scope of the bot?

7. Visual designers spend time on aesthetics and, like them, conversation designers spend a lot of time writing content and functionality that fits the scope and audience of your bot. We do not speak the way we write, so you can't literally turn your website into a bot.

8. Think about the engagement trio, that is, **Attract-Engage-Delight**. Be very crisp and clear about your bot's purpose and core functionality. Surprise your users with **Acuity and Serendipity**.

9. Bots are very **iterative** — you have to keep on improving them as you learn, as well as the users. Build the user's trust and confidence slowly. Expose users to new functionalities continuously; a welcome area with talks about new features is a good idea. Alternatively, suggest new contextual features for original questions.

10. Think of bots as a **gateway** — an interface to services. You still need the backend to fulfill the services — queries et al.

11. Plan for learning from real users and improve your bot. Once your assistant is able to handle a few happy path stories, it is time to let it loose into the real world to steer the direction of development.

12. Follow **Grice's maxims**, viz. the maxim of quality, the maxim of quantity (as informative as required and not more), the maxim of relation (or relevance – be relevant), the maxim of manner (be brief and orderly), and the maxim of smartness.

CREATING A CUSTOM CHATBOT

In this section, we will create a custom chatbot to get stock market quotes using **Amazon Lex**. The bot will listen to our utterances for a valid intent: `GetQuote`. This signals to the bot that, for example, we had to get a stock market quote for a given stock ticker symbol, which will reside in a slot named **ticker**. The bot will then look up the quote for that ticker symbol from a freely available financial API named **IEX**, and will return the information to the user via a conversational response:

> **NOTE**
>
> A stock ticker symbol is the standard way in which stocks that are traded on an exchange, such as the New York Stock Exchange or NASDAQ, are represented. A sequence of alphabetical letters represents the company's stock that is being traded.

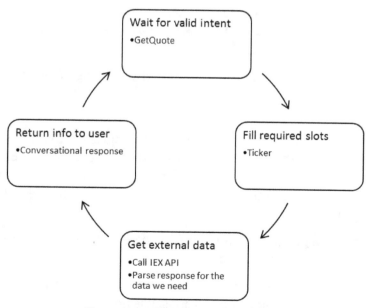

Figure 4.3: The chatbot's workflow

We can create a flowchart for this process, as shown in the following diagram. Let's go over it in further detail:

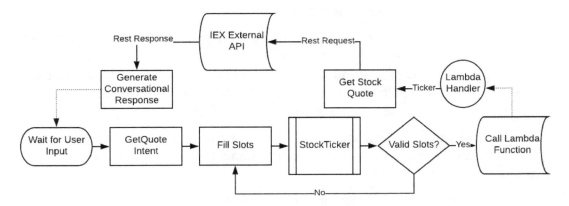

Figure 4.4: Flowchart of the chatbot's workflow

Recognizing the Intent and Filling the Slot Value

As a first step, the bot waits for the user's input in order to recognize a valid intent. When it extracts the **GetQuote** intent as the intent from an utterance posted by the user, it will then try to fill the required slots. In our case, we only have one slot of the **StockTicker** type (which is a custom slot type). The bot will issue a prompt, asking the user to provide the value of the slot and parse the utterance in response, in order to fill the slot value.

Valid slots are those that the system recognizes. If the slot value is not part of the list of permitted values, or if the system does not recognize what is entered for the slot value, it is said to be **invalid**, or **not valid**.

If the slot value is not valid, it will go back to trying to fill the slot (at least up to the number of times we have specified it should try before giving up and going back to the beginning). Once the bot has a slot filled with a valid value, it then proceeds to fulfill the intent.

Fulfilling the Intent with a Lambda Function

While the default fulfillment action is to return the intent and slot value to the user so that they can proceed to work with it within their own application, we will instead choose to set up a Lambda function on AWS that can handle the intent and run the business logic required to fulfill it.

At this point, the bot process running within Lex proceeds to call the **Lambda** function, which we have written and specified for fulfillment:

`Lambda_function.Lambda_handler`

When Lex calls out to the function for fulfillment, it sends a **JSON** payload containing various pieces of information about the sender, as well as the intent and slot value. The **Lambda_handler()** method parses the intent and slot parameter value from the **JSON** payload, and then dispatches another function call to the method, which gets the market quote value that we're looking for from the external API.

Finally, the **Lambda** function also packages the response as another **JSON** string and returns it to Lex. Lex parses the **JSON** response behind the scenes and presents the response message to the user.

We will go through all of these elements in a lot more depth in the next two exercises. In the first exercise, we will set up the new chatbot, and in the second one, we will implement our Lambda handler function so that it returns back to the user the actual value of the market price of the ticker symbol that the user asks the bot for.

A BOT THAT RECOGNIZES AN INTENT AND FILLING A SLOT

In the next exercise, you will create a custom chatbot that recognizes the intent, named **GetQuote**, in order to get a market price quote for a given ticker symbol. The bot will prompt the user for the value of the ticker symbol that the user is interested in, until the slot is filled. You will also learn how to state the intent and fill the slot in the same utterance. This chatbot can be tested via a conversational interface.

EXERCISE 4.01: CREATING A BOT THAT WILL RECOGNIZE AN INTENT AND FILL A SLOT

In this exercise, we will create and test an Amazon Lex-based bot with a custom intent and slot. The steps that have to be performed to create a bot with a custom intent and slot are as follows:

1. The first step is to navigate to **Amazon Lex service** from the Amazon Management Console. Usually, this entails going to aws.amazon.com, then **My account**, and then clicking **AWS Management Console**.

2. You can select **Services** by clicking **Amazon Lex** under **Machine Learning**.

3. The next step is to select the **Create** button. This will take you to the **bot** creation screen:

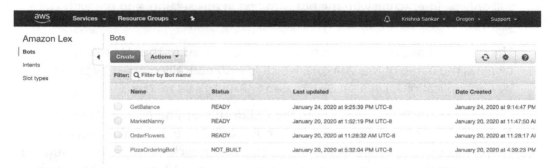

Figure 4.5: Amazon Lex Console

4. At this point, you can create a custom bot by clicking the **Custom bot** option button. This reveals the bot's details, which can be filled out, as shown in the following screenshot:

Figure 4.6: Custom bot option

5. The **bot** name field can be set to **MarketNanny**. The **Output** voice field is set to **None. This is only a text based application**, because we will only be interacting with the bot with text in this section, and not with voice just yet.

   The session timeout can be set to the default of **5 min**. The IAM role field displays the name of the IAM role, which is automatically created by Lex for use by bot applications. Let's set **Sentiment Analysis** to **Yes**.

6. Finally, the **COPPA** field pertains to the **Children's Online Privacy Protection Act**, which is what online applications must conform to. Assuming that no children under 13 are present in the class, you can click **No**. If, however, you are a student under 13 or intend to have someone under 13 use your chatbot, then you should click the **Yes** option instead.

> **NOTE**
>
> A law was passed in 1998 to protect the privacy of children under 13. It states that online sites may not collect personal information from users younger than 13 years of age without parental consent, among other provisions. You can learn more about the COPPA act at https://www.ftc.gov/enforcement/rules/rulemaking-regulatory-reform-proceedings/childrens-online-privacy-protection-rule.

7. Finally, clicking the **Create** button will create the chatbot and bring you to the bot **Editor** screen. This screen will allow you to create and define an intent for the bot, as well as a slot with a custom **Slot type**.

8. Click the **Create Intent** button to bring up an **Add Intent** pop-up dialog window:

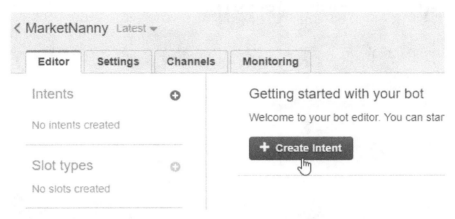

Figure 4.7: MarketNanny bot editor

9. Conversely, if you already have an intent defined, you can create a new one by clicking on the **+** sign next to the **Intents** heading in the left-hand side column on the screen.

10. The **Create Intent** window offers a few options that we can use to add an intent to the bot. The **Import intent** link allows us to import an intent from a **ZIP** file containing one or more **JSON** files with intents in the Lex format.

11. The search for existing intents allows you to reuse the intents that you may have defined or imported previously, as well as the built-in intents defined by **Amazon Lex**.

12. Click on the **Create Intent** link to get to the dialog box shown in the following step.

13. In the **Create intent** dialog box, name your new intent **GetQuote**. The bot will recognize this intent when you let it know that you are interested in a market quote. Click the **Add** button to complete this step:

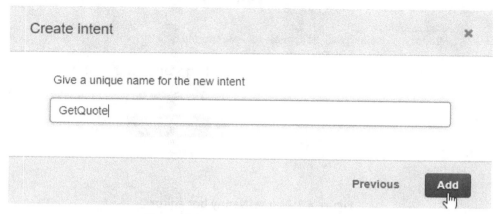

Figure 4.8: Creating an intent screen

14. You should be back at the Editor screen at this point, and you should see the **GetQuote** intent in the left toolbar portion of the screen, as shown in the following screenshot. The Editor screen also contains a number of fields that are used to define and customize the new intent.

15. The first thing to do is to fill in some sample utterances to train the **NLU** system behind Lex to recognize the utterances you will provide to the bot as signaling the **GetQuote** intent:

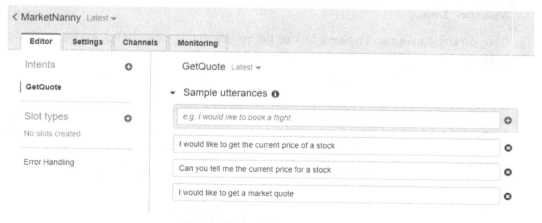

Figure 4.9: Creating the intent

16. After entering some sample utterances, click on the **Build** button near the top of the page in order to initiate the training process for the bot:

Figure 4.10: Building the bot

17. There will be a follow-up dialog box with another **Build** button, which you should also click:

Figure 4.11: Build confirmation

18. After this, you should wait until you see the **MarketNanny build was successful** message box. This might take anything from a few seconds to a couple of minutes:

Figure 4.12: Bot build is successful

You can test your new intent within the bot in the **Test bot** pane, in the upper right-hand corner of the screen.

> **NOTE**
> If the Test bot pane is not visible, you may have to click on an arrow button in order to expand it and make it visible.

19. Type *utterances* into the pane to verify that the bot is able to recognize the correct intent from the utterances:

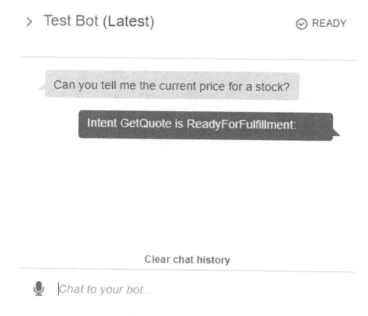

Figure 4.13: Test bot

20. You know that it has recognized the intent correctly when it returns the following response: **Intent GetQuote is ReadyForFulfillment**. Feel free to experiment with different utterances, based on your sample utterances, in order to verify that the **NLU** engine is working correctly.

    At this point, your bot doesn't do anything much apart from try to recognize the **GetQuote** intent and flag that it is ready for fulfillment. This is because we have not added any slots to the intent.

21. Your next step will be to add a slot, along with a custom slot type for the slot:

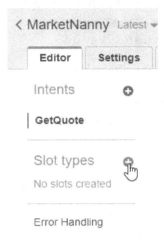

Figure 4.14: Adding a Slot

22. Adding a `slot type`. This can be done by pressing the **+** button next to slot types in the left toolbar section of the Editor screen. This brings up an **Add slot type** dialog box, where we can also choose to import the slot type as before with intents by using the Lex **JSON** structure. However, before we do that, we will click on the **Create slot type** link to create a new slot type:

Figure 4.15: Creating a slot type

23. In the **Add slot type** dialog box that pops up, enter the slot type name as **StockTicker**. This is the name of the slot type that we are defining. Optionally, you can enter a description in the **Description** field and leave the **Slot Resolution** option as **Expand Values**.

24. Under the **Value** field, enter a few **stock ticker** symbols, as shown in the following screenshot, to provide sample values for the **StockTicker** slot type. You can add some of your own, as well, if you wish:

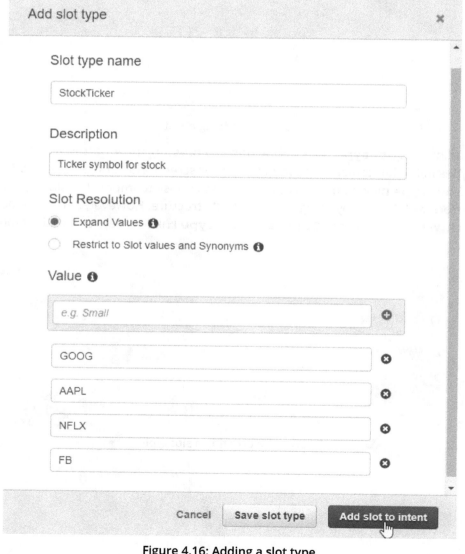

Figure 4.16: Adding a slot type

25. Finally, click on the **Add slot to intent** button in order to add the slot type to the intent, and close the dialog.

26. We could have also clicked on the **Save slot type** button and added the slot to the intent in a separate step, but using the button is the shortcut to accomplishing both actions in a single step.

27. When you close the dialog box, you will find that Lex has added a new slot entry as well, under the slots section. It is helpfully prefilled with the **StockTicker** slot type, and you should change the name of the slot to ticker under the **Name** field for the entry.

28. Click the wheel under the **Prompt** field to expand it to a new dialog box:

Figure 4.17: Editor dialog box

29. The prompts editor dialog box (named ticker Prompts or ticker Settings) allows us to enter prompts for the **Slot**, which the bot will use to store the user **inputs** and corresponding sample **utterances** that the user would typically provide to the bot while the bot is trying to elicit the information from the user with the prompts.

30. The placement of the slot value within the corresponding utterances for the slots is denoted by curly braces **{ }** and the name of the slot within the braces. In this case, since the slot is named **ticker**, it is denoted by **{ticker}** within the sample utterances.

31. Fill in the prompts (a single prompt is fine – if you add more prompts, the bot will use them randomly, for variety) in the **Prompts** section.

32. Then, add some **utterances** to the Corresponding utterances section, denoting the placement of the slot value using the placeholder token of **{ticker}** in each sample statement.

33. Leave the **Maximum number of retries** field as the default value of **2**. This means that it will try to get the value for the slot twice before signaling an **error**:

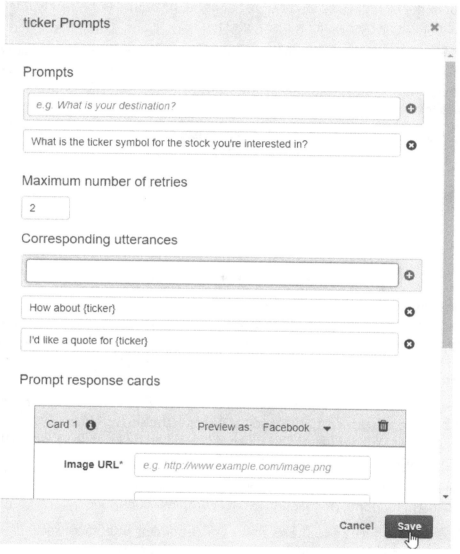

Figure 4.18: Ticker prompt screen

34. Next, click the **Save** button to save the slot prompts and the corresponding utterances definitions.

35. Finally, click the **Save Intent** button at the bottom of the screen, and then the **Build** button at the top of the screen, in order to initiate the training process with the new slot and slot type that we have defined. Wait for the completion dialog to display when the training is done:

Figure 4.19: Saving the Intent

36. Your updated intent is now ready to be tested in the **Test Bot** pane:

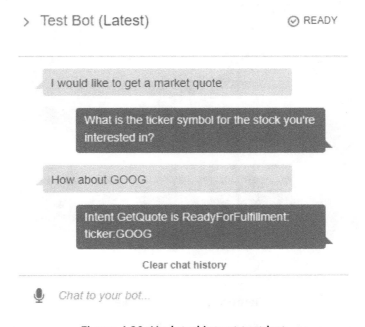

Figure 4.20: Updated intent test bot

37. At the end of the bot flow, when all the information it requires has been filled in, it returns the intent in the same format as before. However, it follows this response line with another line, containing the name and value of the slot parameter:

```
ticker:GOOG
```

38. This indicates that the ticker Slot has been filled with the **GOOG** value. So, that's great; our intent with slot is working.

39. While you're having fun playing around with the bot to verify that the intent and slot are working as they should, why not try something a little bit different? Enter some utterances that are not a part of the sample utterances that you previously entered to train the bot.

40. Type **Can I get a market quote?** as your initial utterance and see whether the bot can recognize the intent. Bear in mind that the sentence, though similar to the sample utterances, is not one of those utterances:

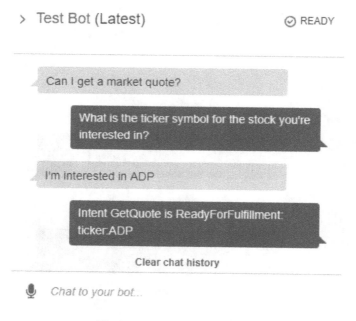

Figure 4.21: Test bot screen

As you can see from the testing shown in the preceding screenshot, not only does Lex recognize the correct intent from an utterance it has not been trained on, but it also recognizes a new symbol that it has not seen before (ADP) correctly as the value for the ticker slot.

41. Now, let's try a conversational form of a corresponding utterance for the slot prompt by inserting a random interjection as a part of the sentence, again using a new ticker symbol (**VZ**) that the bot has not been previously trained on. Again, it is correctly processed and recognized:

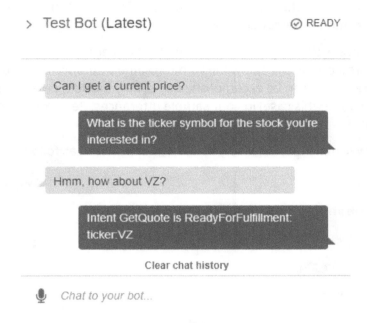

Figure 4.22: Test bot screen

Clearly, quite a bit of flexibility is possible between training and realworld examples of conversational input with an NLU engine.

NATURAL LANGUAGE UNDERSTANDING ENGINE

NLU demonstrates the advantage of using an NLU engine that has been trained on a huge set of conversational sentences and has formed a large inference model.

It is able to connect sentences that are not the same as the ones it has specifically been trained on. In fact, they can be significantly different, but the model is large enough to infer that the semantic meanings are similar.

There is one more trick that you can use to make it easier for the user to interact with your bot. You can fill the slot value with the same utterance as the one that establishes intent. This can be accomplished by simply including the slot placeholder token (`{ticker}`, in this case) in your sample utterances. Perform the following steps to do so:

1. Add a new sample utterance to your **GetQuote** intent, as follows:

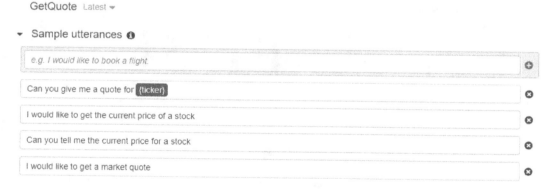

Figure 4.23: GetQuote screen

2. The **ticker** placeholder token denotes that the slot may be filled directly within the initial utterance, and that, in this case, a prompt doesn't need to be generated:

Figure 4.24: Build screen for the bot

3. Click on the **Build** button to train your updated intent as before, and then test it in the **Test Bot** pane, as follows:

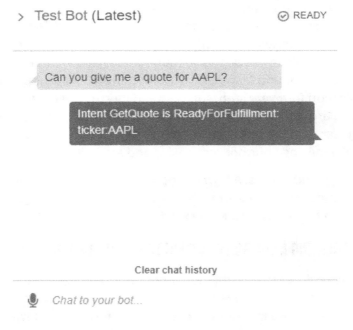

Figure 4.25: Test Bot screen

You can see that the intent is ready for fulfillment and that the slot value is filled appropriately, in a single step.

We have now gone through the process of defining a custom chatbot, complete with a custom intent, slot type, and slot, within Amazon Lex. Furthermore, we have trained and tested the bot to verify that it is able to classify the correct intent and correctly infer the slot values from conversational input to a high degree of accuracy.

Finally, we added a shortcut method to fill in the slot value directly in the initial utterance by inserting the placeholder token for the slot value in the sample utterance to train the NLU engine behind Lex.

LAMBDA FUNCTION – IMPLEMENTING BUSINESS LOGIC

You can create AWS Lambda functions that can be triggered from your Amazon Lex bot. As we discussed in *Chapter 2, Analyzing Documents and Text with Natural Language Processing*, serverless computing and Lambda functions are a good match for implementing the fulfillment and validation functions in your Lex bot. The Lambda functions integrate better and faster and scale better than returning the intent to a backend application for every step, such as validation. Once the intent has been validated and you are satisfied with the parameters, you can call a backend API to fulfill the request. You can implement simple fulfillment requests as Lambda functions, thereby making your bot responsive and scalable.

In the next exercise, you will learn how to implement the business logic behind the bot as a Lambda function in AWS and call a real-world REST API to get information that you can return to the user from an external service.

EXERCISE 4.02: CREATING A LAMBDA FUNCTION TO HANDLE CHATBOT FULFILLMENT

In this exercise, we will handle chatbot fulfillment business logic with a `Lambda` function that is created and deployed on AWS. In the previous exercise, we created a chatbot with a `GetQuote` intent and ticker slot. Perform the following steps to implement business logic:

1. Navigate to the **AWS Lambda** screen via **AWS Management Console – Services** and then **Lambda** under **Compute**.

2. If you have never used Lambda before, you should be presented with a welcome screen:

Figure 4.26: AWS Lambda start up screen

3. Click the **Create a function** button to get started.

4. Select the **Author from scratch** option on the next page:

Figure 4.27: Selecting an author

5. For the runtime, choose **Python 3.6** from the drop-down menu as you will be implementing the handler in the Python language for this exercise. In the **Name** field, fill in **marketNannyHandler**:

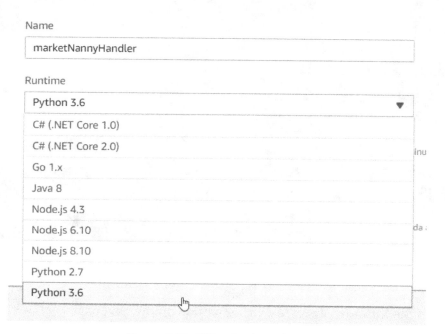

Figure 4.28: Filling in the values

6. Click **Choose or create an execution role** and choose the role field. Then, choose the **Create a new role from AWS policy templates** radio button:

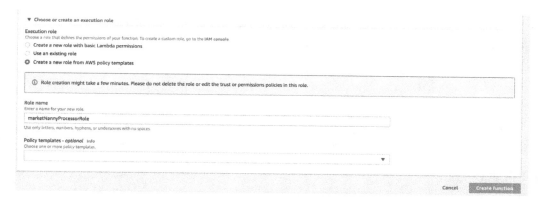

Figure 4.29: Role selection screen

7. Enter the name **marketNannyProcessorRole** in the **Role name** field. Then, click the **Create function** button to create the Lambda function in AWS. You should see a confirmation screen, as follows:

Figure 4.30: Confirmation screen

In this exercise, you learned how to handle chatbot fulfillment business logic with a Lambda function created and deployed on AWS.

IMPLEMENTING THE LAMBDA FUNCTION

Here, you will use the Lambda Function editor entirely in-line, which means that you can enter and modify the code directly without having to upload any files to AWS. The code that you enter will be executed when the Lambda function is invoked:

Figure 4.31: Function code screen

First, let's look at the structure of the Lambda function.

When you created the **marketNannyHandler** function, AWS created a folder with the same name, with a Python file named **Lambda_function.py** within the folder. This file contains a stub for the **Lambda_handler** function, which is the entry point of our Lambda function. The entry point takes two parameters as arguments:

- The event argument provides the value of the payload that is sent to the function from the calling process. It typically takes the form of a Python **dict** type, although it could also be one of **list**, **str**, **int**, **float**, or **NoneType**.

- The context argument is of the **LambdaContext** type and contains runtime information. You will not be using this parameter in this exercise.

The return value of the function can be of any type that is serializable by **JSON**. This value is returned to the calling application after serializing.

INPUT PARAMETER STRUCTURE

Now, let's take a closer look at the structure of the event argument that gets passed to the **Lambda_handler** function. If we are asking for a market quote with a ticker value of **GOOG**, the **JSON** value of the intent section within the parameter will appear as follows:

```
{
    ...
    "currentIntent":
    {
        "name": "GetQuote",
        "slots":
        {
            "ticker": "GOOG"
        },
        ...
    }
}
```

The relevant values that we are interested in for processing are **name** and the single **ticker** value within the **slots** section under **currentIntent**.

Since our **JSON** input gets converted to a Python dictionary, we can obtain these values within the Lambda function as follows:

```
event['currentIntent']['name']
event['currentIntent']['slots']['ticker']
```

IMPLEMENTING THE HIGH-LEVEL HANDLER FUNCTION

> **NOTE**
>
> The **lambda_function.py** file contains the full source code. It is available on GitHub at https://packt.live/2O8TUwA. You can refer to it as you type in the code in the Lambda editor. We have included debugging tips at the end of this example. It might be a good idea to read through the example as well as the tips first before you start implementing.

The first step in implementing our handler is to identify the intent name and call the corresponding function that implements it. The pseudocode for this looks as follows:

```python
import json

def get_quote(request):
    return "Quote handling logic goes here."

def lambda_handler(event, context):
    # TODO implement
    print(event)
    intent = event['currentIntent']['name']
    if intent == 'GetQuote':
        return get_quote(event)
    return {
        'statusCode': 200,
        'body': \
        json.dumps("Sorry, I'm not sure what you have in mind. "\
                "Please try again.")
    }
```

This is sufficiently complete to actually be tested against your chatbot at this point, if you so desire, but let's press on with the implementation.

To test, you should add a test event, as shown in the instructions that follow:

Go to **Configure test events**:

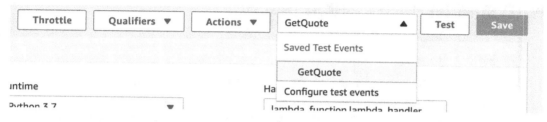

Figure 4.32: Configure test events drop-down box

Edit it as shown here. The Lambda function requires the JSON structure as shown:

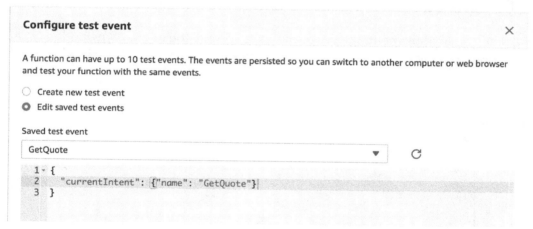

Figure 4.33: Editing the Lambda test event

IMPLEMENTING THE FUNCTION TO RETRIEVE THE MARKET QUOTE

The next step will be to implement the **get_quote** function, which does the work of actually getting the market quote information and returning it to the calling handler function:

```
def get_quote(request):
    Slots = request['currentIntent']['slots']
    ticker = Slots['ticker']
    price = call_quote_api(ticker)
```

Note that we have named the parameter request, so the **object** event to which we send the function is referred to as a request within this function. It contains the same value and structure, just renamed. Therefore, we can get the value of the ticker Slot, as mentioned previously, by getting the value of the item with the **ticker** key under it by using the following code:

```
request['currentIntent']['Slots']
```

Then, we call the **call_quote_api ()** function to retrieve the value of the market quote for the value of the ticker item. We haven't implemented **call_quote_api ()** yet, so let's do this next.

We will implement the **call_quote_api** function as follows:

```
def call_quote_api(ticker):
    response = \
      urlopen('https://www.alphavantage.co/query?'\
            'function=GLOBAL_QUOTE&symbol={}'\
            '&apikey=3WIN88G0AVG7RZPX'.format(ticker))
    response = json.load(response)
    ''' Sample Response: \
        {'Global Quote': {'01. symbol': 'AAPL', \
                          '02. open': '316.2700', \
                          '03. high': '318.7400', \
                          '04. low': '315.0000', \
                          '05. price': '318.7300', \
                          '06. volume': '33454635', \
                          '07. latest trading day': '2020-01-17', \
                          '08. previous close': '315.2400', \
                          '09. change': '3.4900', \
                          '10. change percent': '1.1071%'}} '''
    return response['Global Quote']["05. price"]
```

Here, ticker is the value of the ticker parameter (in this specific example, it would be **GOOG**). We use Alpha Vantage, which provides a static endpoint on the internet at https://www.alphavantage.co/, to retrieve a quote. We have also captured a sample response as an example. You should get your own API key.

Since it is implemented as a simple **GET** request, with the ticker parameter embedded within the **URL**, with the API key, we can simply use the built-in **urlopen** method in the **urllib.request** module (which we will have to remember to import) to receive a response from the URL with the ticker embedded within it.

Since the response is also in **JSON** format, we need to import **json module** and load the response using the **json.load** function. The only field we are interested in within the response is **05. price**, so we return that as the return value from our function.

RETURNING THE INFORMATION TO THE CALLING APP (THE CHATBOT)

Now that we have the market quote value, we can return it to our calling application, which is the chatbot that we implemented. We have to do a couple of small things, however, to return this value. First, we need to format it as a conversational response, as shown in the following string:

```
message = 'The last price (delayed) of ticker {} was {}'\
          .format(ticker, price)
```

This should let the chatbot display the following message:

```
The last price (delayed) of ticker GOOG was 1107.32
```

There is one final step, which is to construct an **Amazon Lex JSON** return format that contains our message and a couple of other items of information. We will use the **close** helper function to do this:

```
return close(message)
```

Our **close** function takes a single parameter, which is the string that we wish to return to the chatbot (in this case, this is the value of the message variable). It generates a **JSON** wrapper around the content, which conforms to the structure that our Lex-based bot is expecting and from which it can extract the content and deliver it to the user. The structure of the wrapper is not important at this stage, but if you are curious, you can look at the implementation of the **close** function. As we mentioned earlier, the **lambda-function.py** file contains the full source code for the lambda function. It is available in GitHub at https://packt.live/2O8TUwA.

The code window should look as follows:

```
import json
from urllib.request import urlopen

def get_quote(request):
    Slots = request['currentIntent']['slots']
    ticker = Slots['ticker']
    price = call_quote_api(ticker)
    message = 'The last price of ticker {} was {}'.format(ticker, price)
    return close(message)

def call_quote_api(ticker):
    response = urlopen('https://www.alphavantage.co/query?function=GLOBAL_QUOTE&symbol={}&apikey=3WIN48G0AVG7RZPX'.format(ticker))
    response = json.load(response)
    ''' Sample Response:
    {'Global Quote': {'01. symbol': 'AAPL', '02. open': '316.2700', '03. high': '318.7400', '04. low': '315.0000', '05. price': '318.7300',
    '06. volume': '33454635', '07. latest trading day': '2020-01-17', '08. previous close': '315.2400', '09. change': '3.4900',
    '10. change percent': '1.1071%'}} '''
    return response['Global Quote']['05. price']

def lambda_handler(event, context):
    intent = event['currentIntent']['name']
    if intent == 'GetQuote':
        return get_quote(event)
    return "Sorry, I'm not sure what you have in mind.  Please try again."

def close(message):
    return {
        'sessionAttributes': {},
        'dialogAction': {
            'type': 'Close',
            'fulfillmentState': 'Fulfilled',
            'message': {
                'contentType': 'PlainText',
                'content': message
            }
        }
    }
```

Figure 4.34: Code window

CONNECTING TO THE CHATBOT

At this point, the only task remaining is to connect the Lambda function to the chatbot and test it. Perform the following steps to do so:

1. Navigate back to the Amazon Lex dashboard and select the **MarketNanny** bot:

Figure 4.35: Connecting to the bot

2. Then, scroll down to the **Fulfillment** section and select the **AWS Lambda function** option. Next, select the **marketNannyHandler** function from the **Lambda function** drop-down menu and leave **Version or alias** as the default value of **Latest**:

Figure 4.36: Confirmation prompt

3. Rebuild the intent by clicking on the **Build** buttons, and test the chatbot together with the Lambda handler in the Test Chatbot pane:

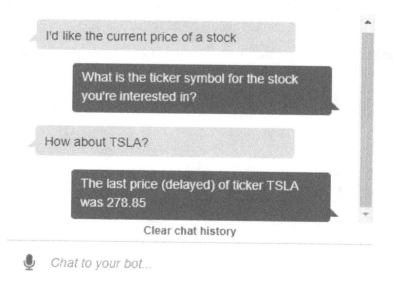

Figure 4.37: Chatbot updated

4. The following screenshot shows the interaction with the bot to find out the current price of AAPL:

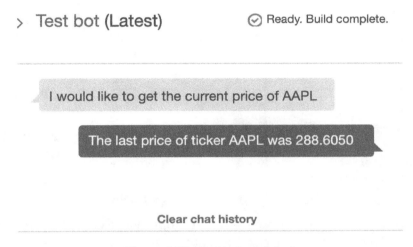

Figure 4.38: Chatbot updated

DEBUGGING TIPS

Here are some debugging tips that will help you:

1. The logs from the monitoring tab on the Lambda pane are very useful:

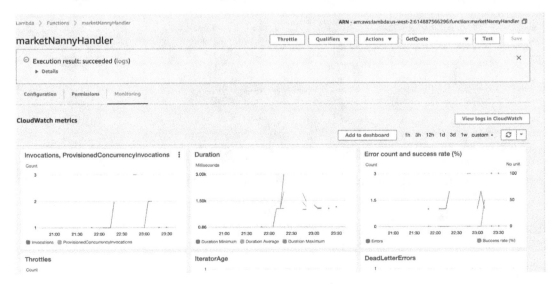

Figure 4.39: CloudWatch metrics

2. The logs are collected at the **CloudWatch** Logs insight:

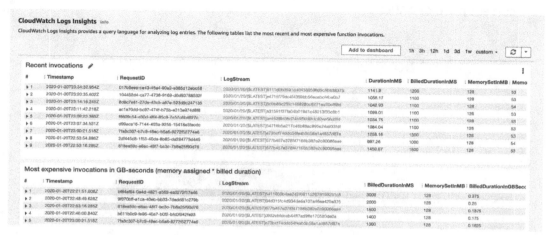

Figure 4.40: CloudWatch logs insights

3. As you can see, this took us quite a few attempts. we used print statements inside the Lambda that print out the contents. A couple of sample logs can be seen in the following screenshot, along with the printout of the request JSON from the Lex bot, as well as the http response from the stock quote API. This makes it easy to see where the various information pieces are nested:

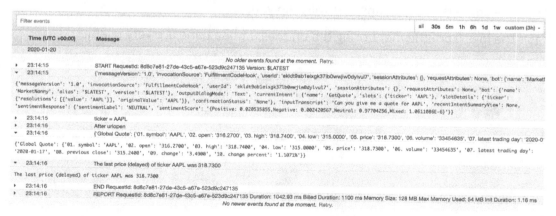

Figure 4.41: CloudWatch logs with output from print statements

4. You can see an error that I encountered in the following screenshot. The stock API returns the values in a nested JSON, so you have to use the **response ['Global Quote'] ["05. price"]**, and not just the response **["05. price"]**:

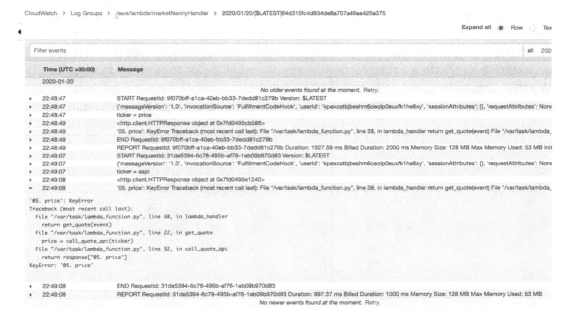

Figure 4.42: CloudWatch logs showing KeyError

5. The Lambda logs are extremely useful and capture the errors. Develop incrementally and test every change. If there are too many moving parts or changes, debugging will be difficult.

6. It will take a little time to get used to the various consoles of the AWS ecosystem, understand the permissions, and so on, but if you persist, you will reap the benefits.

SUMMARY

We started this chapter with an introduction to Conversational Artificial Intelligence and learned how different aspects of this technology help us build a good, useful chatbot. We also learned some core concepts, such as utterances, intents, plots, and so on, that serve as the foundation for building a chatbot. Later, right before we built our first chatbot, we discussed some best practices that come in handy while designing Conversational AI. Equipped with this knowledge, we performed an exercise to create a bot to recognize intent and fill a slot to retrieve stock prices. We then created a Lambda function in AWS to help us implement the business logic behind the bot. In the next chapter, we will learn how to use speech with chatbots.

5

USING SPEECH WITH THE CHATBOT

OVERVIEW

In this chapter, we will learn about the basics of Amazon Connect. We'll look at how to use Amazon Connect, Lex, and Lambda to interact with a chatbot using voice. We will also demonstrate how you can create a personal call center using Amazon Connect. We'll learn how to obtain a free phone number for a personal call center. We will also learn about using Amazon Lex chatbots with Amazon Connect with contact flows and different templates. By the end of this chapter, you will be able to connect the call center to your Lex chatbot.

AMAZON CONNECT BASICS

Amazon Connect is a service from AWS (Amazon Web Services) that allows you to create cloud-based contact centers. This means that people can use a telephone number to contact the service and have conversations with bots or human representatives. In this chapter, we are primarily interested in automating interaction using the chatbot that we built in the previous chapter.

Some key features of Amazon Connect are as follows:

- It is easy to set up and use Connect with workflows that are defined using a graphical editor.

- There is no infrastructure to deploy or manage, so contact centers can be scaled up and down quickly.

- It is a **pay-as-you-go service**, so there is no setup or monthly fees. We will be using the free tier, so we should not have to pay anything to use the service. For commercial usage, charges are based on rates per minute.

- Amazon Connect is deployed in 42 availability zones and within 16 geographic regions.

> ### DISCLAIMER
>
> Unfortunately, Amazon Connect is not available for use in all regions. When setting up Amazon Connect, a local telephone number is provided, and at the time of writing this book (April 2020), this service is only available in the US, UK, Australia, Japan, Germany, and Singapore. The good news is that Amazon is constantly expanding its services. So, by the time you read this book, Amazon Connect might be available where you are. The region table at https://aws.amazon.com/about-aws/global-infrastructure/regional-product-services/.

FREE TIER INFORMATION

Throughout this book, you will only need to use the free tier of the services presented. However, it is important to be aware of the limits of free usage and the pricing of other tiers.

You should refer to the official web page at https://aws.amazon.com/connect/. A single contact center may include a set amount of Amazon Connect service usage and a direct-dial number including 60 minutes of inbound and outbound calls. This can change depending on your regional settings.

> **NOTE**
>
> You shouldn't need to go beyond the services provided by the free tier for this book. If you go beyond the limits of the free tier, you will be charged by Amazon according to the rates published at https://aws.amazon.com/connect/pricing/.

INTERACTING WITH THE CHATBOT

Using Connect to interact with your chatbot by voice requires you to first set up a call center within Connect. The call center receives a free local phone number (or a US toll-free number in the United States). This number can be connected to an **Amazon Lex** chatbot; in our case, this will be the chatbot that we have already created (`MarketNanny`). The chatbot uses the Lambda serverless service to get data from an external API and relay it back to the user on the phone:

Reference for image: https://aws.amazon.com/blogs/aws/new-amazon-connect-and-amazon-lex-integration/

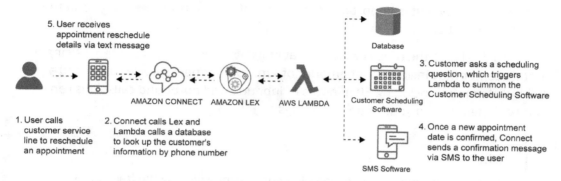

Figure 5.1: A sample voice-based chatbot application using Amazon Connect, Lex, and Lambda

TALKING TO YOUR CHATBOT THROUGH A CALL CENTER USING AMAZON CONNECT

Using Amazon Connect, we can create a call center application that will allow us to connect to the chatbot that we built in the preceding *Chapter 4, Conversational Artificial Intelligence* (**MarketNanny**), using voice commands rather than a textbox.

To create an Amazon Connect call center, you need to make an Amazon Connect instance. Each example contains the majority of the assets and settings identified with your call center instance. You can oversee the settings for your scenario from the Amazon Connect support page.

You can make various instances; however, each example is limited to solely inside the AWS area in which it has been created. The settings, clients, measurements, and details are not shared across Amazon Connect instances.

> **NOTE**
>
> It is mandatory to have an AWS account. Amazon Lex services can be accessed through the Console page.

EXERCISE 5.01: CREATING A PERSONAL CALL CENTER

In this exercise, we will create a personal call center using Amazon Connect, and we will connect your **MarketNanny** chatbot to it. Note that we have already discussed the Amazon Connect service earlier in this chapter:

1. For the first step, navigate to the Amazon Connect service page in the AWS Console. You can select the link to navigate to, or you can go directly to https://console.aws.amazon.com/connect:

Amazon Connect

makes it easy for you to set up and manage a customer contact center and provide reliable customer engag
nect you can deploy a customer contact center with just a few clicks in the AWS management console, on
anywhere, and quickly begin to engage with your customers.

Get started

Get started guide

ect   Test drive   Onboard agents, s

tact Center up and   Answer some test calls and check out Amazon Connect's Contact Control Panel,
                                         metrics, and administrator tools.

Amazon Connect documentation and support

Get started guide | Amazon Connect documentation | Support

Figure 5.2: The Amazon Connect welcome screen

2. Click the **Get started** button to create a new **Call Center** instance. In the screen that follows, keep the default option of **Store users within Amazon Connect**, and then enter a name for your application. The name is unique across AWS and duplicates are not allowed, so you may have to experiment a bit or add numbers to the name until you get a name that is unique.

3. Click on the **Next step** button when you are done:

Amazon Connect resource configuration

Get up and running in a few easy steps

Step 1: Identity management	Identity management
Step 2: Administrator	Amazon Connect can be configured to manage your users directly or to leverage an existing directory. This cannot be changed once your instance is created. Learn more
Step 3: Telephony options	
Step 4: Data storage	⦿ Store users within Amazon Connect
Step 5: Review and create	Users will be created and managed by you within Amazon Connect. Note: you will not be able to share users with other applications.

Access URL   https:// | jarvis42 | .awsapps.com/connect/home ⓘ

○ Link to an existing directory
Amazon Connect will leverage an existing directory. You create users within the directory and then add and configure them within Amazon Connect. Note: you can only associate a directory with a single Amazon Connect instance. Learn more

○ SAML 2.0-based authentication
AWS supports identity federation with SAML 2.0 (Security Assertion Markup Language 2.0), an open standard that many identity providers (IdPs) use. This feature enables federated single sign-on (SSO), so users can log into the AWS Management Console or call the AWS APIs without you having to create an IAM user for everyone in your organization. Learn more

Cancel   Previous   Next step

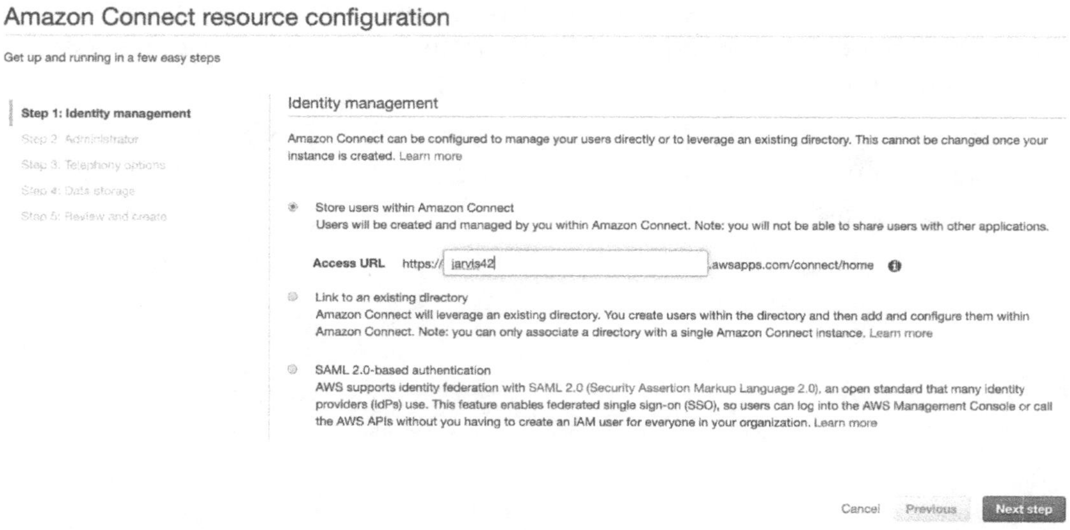

Figure 5.3: Step 1 of the Amazon Connect resource configuration screen

4. In the next step, add the information for a new admin, setting the email address to your email address. Again, click the **Next step** button when you are done:

Amazon Connect resource configuration

Get up and running in a few easy steps

Step 1: Identity management	Create an Administrator
Step 2: Administrator	Specify an administrator for this instance of Amazon Connect; this could be you or someone else. You will be able to manage permissions and add more users from within Amazon Connect.
Step 3: Telephony options	
Step 4: Data storage	⦿ Add a new admin
Step 5: Review and create	

First Name | John
Last Name | Smith
Username | jsmith
Password | ••••••••
Password (verify) | ••••••••
Email Address | jsmith@mydomain.com

☐ Skip this

Cancel   Previous   Next step

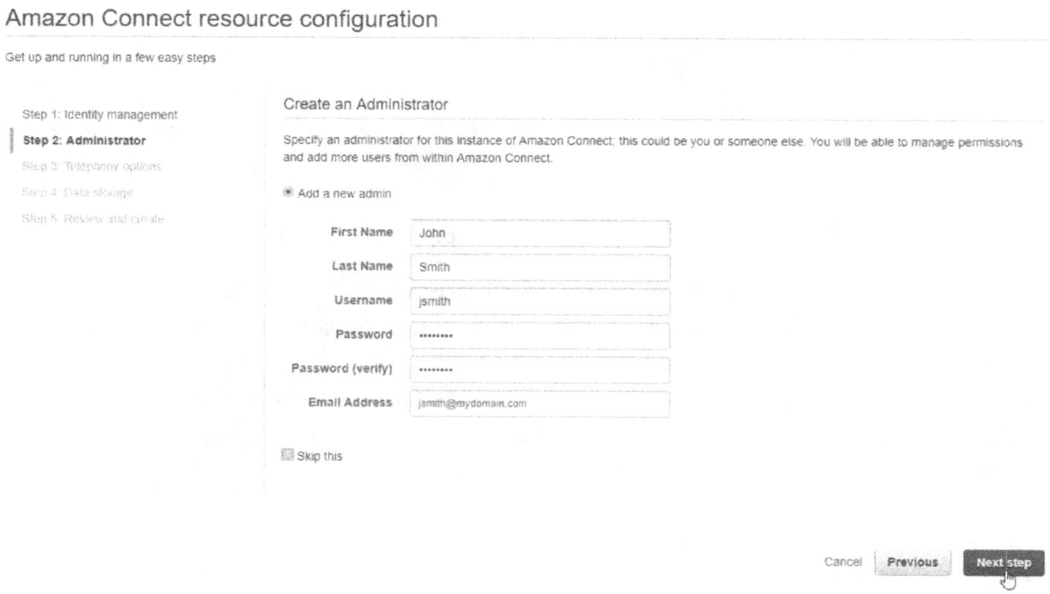

Figure 5.4: Step 2 of the Amazon Connect resource configuration screen

5. In the next step, leave the **Incoming calls** checkbox checked, and uncheck the **Outbound calls** checkbox:

> **NOTE**
>
> In this case, we have no requirement for our bot to initiate a call to anyone, but we do want it to be able to receive calls.

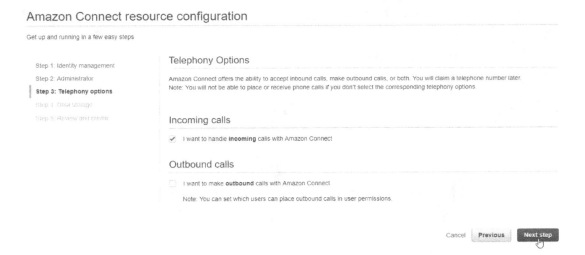

Amazon Connect resource configuration

Get up and running in a few easy steps

Step 1: Identity management
Step 2: Administrator
Step 3: Telephony options
Step 4: Data storage
Step 5: Review and create

Telephony Options

Amazon Connect offers the ability to accept inbound calls, make outbound calls, or both. You will claim a telephone number later.
Note: You will not be able to place or receive phone calls if you don't select the corresponding telephony options.

Incoming calls

☑ I want to handle **incoming** calls with Amazon Connect

Outbound calls

☐ I want to make **outbound** calls with Amazon Connect

Note: You can set which users can place outbound calls in user permissions.

Cancel   Previous   Next step

Figure 5.5: Step 3 of the Amazon Connect resource configuration screen

6. Click the **Next step** button when you are done.

7. Next, you will be presented with an informational screen, letting you know that you are granting the call center application permissions to read and write data to or from your S3 bucket, to encrypt or decrypt data, and to read and write to and from the **CloudWatch** logs.

8. It will also show you the location of the **S3 buckets** where your **data** and Contact flow logs will be stored. Click **Next step**.

> **NOTE**
>
> Note that there is a **Customize settings** link to further customize these locations, but we will not use this now.

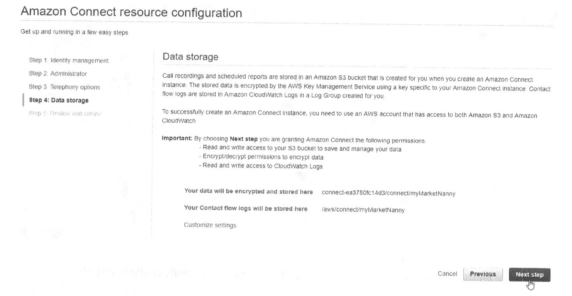

Figure 5.6: Step 4 of the Amazon Connect resource configuration screen

9. This will bring you to the final screen, which will provide you with a review of all of the settings for your Contact center application:

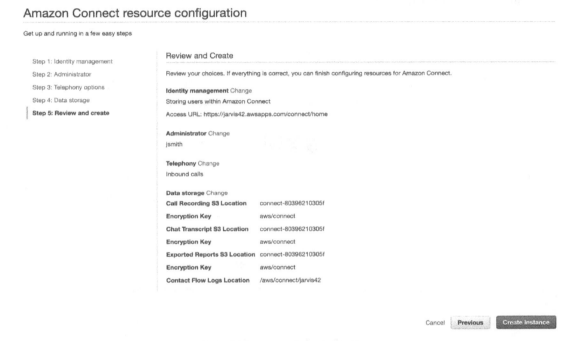

Figure 5.7: Step 5 of the Amazon Connect resource configuration screen

10. Now, click the **Create instance** button to create your application. You should see a dialog window:

Figure 5.8: Setting up Amazon Connect

11. In a minute or two, it will complete the setup process and take you to a **Success!** screen, where you can click on the **Get started** button to go directly to your application:

Success!

Your Amazon Connect has been created.
Now you can begin to choose phone numbers, accept calls, and engage with your customers.

Users can access Amazon Connect at: https://myMarketNanny.awsapps.com/...
Please allow up to 15 minutes for the login page to become accessible.

Configure additional resources such as data streaming and CRM integrations within Amazon Connect AWS console.

Figure 5.9: The Success! screen

> **NOTE**
>
> It may take up to 15 minutes for the application to get set up. So, if you do not succeed in getting to the application page initially, have some patience and try again every once in a while, until it does succeed.

Typically, it should not take very long, and generally, the application page will be accessible right away.

So, you have created a customer contact center, in minutes, that would previously take anywhere between 3 to 6 months. While the creation interface looked very simple, it has masked all the complexity of the underlying infrastructure. This is the power of Amazon AWS Connect.

As you will see in the next exercise, you can actually get a physical phone number in order to call your very own contact center.

EXERCISE 5.02: OBTAINING A FREE PHONE NUMBER FOR YOUR CALL CENTER

In this exercise, we will acquire a free number for our custom call center. The free telephone number can be acquired by the free tier services provided by Amazon Connect. The following are the steps to perform to obtain a free number:

1. The welcome screen for your personal call center should be visible. If it is not, you can access it easily at the URL displayed on the previous screen, right before you click the **Get Started** button:

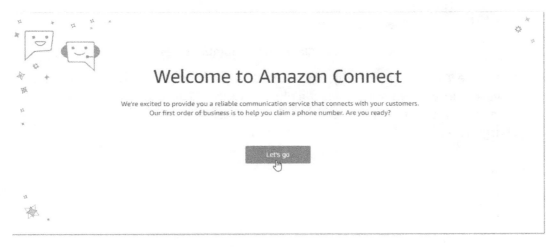

Figure 5.10: The Amazon Connect welcome screen

2. At this point, you can click the **Let's go** button in order to initiate the first step, which is to claim a local phone number for your call center application. On this screen, you can select your country:

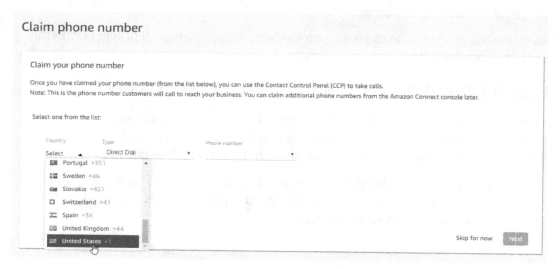

Figure 5.11: The Claim phone number screen

3. Leave the **Type** as the default (**Direct Dial**) option. Then, from the **Phone number** drop-down menu, select a phone number. This should be, in most cases, a number that is local to you. If you choose one that is not, you may be charged based on the cost to dial the number:

Figure 5.12: Phone number selection

4. Click the **Next** button when you are done. This will allow you to test your new phone number by dialing it. You should hear a message that starts with *Hello, thanks for calling*

5. This will be followed by a list of options; you can try them for yourself to see what they do when you have some time. For now, click the **Continue** button, which will bring you to the **Dashboard** screen:

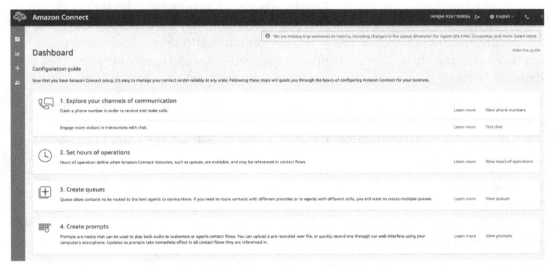

Figure 5.13: The Amazon Connect Dashboard screen

You now have a working call center application on Amazon Connect.

USING AMAZON LEX CHATBOTS WITH AMAZON CONNECT

With Amazon Lex, you can create intelligent chatbots. This can be done by converting contact flows into regular conversations. The Amazon Connect service compliments the previously mentioned feature by enabling the creation of a contact center (cloud-based) along with the generation of dynamic flows. This delivers a personalized experience to your callers. Additionally, **Dual-tone multi-frequency** (DTMF) digits entered by callers during a call can be easily recognized by these chatbots.

With both Amazon Lex and Amazon Connect working in sync, the chatbot can gauge the caller's intent. Furthermore, you can use the AWS Lambda function along with your chatbot to process caller requests, provide information to callers, and query applications. These chatbots are capable of maintaining context by intelligently managing dialogue and reviewing replies based on caller responses on the fly.

In the next section, we will connect your *MarketNanny* chatbot to the call center. This is so that the user can speak into the phone and have their speech automatically converted into a text utterance that will be sent to the Lex chatbot.

UNDERSTANDING CONTACT FLOWS

A **contact flow** defines each step of the experience that customers have when they interact with your call center. Amazon connect has templates for you to create simple and efficient contact flows. You can also create new contact flows using the visual contact flow editor. The editor is a very intuitive and simple tool to create contact flows. But do not let the simplicity fool you—you can create very complex and detailed flows.

The contact flow designer screen provides a way to create contact flows in a drag and drop environment. Contact flows are made of nodes that can be accessed in the left panel, within the designer area (under the **Show additional flow information** link).

Nodes are categorized under the **Interact**, **Set**, **Branch**, **Integrate**, and **Terminate/Transfer** categories. Nodes in each category can be hidden or revealed by clicking on the drop-down icon next to the section name. You will explore some of the nodes that are available by creating the contact flow for your chatbot.

Contact flows are a way for users (typically, supervisors) to progressively refresh the settings for each call entering the framework and ensure that the users hear customized and pertinent choices. While there are a number of predesigned contact flows, you will create a new one for your **MarketNanny** chatbot.

CONTACT FLOW TEMPLATES

The following lists the various templates that are available. Just for information, the complete list is shown in the following screenshot. The ones you create will also show up in the template list. You can click each flow to get more details and learn from them:

Name	Type	Description	Status
Default agent hold	Agent hold	Audio played for the agent when on hold	Published
Default agent transfer	Transfer to agent	Default flow to transfer to an agent.	Published
Default agent whisper	Agent whisper	Default whisper played to the agent.	Published
Default customer hold	Customer hold	Default audio the customer hears while on hold.	Published
Default customer queue	Customer queue	Default audio played when a customer is waiting in queue.	Published
Default customer whisper	Customer whisper	Default whisper played to the customer	Published
Default outbound	Outbound whisper	Default flow for outbound calls.	Published
Default queue transfer	Transfer to queue	Default flow used to transfer to a queue.	Published
GetBalance	Contact flow		Published
MarketNannyFlo	Contact flow		Published
Sample AB test	Contact flow	Performs A/B call distribution	Published
Sample disconnect flow	Contact flow	Enables customer to transfer to another flow even after the first agent has disc…	Published
Sample inbound flow (first contact e…	Contact flow	First contact experience	Published
Sample interruptible queue flow wit…	Customer queue	Plays looping audio and offers a callback to the customer every thirty seconds	Published
Sample Lambda integration	Contact flow	Invokes a lambda function to determine information about the user.	Published
Sample note for screenpop	Contact flow	Screenpop is a Contact control pannel feature that allows loading a web page o…	Published
Sample queue configurations flow	Contact flow	Puts a customer in queue and gives them the option to be first in queue, last in …	Published
Sample queue customer	Contact flow	Places the customer in a queue.	Published
Sample recording behavior	Contact flow	Sample flow to enable recording behavior	Published
Sample secure input with agent	Transfer to queue	Puts agent on hold, enabling the customer to enter digits in private. In a real w…	Published
Sample secure input with no agent	Contact flow	Enables the customer to enter digits in private. In a real world implementation, …	Published

Rows

Figure 5.14: Amazon Connect contact flow templates

In the next topic, we will set up your call center so that it can accept incoming calls, connect your **MarketNanny** chatbot to the call center so that the user can speak into the phone, and have the user's speech automatically converted into a text utterance that will be sent to the Lex chatbot.

The chatbot then continues with processing the utterance, finding the intent and slots, and fulfilling the user request through the Lambda function that you set up in the preceding section.

To connect your call center instance with your chatbot, you will need to go back to the main screen and navigate to the Connect dashboard, as shown in the following screenshot.

Select **Services** > **Customer Engagement** > **Amazon Connect**:

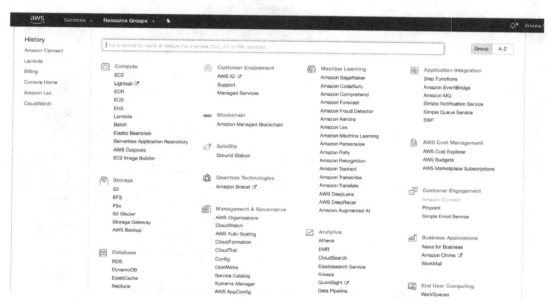

Figure 5.15: Selecting Amazon Connect from the AWS Management Console

Select your Connect instance:

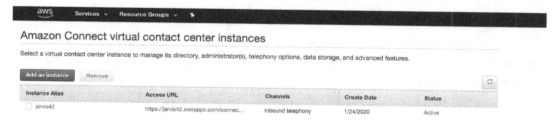

Figure 5.16: Amazon Connect console

EXERCISE 5.03: CONNECTING THE CALL CENTER TO YOUR LEX CHATBOT

In this exercise, you will set up your call center so that it can accept incoming calls, and so that you can connect your **MarketNanny** chatbot to the call center. The following are the steps to complete:

1. From the Amazon Management Console, navigate via **Services** to **Amazon Connect** under **Customer Engagement**. You will see the **Amazon Connect** virtual contact center instances screen; click your instance. Choose **Contact flows** from the left toolbar. Click **Bot**; then click the drop-down menu to find the **MarketNanny** bot entry, select it, and then select the **Add Lex Bot** link to save it:

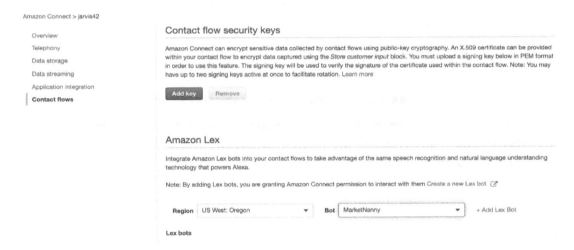

Figure 5.17: The Contact flow screen with the Lex bot's selection drop-down

The following screenshot shows **MarketNanny** added to the Lex bot:

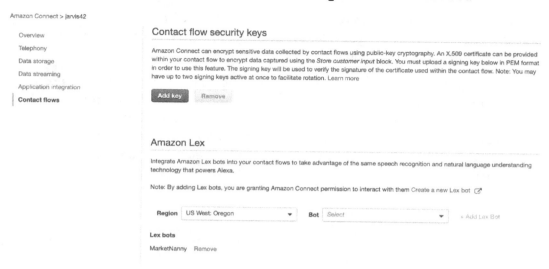

Figure 5.18: Showing the Lex bot under Lex bots

2. Now, you can navigate back to the **Dashboard** screen by selecting the **Overview** link and clicking on the **Login URL** button and then enter the credentials for your Amazon Connect instance. The **Dashboard** screen will open in a new browser tab:

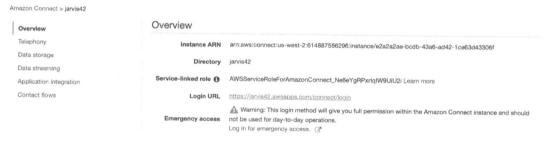

Figure 5.19: The Login overview screen

3. On the **Dashboard** screen, select the **View Contact Flows** icon under **5. Create contact flows**:

Figure 5.20: Selecting routing and contact flows from the Left Panel screen

4. This will bring you to a **Contact flows** screen that is similar to the one we were just on previously. This is the **Contact flow designer** screen, where you can design and create new contact flows:

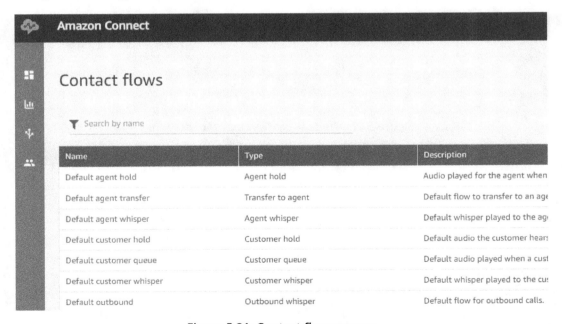

Figure 5.21: Contact flows screen

5. Click the **Create contact flow** button in the upper-right corner of the page to create a new contact flow. Name it **MarketNannyFlow**:

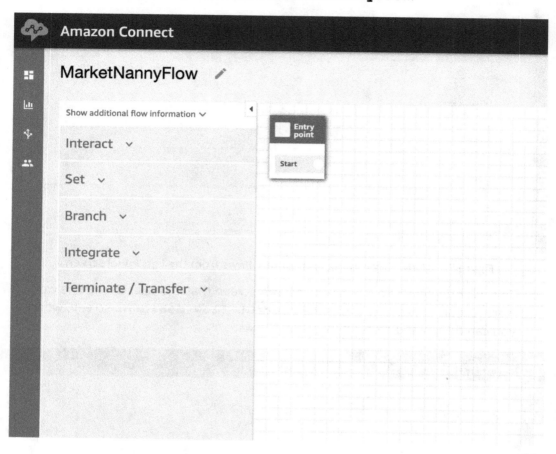

Figure 5.22: The Contact flow designer screen

6. The first node that you will use for your chatbot's contact flow is the **Set voice** node. You can find it under the **Set** category and drag it to the graphical view to the right of the **Entry point** node, which is already in the view.

7. Connect the output of the **Entry point** node to the input of the **Set voice** node by clicking the output circle and dragging it, with your mouse, to the input bump on the left of the **Set voice** node:

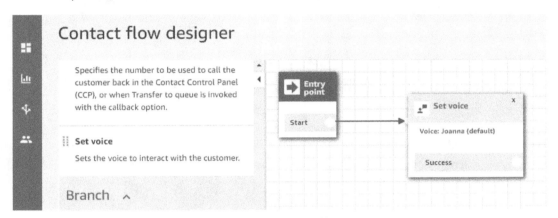

Figure 5.23: The Contact flow designer screen with the Set voice node

8. Next, you can set the *properties of the node* by clicking at the top of the node. This will bring up a panel on the right-hand side of the screen, with the relevant properties that you can set.

9. For this component, it provides **Language** and **Voice** properties, both of which can be set by selecting a value from the dropdown under each property label. You can set the values that are appropriate to your scenario, and then click the **Save** button:

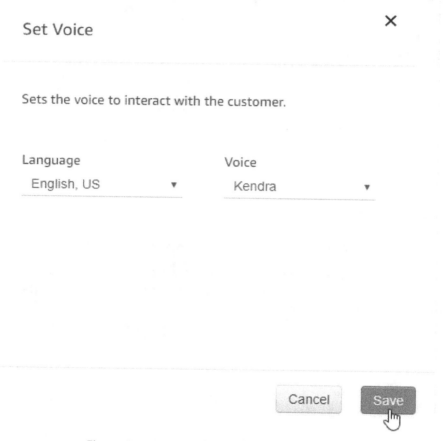

Figure 5.24: Properties for the Set Voice node

10. The next node to add is the **Get customer input** node, which you will find under the **Interact** tab. You can connect the input of this node to the output of the **Set voice** node, just like when you connected **Set voice** to the **Entry point** node:

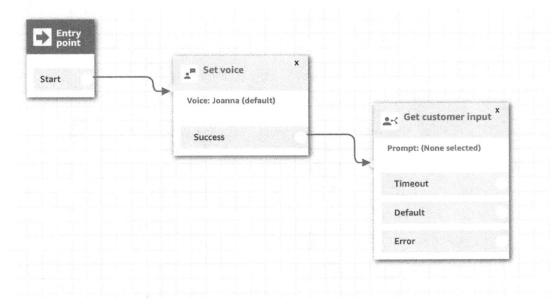

Figure 5.25: Adding the Get customer input node

11. First, click on the properties icon on the **Get customer input** block, select the **Text to speech (Ad hoc)** option, and then click **Enter text** under it. In the input textbox, enter a greeting such as the following:

```
Hi this is the Market Nanny chatbot. How may I help you today?
```

> **NOTE**
>
> Feel free to replace this with some other text that may be more interesting or appropriate for you.

12. This is the text that will be converted into a voice greeting when the **Contact center** application first answers the phone:

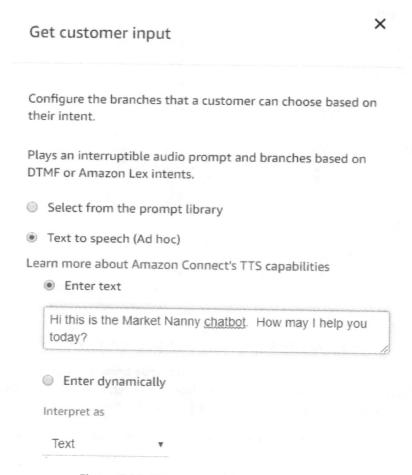

Figure 5.26: Get customer input properties

13. Next, scroll down the settings pane and select the **Amazon Lex** subsection, not the **DTMF** section. Here, you will be able to configure the node to work with your chatbot.

> **NOTE**
>
> The **DTMF** section provides a way to specify interactions with the caller via button presses on their phone, but we will not cover that here. We are much more interested in having our chatbot interact with the caller.

14. In this section, under **Lex bot**, you can enter the name and alias for your chatbot. Under **Name**, enter **MarketNanny**, and under **Alias**, enter **$LATEST**:

15. **$LATEST** is a system-defined alias, which specifies that the contact center will always access the most recently published version of the **MarketNanny** chatbot:

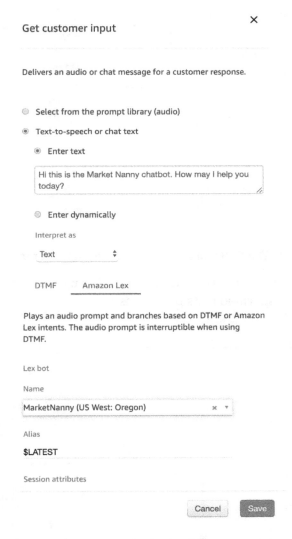

Figure 5.27: Amazon Lex properties in the Get customer input properties

16. Finally, specify the **GetQuote** intent under the **Intents** section. Since that is the only intent we are currently working with, click on the **Save** button:

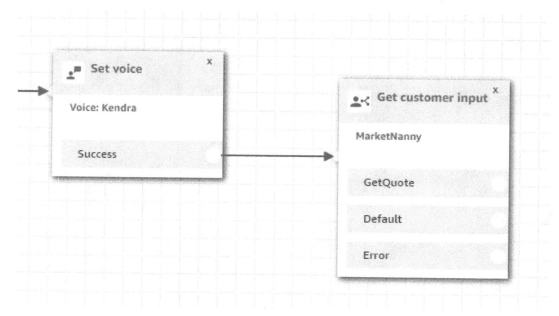

Figure 5.28: The GetQuote intent in the Get customer input node

17. You can now see that the **Get customer input** node has changed to display the intent that we specified in its properties pane:

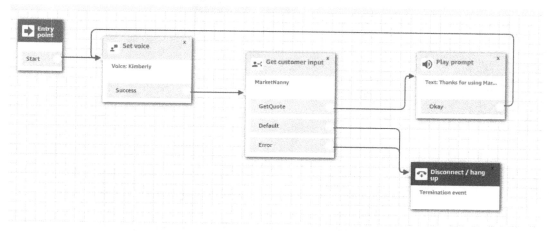

Figure 5.29: Full contact center flow

18. You can finish the flow by adding two more nodes:

- **Play prompt** from the **Interact** section: Set the **Prompt** property to **Text to speech (Ad hoc)** in the property pane, and enter text in the textbox under **Enter text** as follows:

```
"Thanks for using MarketNanny" Feel free to ask me something else.
```

- **Disconnect/hang up** from the **Terminate/Transfer** section. Do not set any properties.

19. Connect the nodes as shown previously. Connect the outputs of the **Default** and **Error** states in **Get customer input** to the input of the **Disconnect/Hang up** node.

20. Connect the **GetQuote** output to the **Play prompt** node.

21. Connect the output from **Play prompt** to the input of **Set voice**. This ensures that you can interact with your chatbot for as long as you keep asking the right questions.

22. Finally, click the **Save** button in the top-right corner of the screen, and then select the **Publish** button to publish the contact flow:

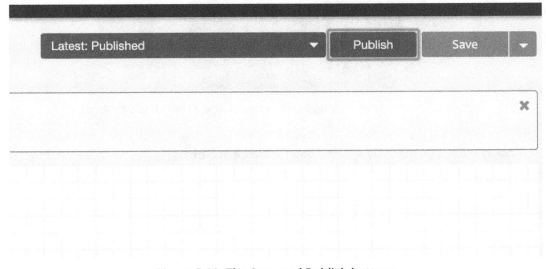

Figure 5.30: The Save and Publish buttons

23. As the final step, you will connect your call center phone number to the new contact flow you have just created.

24. From the menu panel on the left-hand side of the screen, select the **Routing** menu. Then, from that, select the **Phone numbers** item:

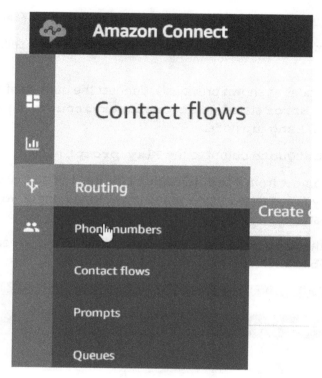

Figure 5.31: Selecting Routing and Phone numbers from the Dashboard

25. This will bring up the **Manage Phone** numbers screen, where you can select the phone number that you wish to use for **MarketNanny**.

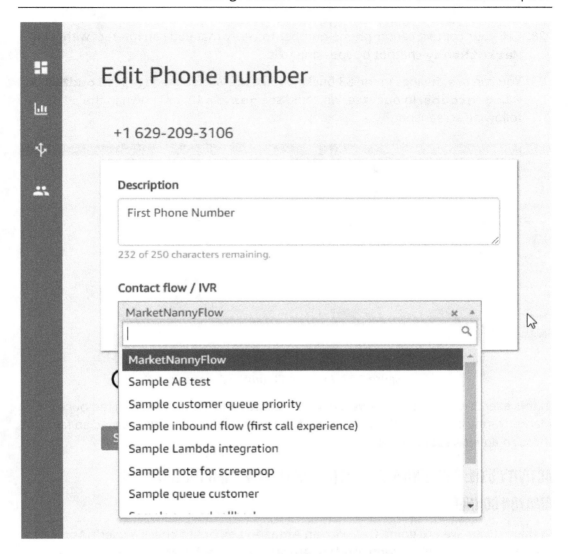

Figure 5.32: The Edit Phone number page

27. Here, click the dropdown under **Contact flow/IVR** and select or type in the name of your new contact flow: **MarketNannyFlow**.

28. Call your contact center phone number to verify that you can interact with your **MarketNanny** chatbot by speaking to it.

29. You can see the logs in the S3 bucket. You can also see the logs in **CloudWatch > Log groups**. In our case, we could see **jarvis42**, as shown in the following screenshot:

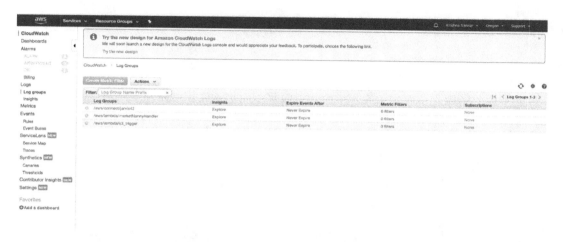

Figure 5.33: Amazon CloudWatch console

In this exercise, we set up our very own call center and we even connected our MarketNanny chatbot to the call center. Now, let's test what we've learned so far through an interesting activity.

ACTIVITY 5.01: CREATING A CUSTOM BOT AND CONNECTING THE BOT WITH AMAZON CONNECT

In this activity, we are going to create an **Amazon Lex** bot to check a user's **Account Balance**. The bot will be controlled via **Automatic Speech Recognition** (**ASR**) and **Natural Language Understanding** (**NLU**) capacities, which are similar innovations that power Amazon's Alexa.

For this activity, we will consider the following user story: as a user, you can check your account balance via the voice user interface using your phone.

Extrapolating, we can see that we need Amazon Connect, a phone number, a Lex bot, and a Lambda to look up the account balance. We will make a simplifying assumption that the user has only one account—otherwise, we would need more prompts to select an account and so on.

The steps to create the Account Balance service via Amazon Connect are as follows:

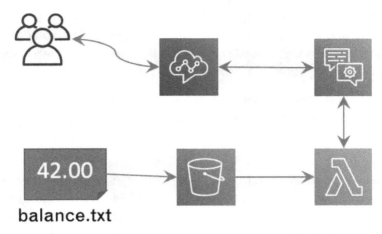

Figure 5.34: Steps to create the Account Balance service via Amazon Connect

1. We will store the account balance in an S3 bucket for simplicity. In real life, the call to a bucket will be replaced by a SQL call to a database, for example, **SELECT account_balance from balance_table WHERE account_number = <account Number>** or something similar.

2. Then, we will create a Lambda to access the bucket and return the balance value.

3. We will then create a Lex bot to get the account balance. That way, we can be omnichannel—a customer can get their account balance via a chatbot or by calling our contact center.

Then, of course, we create a contact flow in Amazon Connect to activate the bot via a call and get the balance via phone.

> **NOTE**
>
> The solution for this activity can be found on page 312.

Hope this activity and this chapter was interesting and that you are motivated to try even more complex and exciting bots that can answer all kind of questions.

SUMMARY

In this chapter, we ventured into the world of voice—we learned about the basics of Amazon Connect, and even looked at the free tier version of Amazon Connect. Later, we explored the sample voice-based chatbot application using Amazon Connect, Lex, and Lambda. Then, we created a personal call center.

You have also learned how to obtain a free phone number for a personal call center, and about using Amazon Lex chatbots with Amazon Connect with contact flows and different templates. Finally, you learned how to connect the call center to your Lex chatbot.

In the next chapter, you will learn how to analyze images with computer vision using Amazon Rekognition services. Amazon Rekognition services are used to detect objects, scenes, and text in images. It is also used to match faces in different images and to compare how closely images are interlinked with each other.

6

COMPUTER VISION AND IMAGE PROCESSING

OVERVIEW

This chapter describes the Amazon Rekognition service for analyzing the content of images using various techniques. You will be introduced to the Rekognition service for image analysis using computer vision, through which you will be able to detect objects and scenes in images. You will learn how to analyze faces and recognize celebrities in images. You will also be able to compare faces in different images to see how closely they match with each other.

By the end of this chapter, you will be able to apply the Amazon vision and image processing AI services in fields such as biology, astronomy, security, and so on.

INTRODUCTION

In the preceding chapters, you have done lots of interesting exercises and activities with the **Amazon Web Services (AWS) Artificial Intelligence (AI)** and **Machine Learning (ML)** services. You combined the serverless computing paradigm and conversational AI to construct chatbots, as well as a fully functional contact center that enables anyone to converse with the chatbots through a voice interface that's available by dialing a local phone number. You also learned about text analysis and topic modeling, all using the AWS services.

In this chapter, you will use the Amazon Rekognition service to perform various image processing tasks. First, you will identify objects and scenes within images. Then, you will test whether images should be flagged as needing content moderation. Next, you will analyze faces using Rekognition. You will also recognize celebrities and well-known people in images. You will compare faces that appear in different images and settings (for example, in groups or isolation) and recognize the same people in different images. Finally, you will extract text from images that might have some text displayed in them.

AMAZON REKOGNITION BASICS

Amazon Rekognition is a deep learning-based visual analysis service from AWS that allows you to perform image analysis on pictures and videos using machine learning. It is built on the same scalable infrastructure as AWS itself and uses deep learning technology to be able to analyze billions of images daily if required. It is also being updated constantly by Amazon and is learning new labels and features.

Some of the use cases for Amazon Rekognition are as follows:

- Searching across a library of image content using text keywords.

- Confirming user identities by comparing live images with reference ones.

- Analyzing trends based on public images, including the sentiments and emotions of the people in the images.

- Detecting explicit or suggestive content and automatically filtering it for your purposes.

- Detecting and retrieving text from images.

> **NOTE**
>
> Amazon Rekognition is also a **HIPAA**-eligible service for healthcare applications. If you wish to protect your data under HIPAA, you will need to contact Amazon customer support and fill out a **Business Associate Addendum** (**BAA**). For more information about HIPAA, go to the following link: https://aws.amazon.com/compliance/hipaa-compliance/.

FREE TIER INFORMATION ON AMAZON REKOGNITION

For this book, you will be using the free tier services of Amazon Rekognition. Be aware of the limits of the free tier services and the pricing options. These are the free services you can use for image processing:

- New Amazon Rekognition clients can break down up to 5,000 pictures a year.

- With the complimentary plan, you can utilize all of Amazon Rekognition's APIs and use up to 1,000 images that have faces free of charge.

> **NOTE**
>
> You should not need to use more than the free tier limits, but if you do go beyond the limits of the free tier, you will get charged by Amazon at the rates published at this link: https://aws.amazon.com/rekognition/pricing/.

REKOGNITION AND DEEP LEARNING

Deep learning is a branch of artificial intelligence and a subfield of machine learning. Deep learning works by inferring high-level abstractions from raw data by using a deep neural network graph with many layers of processing.

Deep learning structures such as **Convolutional Neural Networks (CNNs)** and **Recurrent Neural Networks (RNNs)** have been employed in natural language processing, audio recognition, speech recognition, and computer vision to deliver significant results. **Neural Machine Translation** has replaced all human-curated translation engines, object detection in autonomous cars uses CNN-based architectures extensively, and conversational AI is powering a variety of customer interactions.

The Rekognition service employs deep learning to provide its various features behind the scenes. It uses pre-trained models so that users do not have to train the system. The exact details are proprietary and confidential to Amazon, but we will learn how it works and how to use Rekognition in this chapter. As we mentioned earlier, one interesting aspect of Amazon Rekognition is the fact that the algorithms are monitored and trained periodically to increase their accuracy and capabilities. It can also be extended with custom labels and models trained with your images.

> **NOTE**
>
> For any questions you have, the Amazon Rekognition FAQ page (https://aws.amazon.com/rekognition/faqs/) is an excellent resource.

DETECTING OBJECTS AND SCENES IN IMAGES

Amazon Rekognition provides a feature that can detect objects and scenes in an image and label them. This label may be an object, scene, or concept such as a person, water, sand, a beach (scene), and the outdoors (concept).

Each label comes with a confidence score, which measures, on a scale from 0 to 100, the probability that the service got the correct answer for that label. This allows you or your application to judge the threshold against which to allow or discard results for itself.

Rekognition supports thousands of labels from categories such as those shown in the following table:

Category	Example Labels
People and Events	Wedding, Bride, Baby, Birthday Cake, Guitarist
Food and Drink	Apple, Sandwich, Wine, Cake, Pizza
Nature and Outdoors	Beach, Mountains, Lake, Sunset, Rainbow
Animals and Pets	Dog, Cat, Horse, Tiger, Turtle
Home and Garden	Bed, Table, Backyard, Chandelier, Bedroom
Sports and Leisure	Golf, Basketball, Hockey, Tennis, Hiking
Plants and Flowers	Rose, Tulip, Palm Tree, Forest, Bamboo
Art and Entertainment	Sculpture, Painting, Guitar, Ballet, Mosaic
Transportation and Vehicles	Airplane, Car, Bicycle, Motorcycle, Truck
Electronics	Computer, Mobile Phone, Video Camera, TV, Headphones

Figure 6.1: Labels supported by Amazon Rekognition

Additionally, Amazon is continuously training the system to recognize new ones, and you can request labels that you might wish to use that are not in the system through Amazon customer support.

To create an Amazon Rekognition analysis of a sample image, you can do the following:

1. Navigate to the Amazon Rekognition Service web page in the **AWS Management Console** and click **Services** at the top of the left-hand side. It also has a search box:

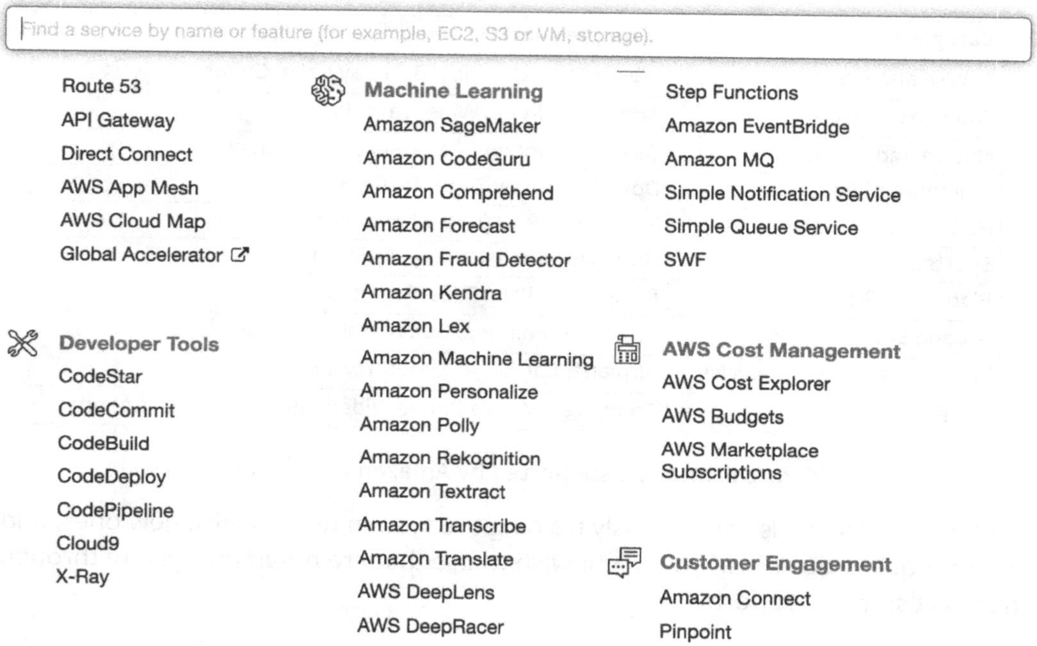

Find a service by name or feature (for example, EC2, S3 or VM, storage).

Route 53
API Gateway
Direct Connect
AWS App Mesh
AWS Cloud Map
Global Accelerator

Developer Tools
CodeStar
CodeCommit
CodeBuild
CodeDeploy
CodePipeline
Cloud9
X-Ray

Machine Learning
Amazon SageMaker
Amazon CodeGuru
Amazon Comprehend
Amazon Forecast
Amazon Fraud Detector
Amazon Kendra
Amazon Lex
Amazon Machine Learning
Amazon Personalize
Amazon Polly
Amazon Rekognition
Amazon Textract
Amazon Transcribe
Amazon Translate
AWS DeepLens
AWS DeepRacer

Step Functions
Amazon EventBridge
Amazon MQ
Simple Notification Service
Simple Queue Service
SWF

AWS Cost Management
AWS Cost Explorer
AWS Budgets
AWS Marketplace Subscriptions

Customer Engagement
Amazon Connect
Pinpoint

Figure 6.2: Selecting the Rekognition service in the AWS Management Console

2. You can find Rekognition under the **Machine Learning** section. When you are on the Rekognition page, click on the **Object and scene detection** link in the left-hand side toolbar to navigate to the **Object and scene detection** page:

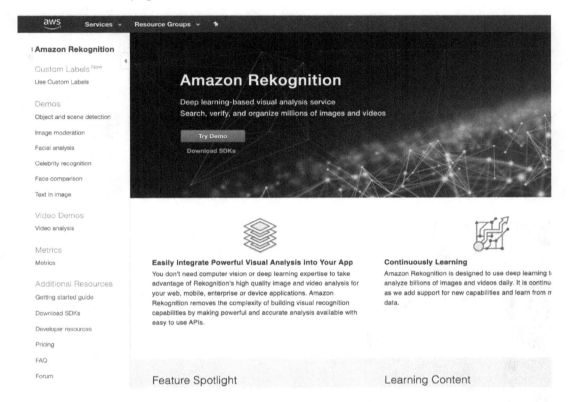

Figure 6.3: Amazon Rekognition service page

3. Next, choose the textbox under the **Use your own image** panel and enter the following URL: https://images.unsplash.com/photo-1540253208288-6a6c32573092?w=800:

Use your own image

Image must be .jpeg or .png format and no larger than 5MB. Your image isn't stored.

⬆ Upload   or drag and drop

Use image URL   Go

Figure 6.4: Use the image URL input textbox

The result for the image is as follows:

Done with the demo?
Learn more

▼ Results

Nature	99.8 %
Outdoors	99.7 %
Sky	98.8 %
Sun	98.5 %
Dawn	94.8 %
Sunset	94.8 %

Show more

▶ Request

▶ Response

Figure 6.5: Results for the sample image

4. You can see that, within the image, the objects that have been detected with greater than 90% confidence are as follows:

   `Nature`

   `Outdoors`

   `Sky`

   `Sun`

   `Dawn`

   `Sunset`

5. Click the **Show more** link to show more results with lower confidence levels. This will show more objects have been detected:

Done with the demo? Learn more	
▾ **Results**	
Nature	99.8 %
Outdoors	99.7 %
Sky	98.8 %
Sun	98.5 %
Dawn	94.8 %
Sunset	94.8 %
Dusk	94.8 %
Red Sky	94.8 %
Sunrise	92.8 %
Sunlight	73.4 %
Mountain	59 %
Show less	
▸ Request	
▸ Response	

Figure 6.6: Full set of labels for our sample image from Object and scene detection

You can choose the threshold amount of the confidence level at which you would like to cut off the results for your application.

EXERCISE 6.01: DETECTING OBJECTS AND SCENES USING YOUR IMAGES

In this exercise, we will detect objects and scenes of custom images using Amazon Rekognition. The custom images can be either taken from online sources, or you can upload them from your local machine. The following are the steps for detecting objects and scenes:

1. Navigate to the Amazon Rekognition service page from the AWS Management Console or go directly to the following URL: https://console.aws.amazon.com/rekognition.

2. Click the **Object and scene detection** link in the toolbar to navigate to the **Object and scene detection** page.

3. Next, choose the textbox under the **Use your own image** panel.

4. Enter the following URL so that you have an image to analyze: https://images.unsplash.com/photo-1522874160750-0faa95a48073?w=800. The following is the image on the Rekognition page. You can see that it was able to zero-in on the image:

Figure 6.7: The first test image for Object and scene detection

NOTE

We have collected images from a stock photo site called https://unsplash. com/, which contains photos that can be downloaded for free and used without restrictions for this book. Always obey copyright laws and be mindful of any restrictions or licensing fees that might apply in the jurisdiction where you reside (if applicable). You may view the license for images from unsplash.com here: https://unsplash.com/license.

5. You may view the results of the object detection under the **Results** panel on the right-hand side of the image. In this case, it is an image of a camera, and the results should look as follows:

▼ **Results**

Electronics	98.5 %
Camera	98.5 %
Strap	93.7 %
Digital Camera	91.5 %

▶ **Request**

▶ **Response**

Figure 6.8: Results for the first test image from Object and scene detection

6. As you can see, the results are quite accurate. Next, you can try the following images and verify that the results are as shown in the tables that immediately follow each image, that is, https://images.unsplash.com/photo-1517941875027-6321f98198ed?w=800 and https://images.unsplash.com/photo-1500111709600-7761aa8216c7?w=800.

The following are the images. This is the second test image:

Figure 6.9: The second test image for Object and scene detection

The following are the results of the second image provided:

▼ Results	
Head	83.7 %
▸ Request	
▸ Response	

Figure 6.10: Results for the second test image from Object and scene detection

This is the third test image:

Figure 6.11: The third test image for Object and scene detection

The following are the results of the third image provided:

▼ Results	
Building	98.6 %
Town	96.9 %
City	96.9 %
Metropolis	96.9 %
Urban	96.9 %
Bridge	96.5 %

Show more

▶ Request

▶ Response

Figure 6.12: Results for the third test image from Object and scene detection

The results for the second image did indicate it was a human head with > **83%** confidence. Looking at the third image of the Golden Gate Bridge, it had more classes before **Bridge** with **96.5%** confidence.

IMAGE MODERATION

In addition to object and scene detection, Rekognition also provides the ability to filter out objectionable content. You can use moderation labels to give point-by-point subclassifications, enabling you to tweak the channels that you use to figure out what sorts of pictures you consider satisfactory or shocking. **Amazon Rekognition Image** provides the **DetectModerationLabels** operation to detect unsafe content in images.

You can utilize this component to enhance photograph-sharing destinations, gatherings, dating applications, content stages for youngsters, online business stages and commercial centers, and more. In this book, we will not use any adult or nude images, but we can show the use of this feature with content that may be considered racy or suggestive in some locales featuring women in revealing clothing such as swimsuits or clubwear.

The images are blurred by default in this section, so you do not have to view them unless you press the **View Content** button.

> **NOTE**
>
> If you find any racy or suggestive images offensive, please skip this section based on your own personal, moral, religious, or cultural norms.

Amazon Rekognition uses a hierarchical taxonomy to label categories of explicit and suggestive content. The two top-level categories are **Explicit Nudity** and **Suggestive**. Each top-level category has many second-level categories. The types of content that are detected and flagged using this feature are as follows:

Top-Level Category	Second-Level Category
Explicit Nudity	Nudity
	Graphic Male Nudity
	Graphic Female Nudity
	Sexual Activity
	Partial Nudity
Suggestive	Female Swimwear Or Underwear
	Male Swimwear Or Underwear
	Revealing Clothes

Figure 6.13: Content type categories

To create an `Image Moderation` of a sample image, you can do the following:

1. Navigate to the Amazon Rekognition service page in the AWS Management Console or go directly to the following URL: https://console.aws.amazon.com/rekognition.

2. Click the `Image Moderation` link in the toolbar to navigate to the **Image Moderation** page.

3. You will see sample images on the bottom left. Click one of them.

4. You will notice right away that the content is blurred, as shown in the following screenshot. The image being analyzed is the first image to the left, which was already selected. You will see that the service has correctly identified **Suggestive** content in the image of the **Female Swimwear Or Underwear** type with a confidence of **94.9%**:

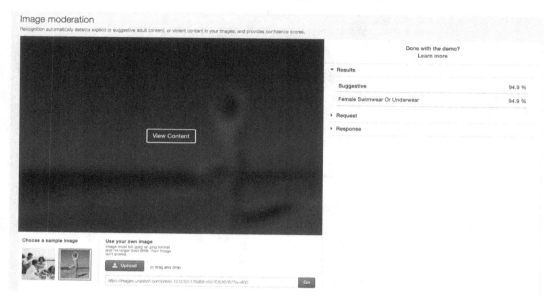

Figure 6.14: Results for image moderation

With this, we've seen how Amazon Rekognition can filter out suggestive content, but let's see how it does when it comes to detecting objectionable content in images.

EXERCISE 6.02: DETECTING OBJECTIONABLE CONTENT IN IMAGES

In this exercise, we will detect objectionable content in images. You can try this service on your images. We have selected three images that we will try out with this feature. Follow these steps to complete this exercise:

1. Copy and paste or type the following URL into the **Use image URL** textbox under the **Use your own image** section at the bottom of the page, and press the **Go** button to receive results from the service – https://images.unsplash.com/photo-1525287957446-e64af7954611?w=800:

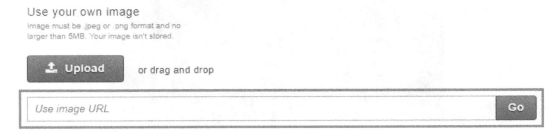

Figure 6.15: Use image URL upload textbox

2. You should receive a result stating that the service has found **Female Swimwear Or Underwear** content with a 99.4% degree of confidence:

Figure 6.16: Result that the image moderation service has found

3. The image **URL** to provide to the service is https://images.unsplash.com/photo-1509670811615-bb8b07cb3caf?w=800.

4. Just as before, enter it in the **Use image URL** textbox and press the **Go** button. This image has no objectionable content:

Figure 6.17: First test image for image moderation

You should see that Rekognition correctly returns no results:

▼ Results

No moderation labels detected

Figure 6.18: Results of the first test image from image moderation

5. Finally, we will use an image that should, again, return some results: https://images.unsplash.com/photo-1518489913881-199b7c7a081d?w=800.

This one should have, once again, correctly been identified as containing content with **Female Swimwear Or Underwear** with a 99.6% degree of confidence:

▾ Results

Suggestive	99.6 %
Female Swimwear Or Underwear	99.6 %

▸ Request

▸ Response

Figure 6.19: Results of the second provided image for image moderation

As you've seen, Amazon Rekognition has powerful image analysis capabilities – including content moderation. As a suggestion, you can try some more images that may or may not be suggestive and check the results. You might find some gaps in the object detection deep learning algorithms.

FACIAL ANALYSIS

Rekognition can perform a more detailed analysis of faces as well. Given an image with a detectable face, it can tell whether the face is male or female, the age range of the face, whether or not the person is smiling and appears to be happy, and whether they are wearing glasses or not.

It can also detect more detailed information, such as whether the eyes and mouth are open or closed, and whether or not the person has a mustache or a beard.

To create a facial analysis of a sample image, you can do the following:

> **NOTE**
>
> Click on the **Facial Analysis** link in the left toolbar to navigate to the **Facial Analysis** page.

1. We will use the upload capability to upload images and analyze the images:

Use your own image

Image must be .jpeg or .png format and no larger than 5MB. Your image isn't stored.

⬆ **Upload**   or drag and drop

Figure 6.20: The image upload button

2. The first image to be analyzed can be found at https://packt.live/3f5ipH0.

You can either save the image onto your disk or download this book's GitHub repository, as we covered in *Chapter 1, An Introduction to AWS*.

3. Click **Upload**; you will be shown the standard explorer window. Navigate to the directory where you have the **Chapter06** folder and select the **Rekognition-05.jpeg** file:

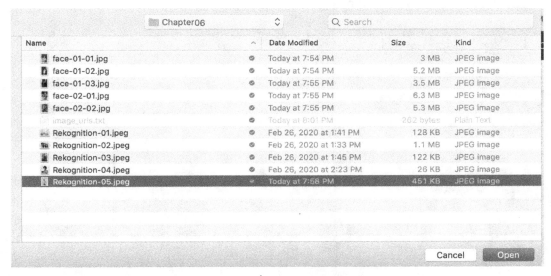

Figure 6.21: The explorer with the upload window

4. For this image, you will see that the main image box displays a bounding rectangle that shows the region in which the face was detected. Within the bounding box, there are also three dots to identify the locations of key facial features – the mouth and nose:

Figure 6.22: First sample image for facial analysis

5. Under the **Results** section to the right of the image, you will see that Rekognition has detected the following attributes of the face in the image:

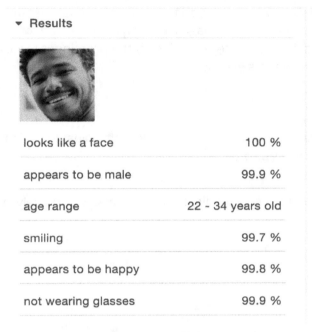

Figure 6.23: Results of the first sample image for facial analysis

You can click the **Show more** link in order to look at the other attributes that have also been identified.

All these identified qualities have an extremely high degree of confidence, showing that the service is very confident about its findings.

EXERCISE 6.03: ANALYZING FACES WITH YOUR OWN IMAGES

In this exercise, you have been provided with three images in the book's GitHub repository (https://packt.live/31X6w1Z) so that you can try out the Amazon Rekognition service with sample images. The images are provided courtesy of https://unsplash.com/ and Pinterest. Let's find out if they can identify the prominent facial attributes. Follow these steps to complete this exercise:

> **NOTE**
>
> Click the **Facial Analysis** link in the left toolbar to navigate to the **Facial Analysis** page.

1. We will use the upload capability to upload images and analyze them:

Use your own image

Image must be .jpeg or .png format and no larger than 5MB. Your image isn't stored.

   or drag and drop

Figure 6.24: The image upload button

2. The first image to be analyzed can be found at https://packt.live/3edZZCx.

    You can either save the image onto your disk or download this book's GitHub repository, as we covered in *Chapter 1, An Introduction to AWS*.

3. Click **Upload** and it will show the standard explorer window. Navigate to the directory where you have the **Chapter06** folder and select the **Rekognition-01.jpeg** file:

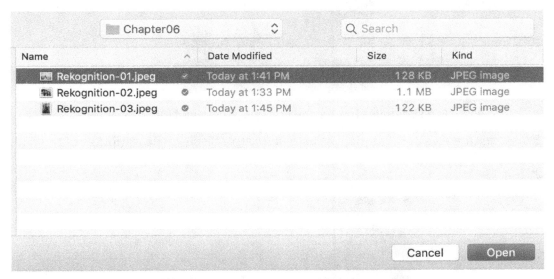

Figure 6.25: The explorer with the upload window

4. You can see from the bounding box and the dots that Rekognition is able to recognize the face easily:

Figure 6.26: Bounding box for the first image provided for facial analysis

5. Under the **Results** section, it quite accurately displays the attributes of the face in the image as well:

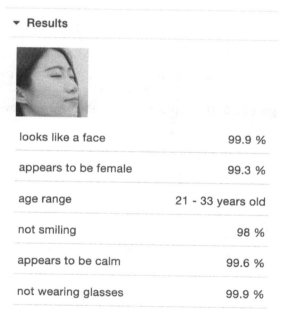

Figure 6.27: Results for the first image provided for facial analysis

6. Let's see if Recognition can detect multiple faces and the facial features of each face. The second image contains multiple faces. The file can be found at https://packt.live/3gDSzu5.

7. Click **Upload** and it will show the standard explorer window. Navigate to the directory where you have the **Chapter06** folder and select the **Rekognition-02.jpeg** file.

8. Rekognition once again does a good job of identifying the faces:

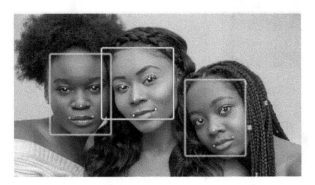

Figure 6.28: Bounding box for the second image provided for facial analysis

9. Now, the **Results** view has a right arrow button and shows the first face:

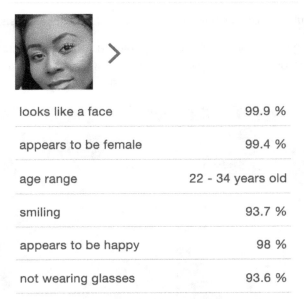

looks like a face	99.9 %
appears to be female	99.4 %
age range	22 - 34 years old
smiling	93.7 %
appears to be happy	98 %
not wearing glasses	93.6 %

Figure 6.29: Results for the second image provided for facial analysis

10. Click the right arrow and you will get the details of the second face:

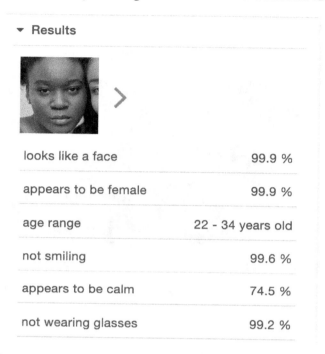

looks like a face	99.9 %
appears to be female	99.9 %
age range	22 - 34 years old
not smiling	99.6 %
appears to be calm	74.5 %
not wearing glasses	99.2 %

Figure 6.30: Results for the second image provided for facial analysis – second face.

11. Finally, we will give Rekognition an image with a neutral emotion to see how it does. We will be using the image at the following link – https://images.unsplash.com/photo-1472099645785-5658abf4ff4e?w=1000:

Figure 6.31: Third image provided for facial analysis

12. As expected, the service can recognize both males and females. It identifies the face with the bounding box:

Figure 6.32: Bounding box for the third image provided for facial analysis

13. It also displays results with a high degree of confidence (**97.7**%) that the face is male. It also updates the age range accordingly:

looks like a face	100 %
appears to be male	97.7 %
age range	39 - 57 years old
not smiling	84.2 %
wearing glasses	97.5 %
not wearing sunglasses	90.2 %

Figure 6.33: Results for the third image provided for facial analysis

It is **84.2%** confident that the man is not smiling, and we can see from the image that he is not smiling very much, if at all. Finally, the service is **97.5%** sure that he is wearing glasses, but it also says with **90.2%** confidence that he is not wearing sunglasses. It shows that there is still room for lots of improvement and we should apply human logic and rules to validate the results from the image detection services. In this case, we can take the one with the larger confidence score (that is, **wearing glasses**) to show that we can use the relative score to evaluate the results.

As we all know, humans are born with extremely good object detection and image analysis capabilities, which we enhance as we grow. But this is very hard for machines as they do not have the capability to reason or perform semantic analysis. The image analysis domain is relatively new, with the bulk of advances coming in the last 5 to 6 years. New algorithms are being researched, new ways of training are being explored, and optimizations are being sought. Therefore, Amazon Rekognition is extremely effective—it has wrapped the algorithms and mechanisms in a set of useful and practical interfaces, masking the underlying algorithmic and computer theoretic complexities, and Rekognition learns and evolves by leveraging the current best practices and research. In this section, you were introduced to the capabilities of Amazon Rekognition's image analysis service. You will see more regarding this service in the following sections.

CELEBRITY RECOGNITION

Rekognition provides us with the ability to recognize and label celebrities and other famous people in images. This includes well-known individuals from a variety of fields, such as sports, business, politics, media, and entertainment.

It is important to remember that Rekognition can only recognize faces that it has been trained on, and so does not cover a full, exhaustive list of celebrities. However, since Amazon continues to train the system, it is constantly adding new faces to the service.

> **NOTE**
>
> Click the **Celebrity recognition** link in the left toolbar to navigate to the **Celebrity recognition** page.

To create a celebrity recognition of a sample image, you can do the following:

1. Click the **Upload** button. We will use a picture whose file can be found at https://packt.live/38CmbVM. You can either save the image onto your disk or download this book's GitHub repository, as described in *Chapter 1, An Introduction to AWS*.

2. It will show the standard explorer window. Navigate to the directory where you have the **Chapter06** folder and select the **Rekognition-04.jpeg** file:

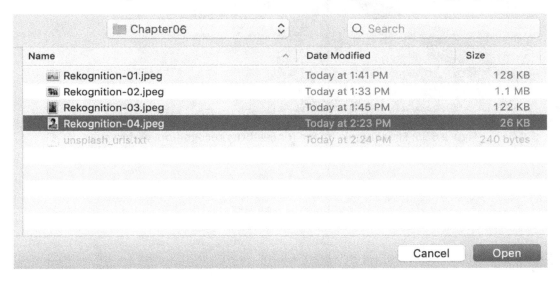

Figure 6.34: The explorer with the upload window

3. Amazon Rekognition does an excellent job of recognizing Nichelle Nichols (famous for playing Lieutenant Nyota Uhura in the Star Trek movies):

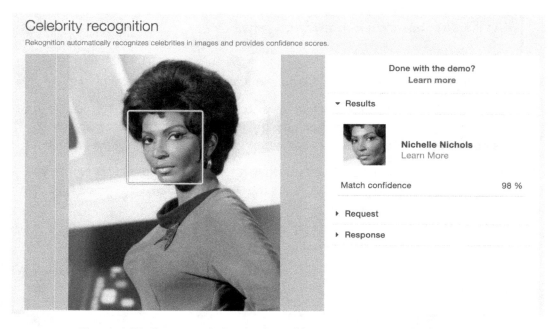

Figure 6.35: First sample image for celebrity recognition, with results

4. Clicking the **Learn More** link in the **Results** box takes you to the IMDb page for Nichelle Nichols:

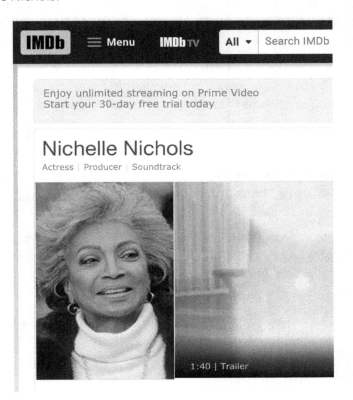

Figure 6.36: The Learn More link for the first sample image

EXERCISE 6.04: RECOGNIZING CELEBRITIES IN YOUR IMAGES

In this exercise, we will use another site that has a larger collection of celebrity images. You can also use these for free without restrictions. You can also try out this service on your own images. We have selected three images that we will try out with this feature.

You may view the license for images from pexels.com here: https://www.pexels.com/creative-commons-images/. Follow these steps to complete this exercise:

> **NOTE**
>
> Click the **Celebrity recognition** link in the left toolbar to navigate to the **Celebrity recognition** page.

1. Copy and paste or type a **URL** into the **Use image URL** textbox under the **Use your own image** section at the bottom of the page, and press the **Go** button to receive results from the service:

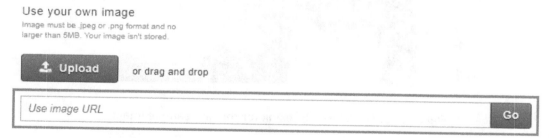

Figure 6.37: The Use image URL input textbox

2. The first URL to enter into the textbox is https://images.pexels.com/photos/276046/pexels-photo-276046.jpeg:

Figure 6.38: First image provided for celebrity recognition

3. This is an image of the well-known actress Charlize Theron. The **Results** section will display her name and a **Learn More** link, which will take you to her IMDb page:

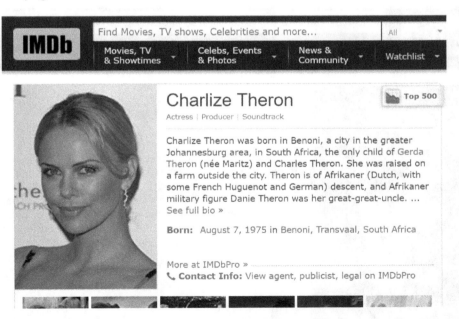

Figure 6.39: The Learn More link for the first image provided for celebrity recognition

4. The second image you can enter in the textbox can be found at https://images. pexels.com/photos/2281/man-person-suit-united-states-of-america.jpg?w=800 and gives us the following image:

Figure 6.40: The second image provided for celebrity recognition

5. This image displays former US President Barack Obama. Rekognition can easily detect him as well and displays his name in the **Results** section. The **Learn More** link, once again, links to his IMDb page:

Figure 6.41: The Learn More link for the second image provided for celebrity recognition

6. The final image contains multiple famous people. Enter the following URL into Rekognition: https://images.pexels.com/photos/70550/pope-benedict-xvi-president-george-bush-laura-bush-andrews-afb-70550.jpeg?w=800. This gives us the following image:

Figure 6.42: The third image provided for celebrity recognition, with three bounding boxes

7. In the **Results** section, you can see that Rekognition recognizes all three famous people in the image:

- George W Bush

- Pope Benedict XVI

- Laura Bush

The following image shows the result of celebrity recognition:

George W. Bush
Learn More

Match confidence   100 %

Pope Benedict XVI
Learn More

Match confidence   100 %

Laura Bush
Learn More

Match confidence   100 %

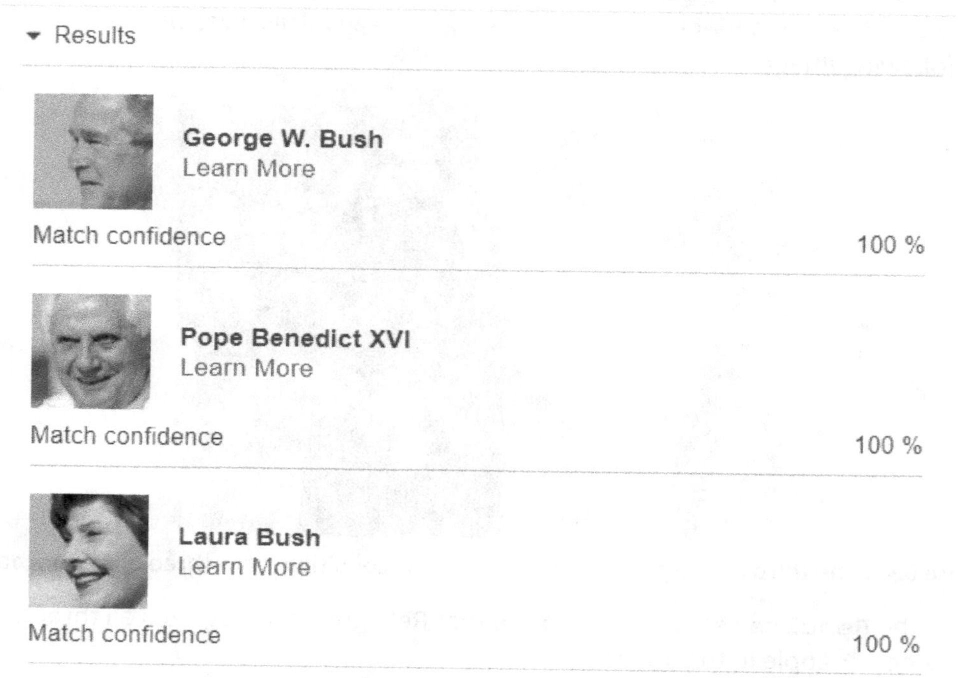

Figure 6.43: Results of the third image provided for celebrity recognition

The **Learn More** links under their names go to their respective IMDb pages. As we have done previously, we can verify this by clicking on them.

FACE COMPARISON

Rekognition allows you to compare faces in two images. This is mainly for the purpose of identifying which faces are the same in both images. As an example use case, this can also be used for comparing images with people against their personnel photo.

This section demonstrates industry standards so that you can utilize Amazon Rekognition to analyze faces inside an arrangement of pictures with different faces in them. When you indicate a **Reference face** (source) and a **Comparison face** (target) picture, Rekognition thinks about the biggest face in the source picture (that is, the reference) with up to 100 countenances recognized in the objective picture (that is, the examination images) and, after that, discovers how intently the face in the source picture matches with the appearances in the target picture. The closeness score for every examination is shown in the **Results** sheet.

Some restrictions on the usage of this feature are as follows:

- If the source image contains multiple faces, the largest face is used to compare against the target image.

- The target image can contain up to 15 faces. The detected face in the source image is compared against each of the faces detected in the target image.

> **NOTE**
>
> Click the **Face comparison** link in the left toolbar to navigate to the **Face comparison** page.

With the face comparison feature, there are two sections with images, side by side. You can choose to compare images in the left-hand section with images in the right-hand section. To create a facial analysis of a sample image, you can do the following:

1. Go to the textbox under the **Use your own image** panel on the left-hand side.

2. Enter the following URL to get an image to analyze: https://images.unsplash.com/photo-1524788038240-5fa05b5ee256?w=800.

3. Go to the textbox under the **Use your own image** panel on the right-hand side.

4. Enter the following URL to get an image to analyze – https://images.unsplash.com/photo-1524290266577-e90173d9072a?w=800.

Figure 6.44: First sample images provided for face comparison

5. With the default selections, in the **Results** section, you will see that it identifies the girl in the left image on the right-hand side with a **99.8%** degree of confidence, as shown here:

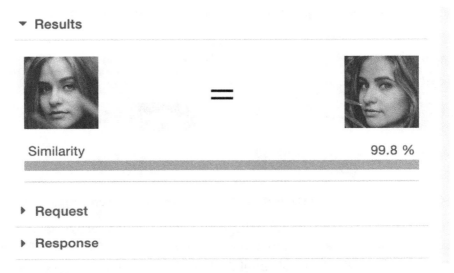

Figure 6.45: Results for the first sample images provided for face comparison

ACTIVITY 6.01: CREATING AND ANALYZING DIFFERENT FACES IN REKOGNITION

In this activity, you can try out Rekognition with your own images. For example, we have provided links to two sets of images that display the same people. You can enter the sets of images into the left- (comparison) and right-hand (comparison) sides by using the **Upload** button. Remember that there are two this time, so there are two **Go** buttons to press as well. Follow these steps to complete this activity:

1. Navigate to the Amazon Recognition service from the Amazon Management Console and choose **Face comparison** from the left toolbar.

2. You will see two sets of **Upload** buttons, as shown in the following screenshot:

Figure 6.46: Upload buttons for face comparison

3. Upload the first set of images to Rekognition so that it can recognize and compare the faces. We have three images, **face-01-01**, **face-02-02**, and **face-01-03**, under different lighting conditions and angles. Interestingly, Rekognition can detect that they are all the same face!

The images to be analyzed can be found in the https://packt.live/31X6IP6 and https://packt.live/3ebuSYz, https://packt.live/2ZLseUd files.

You can either save the images onto your disk or download this book's GitHub repository, as we covered in Chapter 1, An Introduction to AWS:

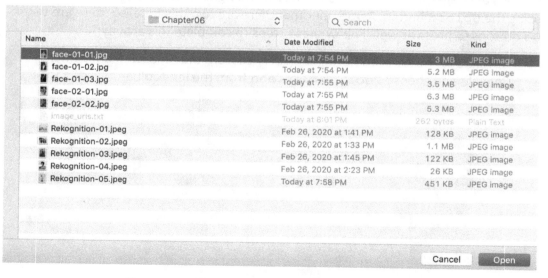

Figure 6.47: The explorer with the upload window

4. Upload https://packt.live/31X6IP6 and https://packt.live/2ZLseUd.

5. Compare the first set of images with the following parameters:

- Degree of confidence

- Comparing with different angles

- Lighting

- Position of glasses on the face

6. Compare the second set of images for face similarity parameters.

> **ADDITIONAL CHALLENGE**
>
> As an additional challenge you can try the same steps on these two images from Unsplash as well: https://images.unsplash.com/photo-1526510747491-58f928ec870f and https://images.unsplash.com/photo-1529946179074-87642f6204d7:

The expected output is the degree of confidence that the corresponding two images from the image sets are of the same person, even with different angles, lighting, and the position of the face. You will see that in the results section. This activity shows the image analysis capabilities of the Amazon Rekognition service.

> **NOTE**
>
> The solution for this activity can be found on page 348.

TEXT IN IMAGES

In the previous chapters, you learned how to extract text from scanned documents such as tax returns and company statements. Amazon Rekognition can detect and extract text from images as well—for example, street signs, posters, product names, and license plates. Of course, this feature is made to work with real-world images instead of document images. The **Text in image** link, which is accessible from the left toolbar, is where this capability resides in Amazon Rekognition.

For each image provided, the service returns a text label and bounding box, along with a confidence score. This can be extremely useful for searching text across a collection of images. Each image can be tagged with the corresponding text metadata based on the results from this and other capabilities of the service.

For now, the only texts that are supported are Latin scripts and numbers (Western script). Up to 50 sequences of characters can be recognized per image. The text must be horizontal with +/- 90 degrees rotation.

> **NOTE**
>
> Click on the **Text in image** link in the left toolbar to navigate to the **Text in image** page.

To identify a "text in image" of a sample image, you can do the following:

1. Go to the textbox under the **Use your own image** panel on the left-hand side.

2. Enter the following URL of an image to analyze: https://images.unsplash.com/photo-1527174744973-fc9ce02c141d?w=800. You will see the following image:

Figure 6.48: The first sample image provided for text in image

Rekognition surrounds the detected text with borders so that you can identify which text regions it has recognized. You can see the results of text extraction in the **Results** section:

Figure 6.49: Results for the first sample image provided for text in image

Rekognition was able to find text in the image and put a box around it; then, it was able to "read" the text and even understand that there are two words! The Rekognition service has extracted text from the image with separators (|) between words in separate regions. Even though the sign's font is unique, with shadows, it was still able to extract the text.

Next, let's try out this capability with our own images from different real-life situations such as storefronts and license plates at different angles. As you will see, Amazon Rekognition does very well on photos taken from below store signs, as well as on photos taken at an angle above license plates.

EXERCISE 6.05: EXTRACTING TEXT FROM YOUR OWN IMAGES

In this exercise, you will extract text from your own images. Let's see how well Amazon Rekognition works with a variety of different text in images. We have provided three royalty-free images for you to use. Follow these steps to complete this exercise:

1. Click on the **Text in image** link in the left toolbar to navigate to the **Text in image** page.

2. Copy and paste or type the following URL into the **Use image URL** textbox under the **Use your own image** section at the bottom of the page: https://images.unsplash.com/photo-1521431974017-2521d1cdcd65?w=800. You will see the following image:

Figure 6.50: The first image provided for text in image

NOTE

Your results may not be as precise as the ones that we've got here.

You can see the bounding boxes around the image, which signify that Rekognition has recognized the text in the image. The results can be viewed in the **Results** panel to the right of the image. It did miss one hyphen between N and OUT, but didn't miss the I in IN, which is barely in the picture and slanted:

▼ Results   US English only

| IN-NOUT |
| BURGER |

Figure 6.51: Results of the first image provided for text in image

3. The next image can be found at the following URL. Copy and paste or type it into the **Use image URL** textbox as before: https://images.unsplash.com/photo-1528481958642-cd4b4efb1ae1?w=800. You will see the following image:

Figure 6.52: The second image provided for text in image

You can see that Rekognition has recognized the main text in the window of the shop: **OCEAN GIFTS SPORTFISHING WHALE WATCHING** and the separation between the words:

▼ Results   US English only

| OCEAN | GIFTS |
| SPORTFISHING |
| WHALE |
| WATCHING |

▶ Request

Figure 6.53: Results of the second image provided for text in image

Even though the results are extremely good, Rekognition can get confused. This is something you should be aware of and watch out for in your results. It is possible for Rekognition to get confused and return spurious results.

4. Finally, copy and paste or type the following URL into the **Use image URL** textbox: https://images.unsplash.com/photo-1456668609474-b579f17cf693?w=800. You will see the following image:

Figure 6.54: The third image provided for text in image

This is another example of a license plate. The results are as follows:

▼ **Results**   US English only

| P052724 |

Figure 6.55: Results of the third image provided for text in image

It has done a good job isolating the number plate.

In this exercise, we learned that Amazon Rekognition can pick out text from images, even with different angles, fonts, shadows, and so forth. You should try this feature out with multiple images with different angles, lighting, and sizes.

SUMMARY

In this chapter, you learned how to use various features of the Amazon Rekognition service and applied this to images. First, you used the service to recognize objects and scenes in images. Next, you moderated images that might have objectionable content by using Rekognition to recognize the objectionable content in the images.

You were able to analyze faces with Rekognition and were also able to identify their gender, age range, whether they were smiling, and whether they were wearing glasses.

You also recognized celebrities and famous people with the service and compared faces in different images to see whether they were the same. Finally, you were able to extract text that was displayed in images.

With this, we have come to the end of this chapter and this book. We hope it was an interesting journey discovering the enormous capabilities of serverless computing, Amazon AI and ML services, text analysis, image analysis, and so forth.

These types of features would have seemed unbelievable just a few years ago. The nature of machine learning and artificial intelligence is such that immense strides have been made, and will continue to be made, in the foreseeable future, in terms of what computers are going to be able to do—and AWS will be able to provide these services for you and your applications.

APPENDIX

CHAPTER 1: AN INTRODUCTION TO AWS

ACTIVITY 1.01: PUTTING THE DATA INTO S3 WITH THE CLI

Solution:

1. Verify the configuration is correct by executing **aws s3 ls** to output your bucket name (the bucket name will be unique):

```
[(base) USS-Defiant-2:aws_book ksankar$ aws s3 ls
2020-01-24 19:11:49 account-balance-202001241911
2020-01-18 13:15:22 aws-ml-s3-trigger-202001181023
2020-01-24 17:03:24 connect-80396210305f
2018-07-15 18:24:27 spark-training
(base) USS-Defiant-2:aws_book ksankar$
```

Figure 1.46: Command line showing the list of files in an S3 bucket

> **NOTE**
>
> The list you will see maybe a little different from the preceding screenshot. It depends on what activities or exercises you have done; you might see a few more files in S3.

2. Let's create a new S3 bucket. **mb** is the command for creating a bucket:

```
aws s3 mb s3://lesson1-text-files-20200217
```

```
[(base) USS-Defiant-2:aws_book ksankar$ aws s3 help
[(base) USS-Defiant-2:aws_book ksankar$ aws s3 mb s3://lesson1-text-files-20200217
make_bucket: lesson1-text-files-20200217
(base) USS-Defiant-2:aws_book ksankar$
```

Figure 1.47: Command to create an S3 bucket

If it is successful, you will see the **make_bucket : message**.

> **NOTE**
>
> Your bucket name needs to be unique, so it is easier to append YYYYMMDD to the name (or something similar) to make it so. You will see this technique in later chapters as well. If you take a look at the earlier **ls** command, you will see the bucket names used — even used YYYYMMDDHHMM to ensure the names were unique. Refer to the S3 "Rules for Bucket Naming" for specific details https://docs.aws.amazon.com/awscloudtrail/latest/userguide/cloudtrail-s3-bucket-naming-requirements.html).

3. Import your text file into the S3 bucket.

   For these exercises, we have prepared some fun-sounding text excerpts for you from Dracula and Peter Pan. These files are on GitHub https://packt.live/31WESlK Assuming you have cloned the repository locally, navigate to the local directory using the command line. In our case, the files are in **~/Documents/aws-book**:

```
(base) USS-Defiant-2:aws_book ksankar$ cd ~/Documents/aws_book/Artificial-Intelligence-and-Natural-Language-Processing-with-AWS/
(base) USS-Defiant-2:Artificial-Intelligence-and-Natural-Language-Processing-with-AWS ksankar$ ls
Chapter01      Chapter04      README.md      lesson2      lesson4      text_files
Chapter02      LICENSE        lesson1        lesson3      old
(base) USS-Defiant-2:Artificial-Intelligence-and-Natural-Language-Processing-with-AWS ksankar$ cd Chapter01
(base) USS-Defiant-2:Chapter01 ksankar$ ls
text_files
(base) USS-Defiant-2:Chapter01 ksankar$ cd text_files/
(base) USS-Defiant-2:text_files ksankar$ ls
neg_sentiment__dracula.txt           peter_pan.txt                    pos_sentiment__leaves_of_grass.txt
(base) USS-Defiant-2:text_files ksankar$ aws s3 cp pos_sentiment__leaves_of_grass.txt s3://lesson1-text-files-20200217
upload: ./pos_sentiment__leaves_of_grass.txt to s3://lesson1-text-files-20200217/pos_sentiment__leaves_of_grass.txt
(base) USS-Defiant-2:text_files ksankar$
```

Figure 1.48: Navigating to the local directory in the command line

4. To copy the files from the local directory to S3, use the command **aws s3 cp pos_sentiment__leaves_of_grass.txt s3://lesson1-text-files-20200217** to import the text file into your S3 bucket as shown at the end of *Figure 1.48*:

5. Similarly, export the **neg_sentiment__dracula.txt** and **peter_pan.txt** files to the S3 bucket:

```
(base) USS-Defiant-2:text_files ksankar$ aws s3 cp peter_pan.txt s3://lesson1-text-files-20200217
upload: ./peter_pan.txt to s3://lesson1-text-files-20200217/peter_pan.txt
(base) USS-Defiant-2:text_files ksankar$ aws s3 cp neg_sentiment__dracula.txt s3://lesson1-text-files-20200217
upload: ./neg_sentiment__dracula.txt to s3://lesson1-text-files-20200217/neg_sentiment__dracula.txt
(base) USS-Defiant-2:text_files ksankar$
```

Figure 1.49: Copying the file from the local directory in the command line

6. Navigate to your desktop in the command line. Create a new local folder named **s3_exported_files** with the **mkdir s3_exported_files** command:

```
[(base) USS-Defiant-2:Desktop ksankar$ mkdir s3_exported_files
[(base) USS-Defiant-2:Desktop ksankar$ ccd s3_exported_files/
-bash: ccd: command not found
[(base) USS-Defiant-2:Desktop ksankar$ cd s3_exported_files/
(base) USS-Defiant-2:s3_exported_files ksankar$ 
```

Figure 1.50: Navigating to the desktop in the command line

7. Next, recursively export both files (**neg_sentiment__dracula.txt** and **peter_pan.txt**) from the S3 bucket to your local directory with the **--recursive** parameter. The following is the output of the command:

```
[(base) USS-Defiant-2:s3_exported_files ksankar$ aws s3 cp s3://lesson1-text-files-20200217 . --recursive
download: s3://lesson1-text-files-20200217/peter_pan.txt to ./peter_pan.txt
download: s3://lesson1-text-files-20200217/pos_sentiment__leaves_of_grass.txt to ./pos_sentiment__leaves_of_grass.txt
download: s3://lesson1-text-files-20200217/neg_sentiment__dracula.txt to ./neg_sentiment__dracula.txt
```

Figure 1.51: Command line to copy files from an S3 bucket

8. Verify the objects were exported successfully to your local folder with the **dir** or **ls** command, as shown in the following screenshot. This is the expected output:

```
[(base) USS-Defiant-2:s3_exported_files ksankar$ ls -la
total 3616
drwxr-xr-x   5 ksankar  staff     160 Feb 17 16:23 .
drwx------+ 18 ksankar  staff     576 Feb 17 16:21 ..
-rw-r--r--   1 ksankar  staff  842169 Feb 17 16:19 neg_sentiment__dracula.txt
-rw-r--r--   1 ksankar  staff  262704 Feb 17 16:19 peter_pan.txt
-rw-r--r--   1 ksankar  staff  738054 Feb 17 16:14 pos_sentiment__leaves_of_grass.txt
(base) USS-Defiant-2:s3_exported_files ksankar$ 
```

Figure 1.52: Output of the multi-file copy from the S3 bucket

CHAPTER 2: ANALYZING DOCUMENTS AND TEXT WITH NATURAL LANGUAGE PROCESSING

ACTIVITY 2.01: INTEGRATING LAMBDA WITH AMAZON COMPREHEND TO PERFORM TEXT ANALYSIS

Solution:

1. Upload the **test_s3trigger_configured.txt** file to our S3 bucket to verify the Lambda **s3_trigger** function was configured successfully.

2. Navigate to the S3 page: https://console.aws.amazon.com/s3/.

3. Click the bucket name you are using to test the **s3_trigger** function (in my case, **aws-ml-s3-trigger-202001181023**):

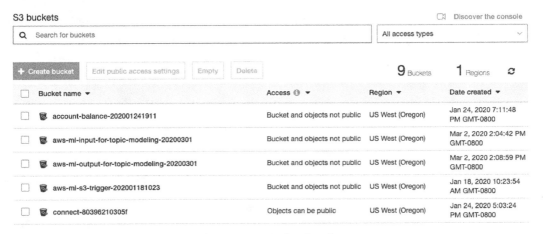

Figure 2.55: S3 bucket list

4. Click **Upload**:

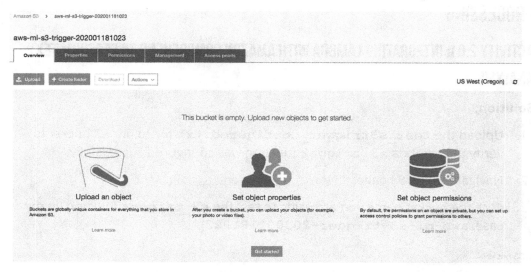

Figure 2.56: S3 bucket list upload screen

The following screen will display:

Figure 2.57: S3 Upload bucket Add files screen

5. Click **Add files**:

Figure 2.58: S3 Add files selection screen

6. Navigate to the **test_s3trigger_configured.txt** file location. Select the file.

   The file contains the following text:

```
I am a test file to verify the s3 trigger was successfully configured
on 1/20/2020 at 1:34 PM and tried 3 times!
```

Before we execute the **s3_trigger**, consider the output based on the following aspects of the text: sentiment (positive, negative, or neutral), entities (quantity, person, place, and so on), and key phrases.

> **NOTE**
>
> **test_s3trigger_configured.txt** is available at the following GitHub repository: https://packt.live/3gAxqku.

7. Click **Upload**, then **Next**:

Figure 2.59: S3 file added to the bucket for the Lambda trigger test

8. Click **Next** in the Set Permissions tab:

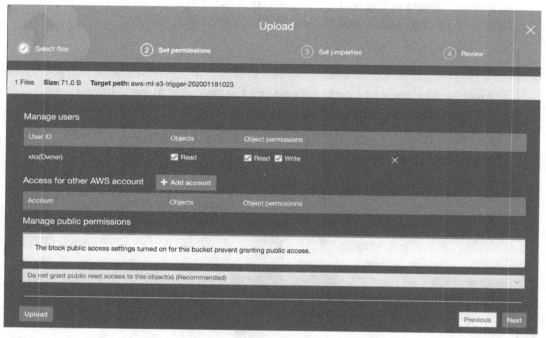

Figure 2.60: S3 file added to the bucket for the Lambda trigger test—object permissions

9. Keep the default **Standard Storage class** and click **Next**:

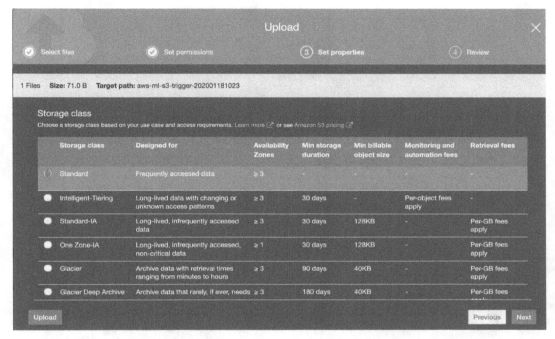

Figure 2.61: S3 file added to the bucket for the Lambda trigger test—Storage class

10. Select **Upload**:

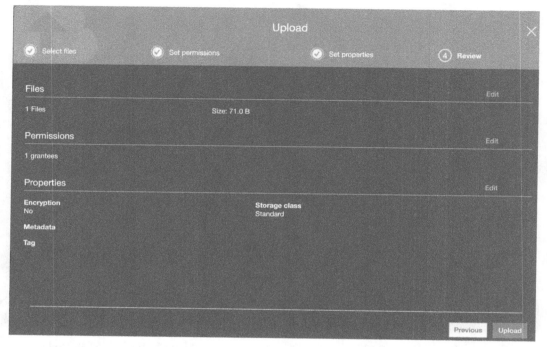

Figure 2.62: S3 file added to the bucket for the Lambda trigger test—Upload

11. You will see the file in the file list:

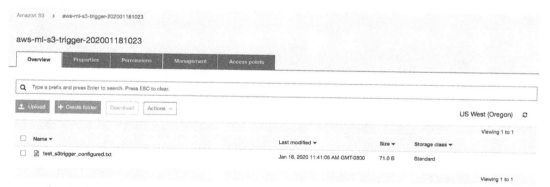

Figure 2.63: S3 file added to the bucket for the Lambda trigger test – file list

12. Now let's see if our Lambda was triggered. Navigate back to the Lambda via **Services>Compute>Lambda>Functions>s3_trigger**. Click **Monitoring**:

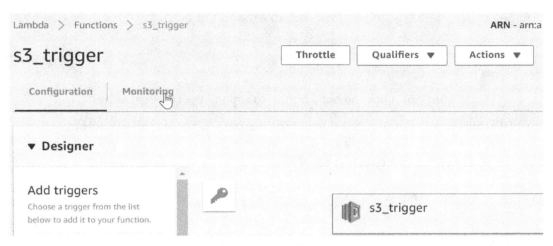

Figure 2.64: Select the Monitoring tab

13. Click **View logs in CloudWatch**:

Figure 2.65: Select View logs in CloudWatch

14. Click the log stream:

CloudWatch > Log Groups > Streams for /aws/lambda/s3_trigger

	Log Streams		Last Event Time
☐	5/[$LATEST]330dd67e.5c5485496f294b7549162d0		16:33 UTC-4

Search Log Group | **Create Log Stream** | **Delete Log Stream**

Filter: Log Stream Name Prefix ✕

Figure 2.66: Select the log stream

15. Select the radio button next to **Text** to expand the output:

CloudWatch > Log Groups > /aws/lambda/s3_trigger > ▓▓▓▓▓/[$LATEST]330dd67ed5c5485496f294b7549162d0

Expand all ● Row ○ Text ⟳

Figure 2.67: Click the radio button to expand the Lambda output

The following is the first few lines of the output. To see the entire output, you need to scroll down to view all of the results (see the following). We will interpret the total output in the next step:

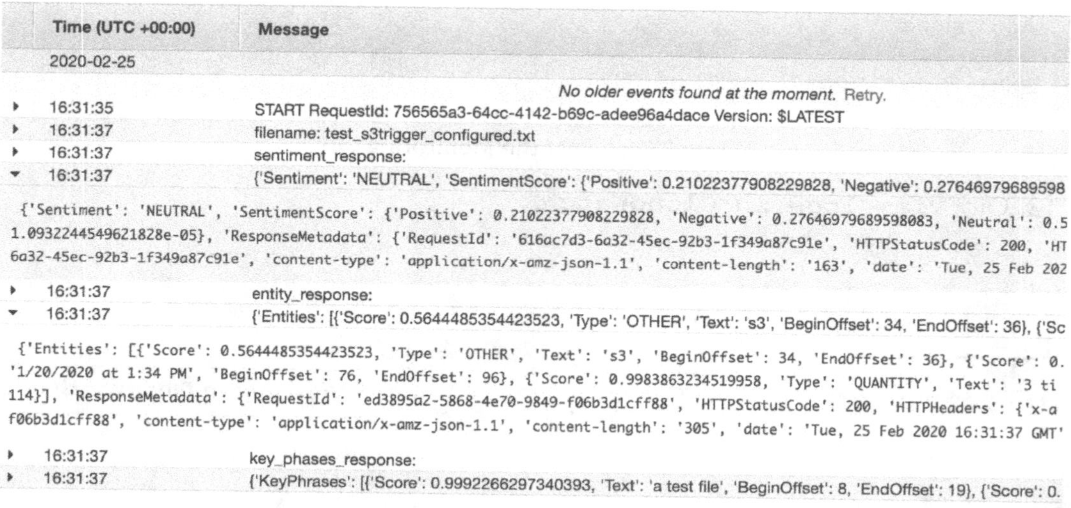

Time (UTC +00:00)	Message
2020-02-25	
	No older events found at the moment. Retry.
▸ 16:31:35	START RequestId: 756565a3-64cc-4142-b69c-adee96a4dace Version: $LATEST
▸ 16:31:37	filename: test_s3trigger_configured.txt
▸ 16:31:37	sentiment_response:
▾ 16:31:37	{'Sentiment': 'NEUTRAL', 'SentimentScore': {'Positive': 0.21022377908229828, 'Negative': 0.27646979689598

{'Sentiment': 'NEUTRAL', 'SentimentScore': {'Positive': 0.21022377908229828, 'Negative': 0.27646979689598083, 'Neutral': 0.5 1.0932244549621828e-05}, 'ResponseMetadata': {'RequestId': '616ac7d3-6a32-45ec-92b3-1f349a87c91e', 'HTTPStatusCode': 200, 'HT 6a32-45ec-92b3-1f349a87c91e', 'content-type': 'application/x-amz-json-1.1', 'content-length': '163', 'date': 'Tue, 25 Feb 202

| ▸ 16:31:37 | entity_response: |
| ▾ 16:31:37 | {'Entities': [{'Score': 0.5644485354423523, 'Type': 'OTHER', 'Text': 's3', 'BeginOffset': 34, 'EndOffset': 36}, {'Sc |

{'Entities': [{'Score': 0.5644485354423523, 'Type': 'OTHER', 'Text': 's3', 'BeginOffset': 34, 'EndOffset': 36}, {'Score': 0. '1/20/2020 at 1:34 PM', 'BeginOffset': 76, 'EndOffset': 96}, {'Score': 0.9983863234519958, 'Type': 'QUANTITY', 'Text': '3 ti 114}], 'ResponseMetadata': {'RequestId': 'ed3895a2-5868-4e70-9849-f06b3d1cff88', 'HTTPStatusCode': 200, 'HTTPHeaders': {'x-a f06b3d1cff88', 'content-type': 'application/x-amz-json-1.1', 'content-length': '305', 'date': 'Tue, 25 Feb 2020 16:31:37 GMT'

| ▸ 16:31:37 | key_phases_response: |
| ▸ 16:31:37 | {'KeyPhrases': [{'Score': 0.9992266297340393, 'Text': 'a test file', 'BeginOffset': 8, 'EndOffset': 19}, {'Score': 0. |

Figure 2.68: The top portion of the s3_trigger output

> **NOTE**
>
> If you encounter permission errors, check the permissions for
> **s3TriggerRole** from **Services>Security, Identity, &
> Compliance-IAM-Roles**. The policy list should look as follows. If one
> of them is missing, you can add them.

16. Also, if you delete and recreate your Lambda, you can reuse the role—just select **Use an existing role** instead of **Create a new role**. It is always good to play around with the various configurations and understand how they all fit together:

Figure 2.69: The policies for s3TriggerRole

17. Now let's examine the results of our Lambda from AWS Comprehend. You might see slightly different confidence levels because Amazon trains its algorithms periodically.

Sentiment_response -> Classified as **51.0**% likely to be neutral. This is a statement, so neutral is fine.

Sentiment_response:

```
{ {'Sentiment': 'NEUTRAL',
    'SentimentScore': {'Positive': 0.21022377908229828,
                       'Negative': 0.27646979689598083,
                       'Neutral': 0.5132954716682434,
                       'Mixed': 1.0932244549621828e-05},
```

entity_response -> It did find the date and the quantity from the text

entity_response:

```
{ 'Entities': [{'Score': 0.9891313314437866,
               'Type': 'DATE', 'Text': '1/20/2020 at 1:34 PM',
               'BeginOffset': 76, 'EndOffset': 96},
              {'Score': 0.9999986290931702, 'Type': 'QUANTITY',
               'Text': '3 times', 'BeginOffset': 107,
               'EndOffset': 114}],
```

key_phases_response -> It found the key phrases and the scores are close to 100% confidence

key_phases_response:

```
{'KeyPhrases': [{'Score': 0.9992266297340393,
                'Text': 'a test file', 'BeginOffset': 8,
                'EndOffset': 19},
               {'Score': 0.9999999403953552,
                'Text': 'the s3 trigger', 'BeginOffset': 30,
                'EndOffset': 44},
               {'Score': 0.9999963045120239,
                'Text': '1/20/2020', 'BeginOffset': 76,
                'EndOffset': 85},
               {'Score': 0.9960731863975525,
                'Text': '1:34 PM', 'BeginOffset': 89,
                'EndOffset': 96},
               {'Score': 0.9999966621398926, 'Text': '3 times',
                'BeginOffset': 107, 'EndOffset': 114}],
```

CHAPTER 3: TOPIC MODELING AND THEME EXTRACTION

ACTIVITY 3.01: PERFORMING TOPIC MODELING ON A SET OF DOCUMENTS WITH UNKNOWN TOPICS

Solution:

1. For this activity, we are going to use 1,000 movie review files. Navigate to the following link (or to your local directory where you have downloaded the GitHub files) to obtain the text data files that contain movie review comments: https://packt.live/3gISDZL. It is definitely better to download the GitHub repository rather than download 1,000 files by hand.

2. Navigate to the S3 dashboard at https://s3.console.aws.amazon.com/s3/home.

3. Click the bucket that you created earlier (in my case, it is "**aws-ml-input-for-topic-modeling-20200301**"):

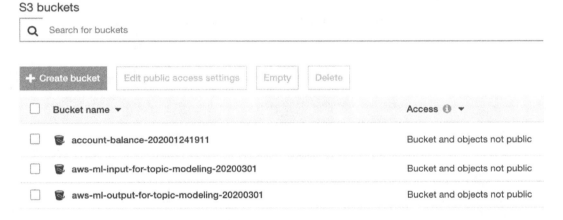

Figure 3.50: The S3 home screen for 'input-for-topic-modeling'

4. Click **Create folder**:

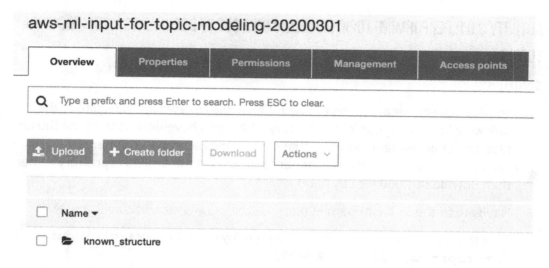

Figure 3.51: Clicking on Create folder

5. Type **movie_review_files** and click **Save**:

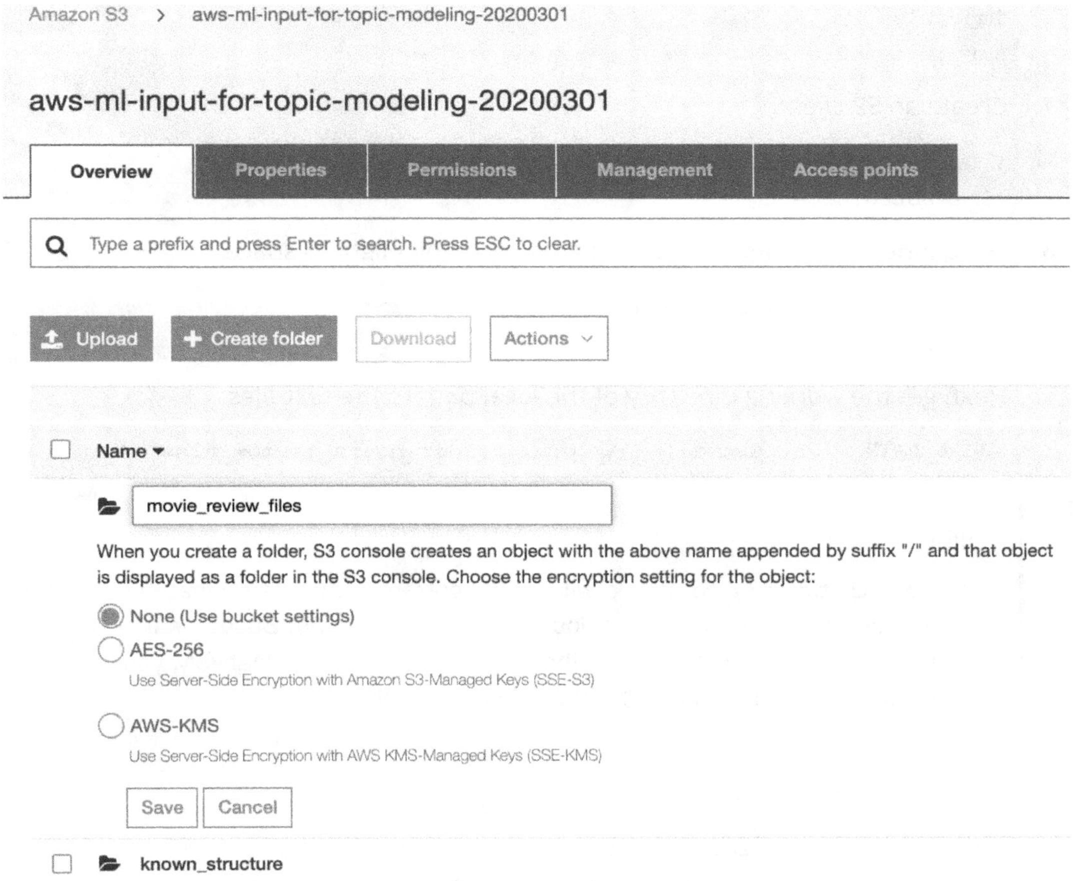

Amazon S3 > aws-ml-input-for-topic-modeling-20200301

aws-ml-input-for-topic-modeling-20200301

Overview	Properties	Permissions	Management	Access points

Q Type a prefix and press Enter to search. Press ESC to clear.

⬆ Upload   **➕ Create folder**   Download   Actions ⌄

☐ Name ▾

📁 movie_review_files

When you create a folder, S3 console creates an object with the above name appended by suffix "/" and that object is displayed as a folder in the S3 console. Choose the encryption setting for the object:

🔘 None (Use bucket settings)

⭕ AES-256
   Use Server-Side Encryption with Amazon S3-Managed Keys (SSE-S3)

⭕ AWS-KMS
   Use Server-Side Encryption with AWS KMS-Managed Keys (SSE-KMS)

   Save   Cancel

☐ 📁 known_structure

Figure 3.52: Clicking Save

> **NOTE**
>
> For this step, you may either follow along with the exercise and type in the code in a Jupyter notebook or obtain the notebook file (**text_files_ to_s3.ipynb**) from the source code folder for this chapter: https://packt. live/2W077MR. Copy the file and paste it into the editor.

6. First, you will import the **os** and **boto3** packages using the following command:

```
import os
import boto3
```

7. Create an S3 client:

```
# Create an S3 client
s3 = boto3.client('s3')
```

8. Next, type in your unique bucket name in the highlighted space:

```
BUCKET_NAME = '<insert a unique bucket name>'
BUCKET_FOLDER = 'movie_review_files/'
```

9. Next, get the working directory of the local path to the text files:

```
LOCAL_PATH = os.getcwd() +'\\local_folder_movie_review_files\\'
```

> **NOTE**
>
> The **os.getcwd()** command will get the current path. Ensure that the movie review files are in a folder located at the same path. Based on the folder name, you have to change the highlighted value. Alternatively, you can assign a custom path to **LOCAL_PATH** as well.

10. Create a list of all the text files:

```
text_files_list = [f for f in os.listdir(LOCAL_PATH) \
                   if f.endswith('.txt')]
```

11. Iterate on all files, and upload each to **s3**:

```
file_count = 0
for filename in text_files_list:
  # print(filename)
  file_count += 1
  s3.upload_file(LOCAL_PATH + filename, BUCKET_NAME, \
              BUCKET_FOLDER + filename)
print(F"Completed uploading {file_count} files.")
```

12. Press *Shift* + *Enter* to run the cell.

13. This will take a few minutes. The result is 1,000 text files uploaded to the S3 **movie_review_files** folder:

```
file_count = 0
for filename in text_files_list:
    # print(filename)
    file_count += 1
    s3.upload_file(LOCAL_PATH + filename, BUCKET_NAME, BUCKET_FOLDER + filename)

print(F"Completed uploading {file_count} files.")
```

Completed uploading 1000 files.

Figure 3.53: movie_review_files uploaded to S3

14. Refer to the following figure for the top few lines of the S3 output:

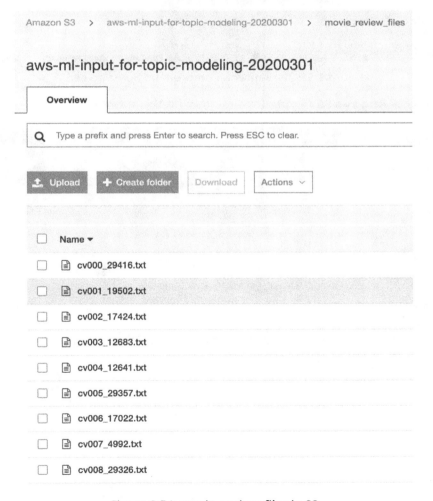

Figure 3.54: movie_review_files in S3

15. Next, navigate to AWS Comprehend via the Comprehend link: https://aws.amazon.com/comprehend/. You can also get there from https://aws.amazon.com/, then clicking **My account** and selecting **AWS Management Console**. In the console, select **services** and then click **Amazon Comprehend** in the machine learning category.

16. Then, click **Launch Amazon Comprehend**:

Figure 3.55: The Amazon Comprehend home screen

17. Now, click **Analysis jobs**, the first item on the left-hand toolbar:

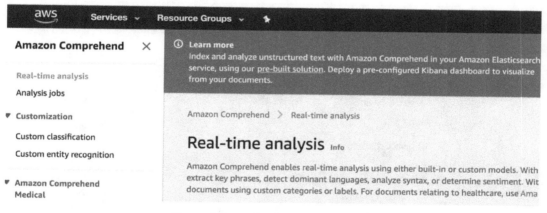

Figure 3.56: Selecting Analysis jobs

18. Now, click **Create job**:

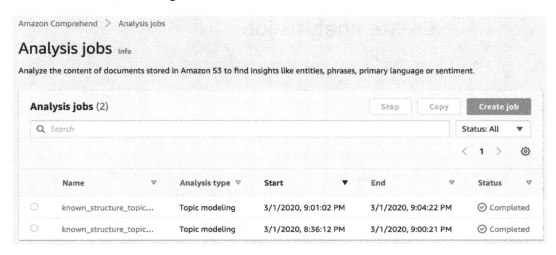

Figure 3.57: Clicking Create job

19. Now, type **unknown_topic_structure_job** in the **Name** input field:

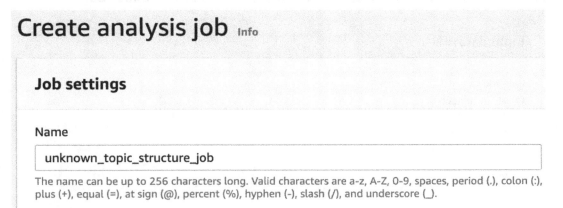

Figure 3.58: Entering unknown_topic_structure_job

20. Select **Topic modeling** in the analysis type drop-down box:

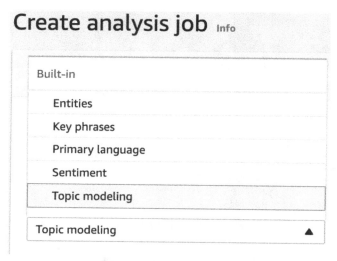

Figure 3.59: Choosing the Topic Modeling analysis type

21. Now, scroll down to the **Input data** section and click **Browse S3**:

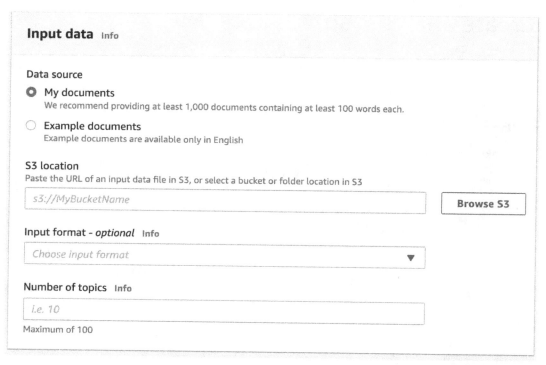

Figure 3.60: Selecting the Browse S3 button

22. Click the radio button next to the bucket you selected to input files for Topic Modeling (**aws-ml-input-for-topic-modeling-20200301**) and then click the bucket name:

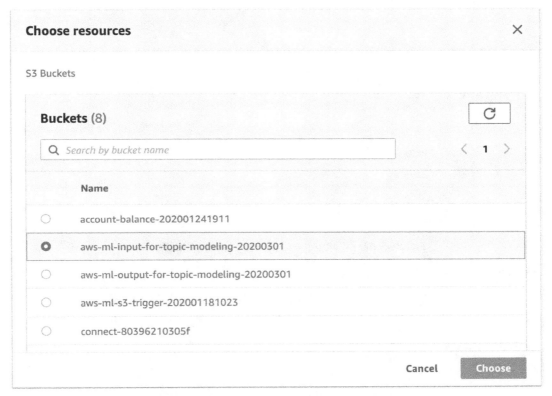

Figure 3.61: Expanding the S3 bucket sub-folders

23. Click the radio button next to the "`movie_review_files`" folder:

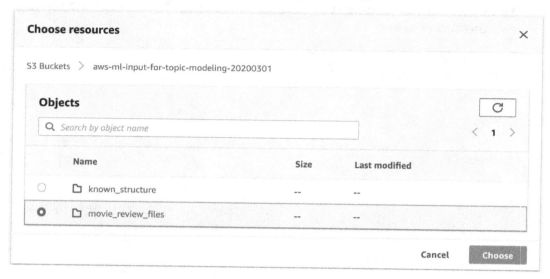

Figure 3.62: Selecting the movie_review_files folder

24. Now, click the **Choose** button.

The following figure shows the S3 location for the input data selected:

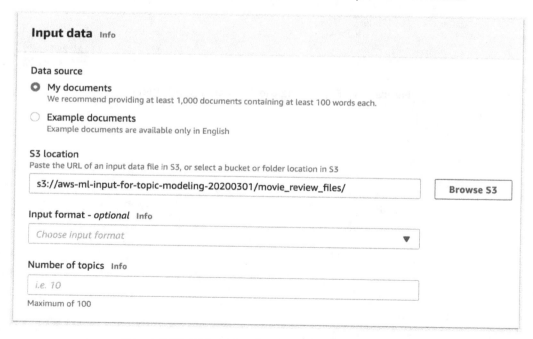

Figure 3.63: S3 location for the input data selected

25. Select **One document per file** from the **Input format** dropdown:

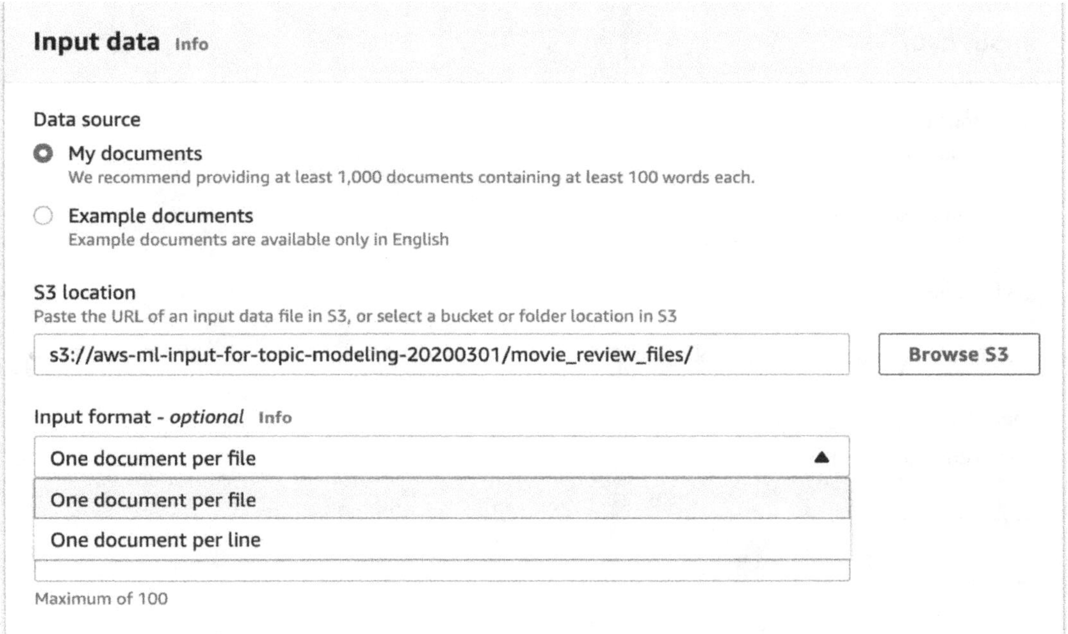

Figure 3.64: Selecting the One document per file option

26. Next, enter **40** in the `Number of topics` input field:

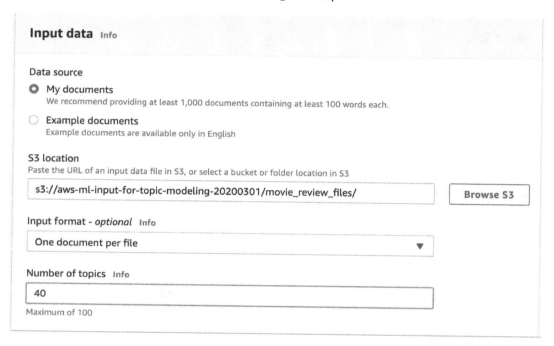

Figure 3.65: Entering 40 topics

27. Scroll down to choose the output location, and then click `Browse S3`:

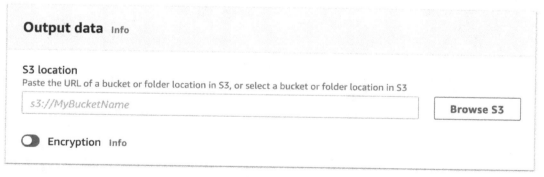

Figure 3.66: Clicking Browse S3

28. Select the output bucket you uniquely named for the Topic Modeling output and click on **Choose**:

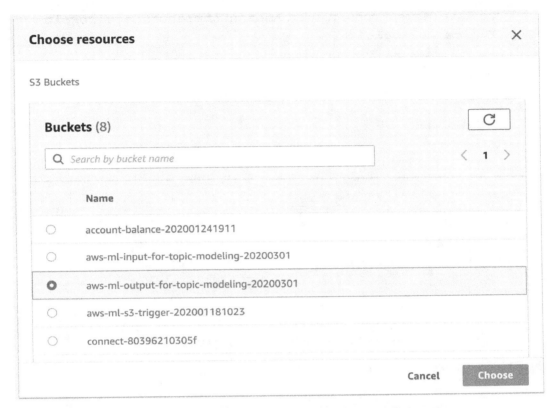

Figure 3.67: Selecting the S3 bucket for the Topic Modeling output

29. Scroll down to **Access Permissions** and select **Use an existing IAM role**, as shown:

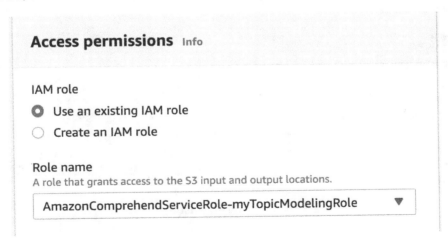

Figure 3.68: Selecting Use an existing IAM role in Access permissions

30. In the **Role Name** dropdown, select **AmazonComprehendServiceRole-myTopicModelingRole**:

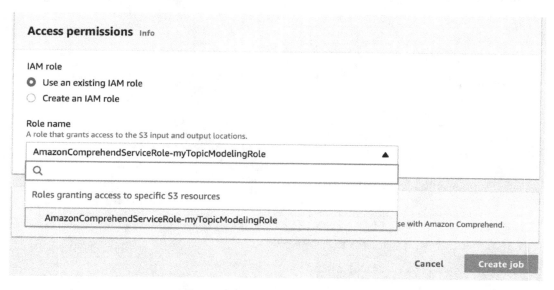

Figure 3.69: Selecting an existing IAM role

31. The final screen should look like the following:

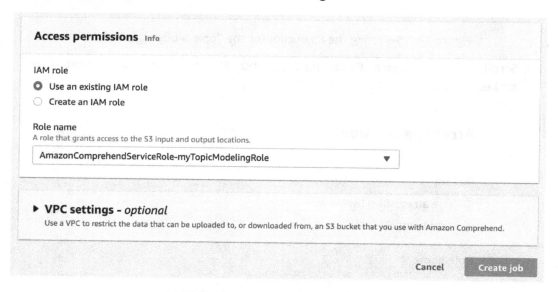

Figure 3.70: Selecting an existing IAM role

32. Click the **Create job** button. The Topic Modeling job status will first display **Submitted**:

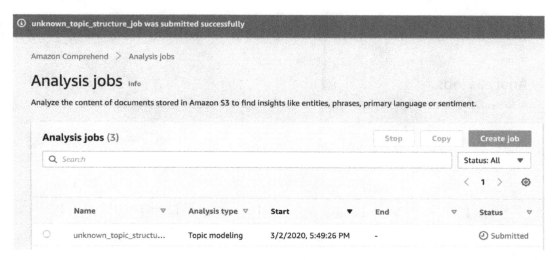

Figure 3.71: Status as Submitted

33. The Topic Modeling job status will next display **In progress**. The Topic Modeling job takes about 20 minutes:

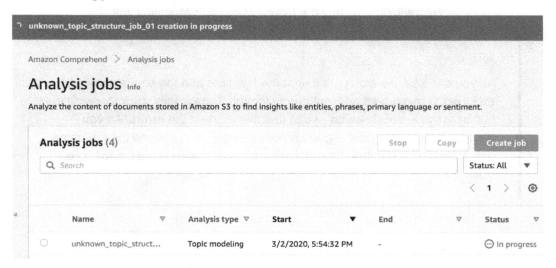

Figure 3.72: Status as In progress

34. When the status changes to **Completed**, click the **unknown_topic_ structure_job** link:

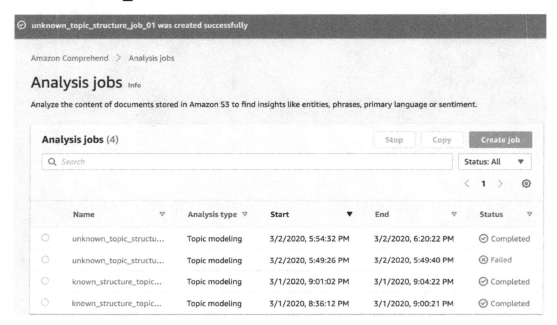

Figure 3.73: Selecting the hyperlinked Topic Modeling link

> **NOTE**
>
> As you can see, we didn't get it right the first time and the status showed **Failed**. It might take a few attempts for you. If a job fails, click **Copy** (the button to the left of **Create job**) and then correct the errors. As you can't have duplicate jobs, a good process would be to append the job name with a sequence number, for example, **unknown_topic_structure_ job_01**.

35. Scroll down and click the Topic Modeling output hyperlink (yours will display a different unique Topic Modeling job alphanumeric character string):

Figure 3.74: Clicking the Topic Modeling output S3 location

36. You will be directed to the actual file in the S3 output folder for the Topic Modeling job. Click **Download**:

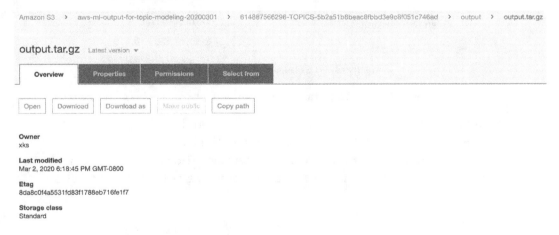

Figure 3.75: Clicking Download on the output file

37. Save the file to a local directory; usually, the **Downloads** folder or the desktop is fine:

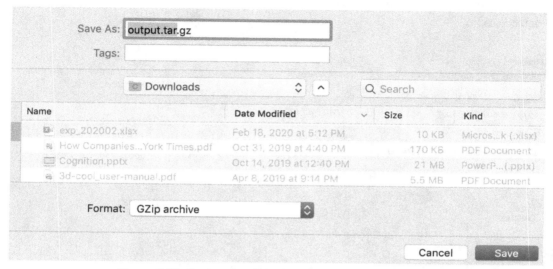

Figure 3.76: Saving the downloaded output file from S3

38. Navigate to the directory where you have downloaded the file and extract the CSV files by double-clicking. In Windows, right-click the **output.tar.gz** file and select **Extract Here**:

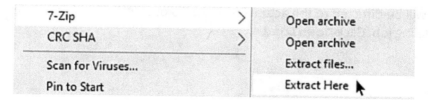

Figure 3.77: Selecting Extract Here

The result is two CSV files: **doc-topics.csv** and **topic-terms.csv**.

For reference, the extracted CSV files are available in the following GitHub directories and where you downloaded them in the local directory (in my case, this is **/Users/ksankar/Documents/aws_book/The-Applied-AI-and-Natural-Language-Processing-with-AWS/Chapter03/Activity3.01**):

https://packt.live/2AIccSw.

https://packt.live/3eaGdry.

We have completed Part 1: Performing Topic Modeling, for this activity. Now, let's move to Part 2: Analysis of Unknown Topics.

> **NOTE**
>
> For this step, you may either follow along with the exercise and type in the code on a Jupyter notebook or obtain the **local_csv_to_ s3_for_analysis.ipynb** file from the GitHub folder where you have downloaded the repository and paste it into the Jupyter editor. For reference, the source code is available via GitHub in the following repository: https://packt.live/3gDErks.

39. Firstly, we will import **boto3**:

```
import boto3
```

40. Next, import **pandas**:

```
import pandas as pd
```

41. Create the S3 client object.

```
region = 'us-west-2'
s3 = boto3.client('s3',region_name = region)
```

42. Next, create a unique name for the S3 bucket to store your source CSV files. Here, the bucket is named **unknown-tm-analysis-20200302**, but you will need to create a unique name:

```
#'<insert a unique bucket name>'
bucket_name = 'unknown-tm-analysis-20200302'
```

43. Next, create a new bucket:

```
# Create a location Constraint
location = {'LocationConstraint': region}
# Creates a new bucket
s3.create_bucket(Bucket=bucket_name,\
                 CreateBucketConfiguration=location)
```

44. Create a list of the CSV filenames to import:

```
filenames_list = ['doc-topics.csv', 'topic-terms.csv']
```

45. Iterate on each file to upload to S3:

```
for filename in filenames_list:
    s3.upload_file(filename, bucket_name, filename)
```

46. Next, check whether the filename is **'doc-topics.csv'**:

```
if filename == 'doc-topics.csv':
```

47. Now, get the **doc-topics.csv** file object and assign it to the **obj** variable:

```
obj = s3.get_object(Bucket=bucket_name, Key=filename)
```

48. Next, read the **csv** object and assign it to the **doc_topics variable**:

```
doc_topics = pd.read_csv(obj['Body']) else:
obj = s3.get_object(Bucket=bucket_name, Key=filename) \
                    topic_terms = pd.read_csv(obj['Body'])
```

49. Merge files on the Topic column to obtain the most common terms for each document:

```
merged_df = pd.merge(doc_topics, topic_terms, on='topic')
```

50. Print the **merged_df** to the console:

```
print(merged_df)
```

51. Next, execute the notebook cells using *Shift + Enter*.

52. The console output is a merged DataFrame that provides the docnames with their respective terms and the terms' weights (refer to the following):

```
# Creates a new bucket
s3.create_bucket(Bucket=bucket_name,CreateBucketConfiguration=location)
```

[2]: {'ResponseMetadata': {'RequestId': '335FE0842237CD71',
      'HostId': 'A80wI6gGBaQrUWuk4tSUMJYOep7ZAcIuD6myH2+em5p+ClqI4Qm1GMqGMZvTAc9PvejnR6eiivg=',
      'HTTPStatusCode': 200,
      'HTTPHeaders': {'x-amz-id-2': 'A80wI6gGBaQrUWuk4tSUMJYOep7ZAcIuD6myH2+em5p+ClqI4Qm1GMqGMZvTAc9P
    vejnR6eiivg=',
       'x-amz-request-id': '335FE0842237CD71',
       'date': 'Tue, 03 Mar 2020 03:26:03 GMT',
       'location': 'http://unknown-tm-analysis-20200302.s3.amazonaws.com/',
       'content-length': '0',
       'server': 'AmazonS3'},
      'RetryAttempts': 0},
     'Location': 'http://unknown-tm-analysis-20200302.s3.amazonaws.com/'}
```

Figure 3.78: Output from the S3 Create bucket call

```
# print the merged_df to the console
print(merged_df)

            docname   topic   proportion       term    weight
0       cv125_9636.txt      5     0.791506       time  0.010082
1       cv125_9636.txt      5     0.791506      jones  0.005874
2       cv125_9636.txt      5     0.791506   fugitive  0.003999
3       cv125_9636.txt      5     0.791506        lee  0.004330
4       cv125_9636.txt      5     0.791506       plot  0.007428
...                ...    ...          ...        ...       ...
43985   cv533_9843.txt     36     0.094384       hack  0.013879
43986   cv533_9843.txt     36     0.094384      young  0.013752
43987   cv533_9843.txt     36     0.094384      movie  0.029418
43988   cv533_9843.txt     36     0.094384     murphy  0.010977
43989   cv533_9843.txt     36     0.094384       time  0.015294

[43990 rows x 5 columns]
```

Figure 3.79: Activity merged Topic Modeling output
```

CHAPTER 5: USING SPEECH WITH THE CHATBOT

ACTIVITY 5.01: CREATING A CUSTOM BOT AND CONNECTING THE BOT WITH AMAZON CONNECT

Solution:

This is an activity that combines what we learned in the previous chapters. Try to complete the activity on your own and refer to the solution as needed. You will make mistakes and will encounter things that do not seem to work. This is all part of learning an interesting domain. If you build and test it incrementally, the development will be easier and there will be fewer moving parts.

Step 1: Creating an S3 Bucket and storing balance.txt

1. First, navigate to the Amazon S3 service from https://aws.amazon.com/, and then navigate to `My Account - AWS management Console-Services-Storage-S3`. Click `Create bucket`:

Figure 5.35: S3 bucket creation for user account balance

For the `Bucket name`, type in `account-balance`, and then click `Create`.

> **NOTE**
>
> The bucket names in AWS have to be unique. Otherwise, you will get a `Bucket name already exists` error. One easy way to get a unique name is to append the bucket name with today's date plus the time, say, YYYYMMDDHHMM. While writing this chapter, we created an `account-balance-202001241911` bucket and it worked.

2. Your bucket will be created, and you will be redirected to the bucket list:

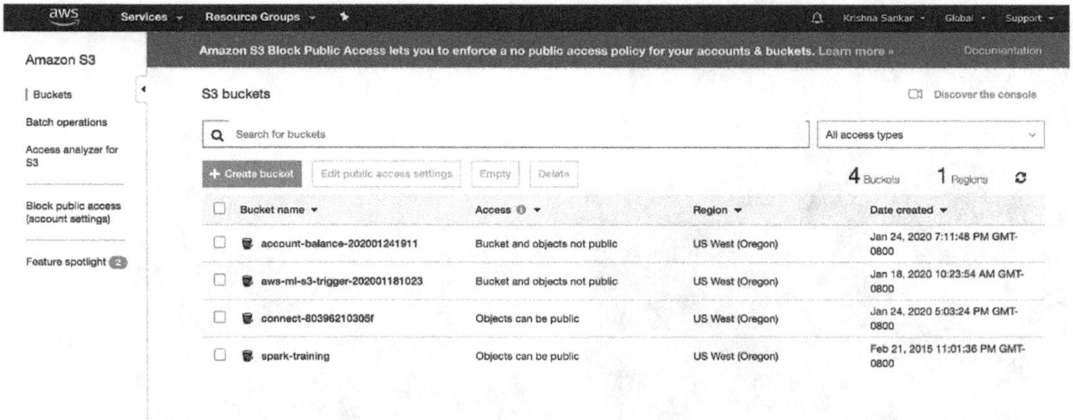

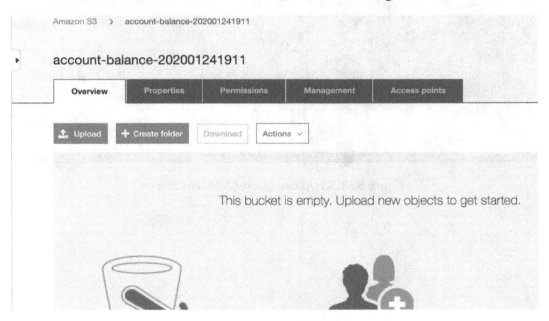

Figure 5.36: S3 bucket list screen

3. Click the bucket name you are using (in our case, **account-balance-202001241911**) and then click **Upload**:

Figure 5.37: S3 bucket list on the Upload screen

The following screen will display:

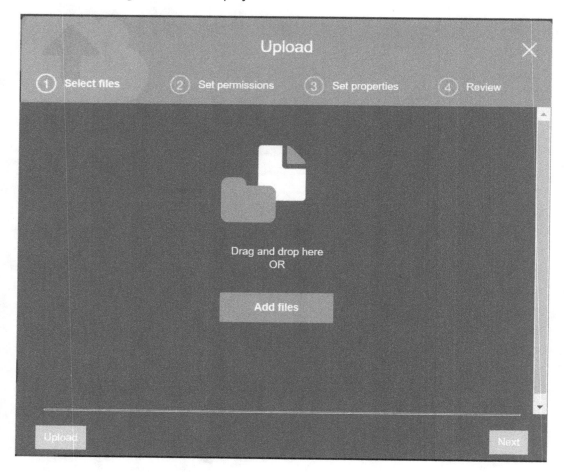

Figure 5.38: S3 Upload bucket Add files screen

4. Click **Add files**:

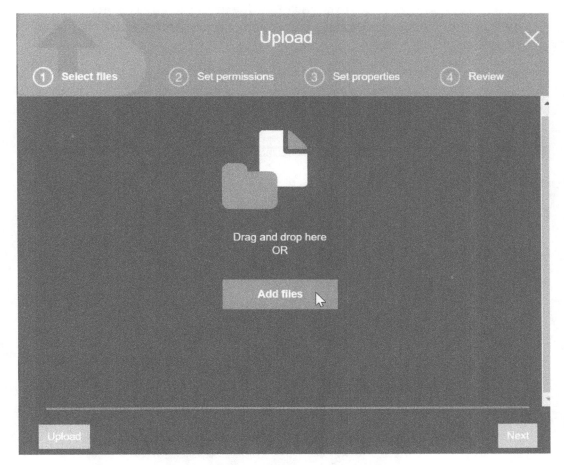

Figure 5.39: S3 Add files selection screen

5. Navigate to the **balance.txt** file location. Select the file.

> **NOTE**
>
> The **balance.txt** file is available from the following GitHub repository:
> https://packt.live/38CipvB.

As we mentioned in *Chapter 1, An Introduction to AWS*, you should have downloaded the GitHub files into a local subdirectory.

As an example, download the files into the **Documents/aws-book/ The-Applied-AI-and-Natural-Language-Processing-with- AWS** directory. As you might have guessed, the files for this exercise are in the **Chapter05** subdirectory.

6. Once the files have been selected, click the **Open** button to upload the files:

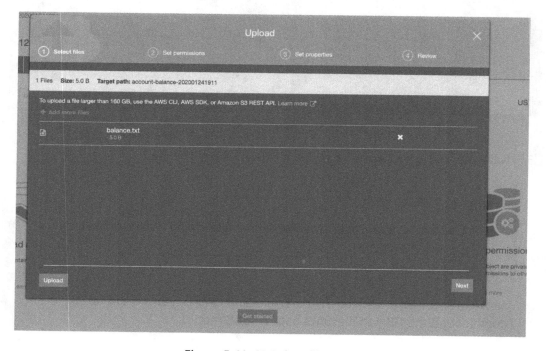

Chapter05			
Name	Date Modified	Size	Kind
fetch_balance.py	Jan 24, 2020 at 9:29 PM	937 bytes	BBEdit...cument
balance.txt	Jan 24, 2020 at 7:15 PM	5 bytes	Plain Text
test_response.json	Jan 18, 2020 at 4:23 PM	250 bytes	BBEdit...cument
test_event.json	Jan 18, 2020 at 4:23 PM	772 bytes	BBEdit...cument

Figure 5.40: File selection window in Explorer

7. Click **Next**:

Figure 5.41: S3 Select files tab

8. Set the permissions to those that are shown in the following screenshot:

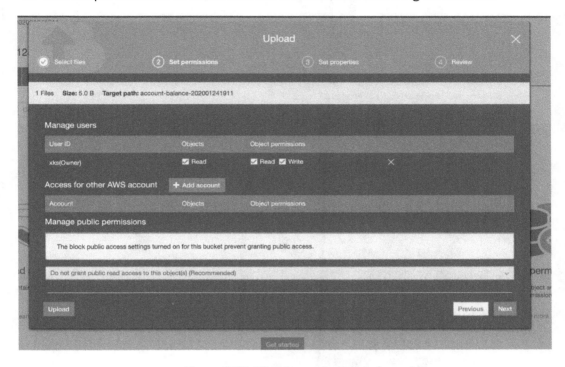

Figure 5.42: S3 Set permissions tab

9. Keep the default **Standard** option under **Storage class** and click **Next**:

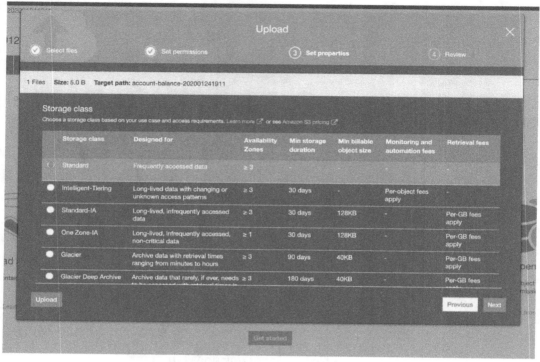

Figure 5.43: S3 Set properties tab

10. Select **Upload** in the **Review** tab:

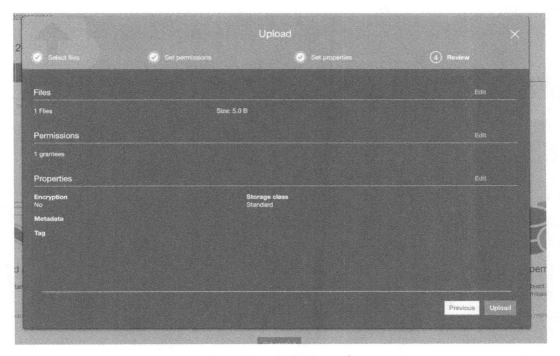

Figure 5.44: S3 Review tab

11. You will see the file in the file list:

Figure 5.45: S3 file list

Step 2: Creating a Lambda function to access the S3 Bucket and read the account balance

1. Navigate to Amazon Lambda, then **Services**, and click **Lambda** under **Compute**:

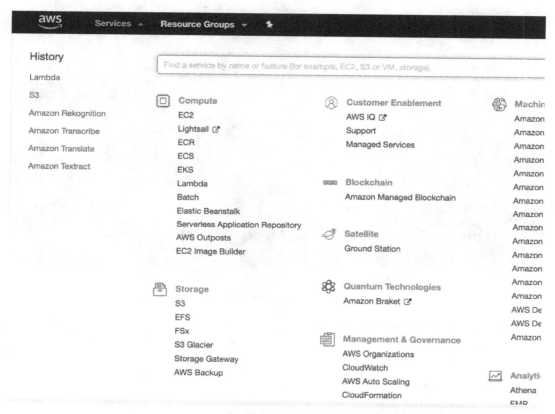

Figure 5.46: Services > Compute > Lambda

You will see the **Lambda** console as follows:

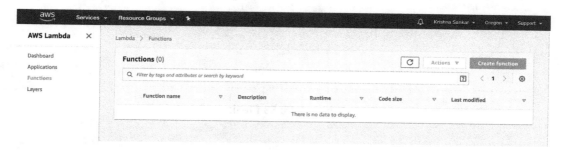

Figure 5.47: Lambda console

2. On the **Lambda** console, click **Create function**.

3. Choose **Author from scratch** from the available options. For **Function name**, type in **fetch_balance**:

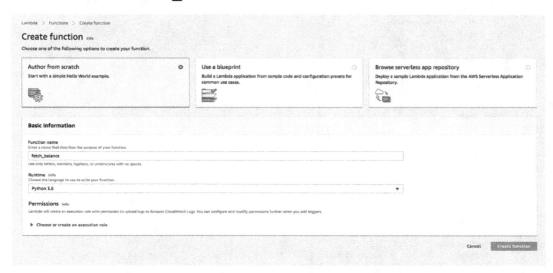

Figure 5.48: AWS Lambda – creating a function with the Author from scratch selection

4. For the **Runtime** option, choose **Python 3.6** from the list:

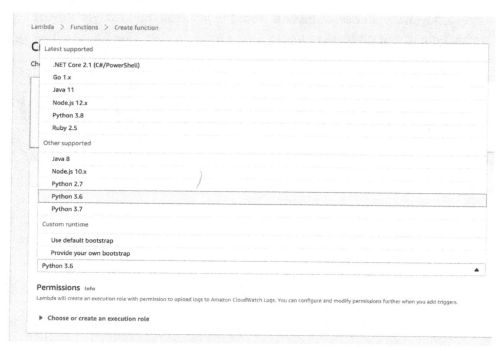

Figure 5.49: AWS Lambda—Python 3.6 selection

5. Click on **Choose or create an execution role** and select **Create a new role from AWS policy templates**. Then, enter the name **readBalanceRole** in the **Role name** field.

6. Click the drop-down menu under **Policy templates** and select **Amazon S3 object read-only permissions**.

7. Then, click the **`Create function`** button to create the Lambda function in AWS:

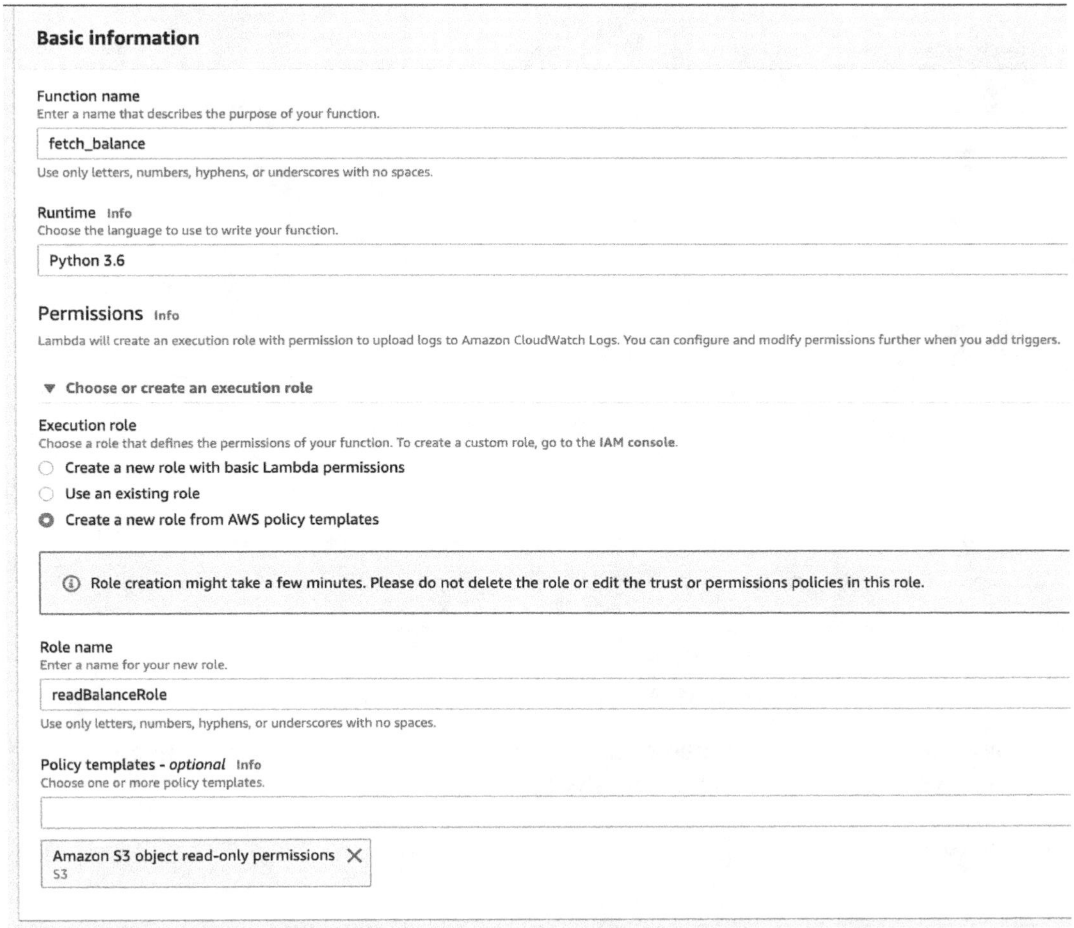

Basic information

Function name
Enter a name that describes the purpose of your function.

> fetch_balance

Use only letters, numbers, hyphens, or underscores with no spaces.

Runtime Info
Choose the language to use to write your function.

> Python 3.6

Permissions Info
Lambda will create an execution role with permission to upload logs to Amazon CloudWatch Logs. You can configure and modify permissions further when you add triggers.

▼ **Choose or create an execution role**

Execution role
Choose a role that defines the permissions of your function. To create a custom role, go to the IAM console.

○ **Create a new role with basic Lambda permissions**

○ Use an existing role

⦿ Create a new role from AWS policy templates

> ⓘ Role creation might take a few minutes. Please do not delete the role or edit the trust or permissions policies in this role.

Role name
Enter a name for your new role.

> readBalanceRole

Use only letters, numbers, hyphens, or underscores with no spaces.

Policy templates - *optional* Info
Choose one or more policy templates.

>

> Amazon S3 object read-only permissions ✕
> S3

Figure 5.50: AWS Lambda—create function screen

You will see the Lambda function designer. There is a lot of information there. Let's focus on the essentials for this activity:

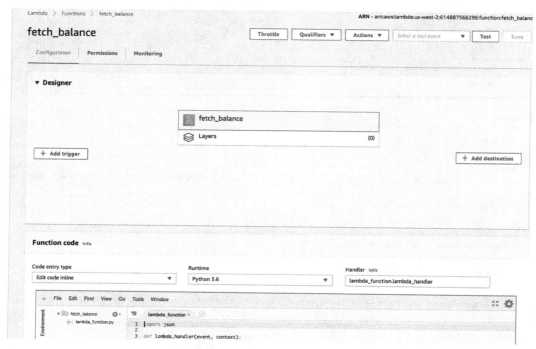

Figure 5.51: AWS Lambda—function designer

8. Next, scroll down the screen to the **Function code** section. The default code will be the same as, or similar to, the following:

Figure 5.52: AWS Lambda—the default lambda_function screen

9. Here, we can enter and edit our code entirely within the **lambda_function** tab (as long as **Code entry type** is set to **Edit code inline**, which is the default value in the drop-down menu):

> **NOTE**
>
> For this step, you may either follow along and type in the code or you can obtain it from the source code folder in your local disk where you downloaded the files from GitHub or https://packt.live/2ZOSJbd.

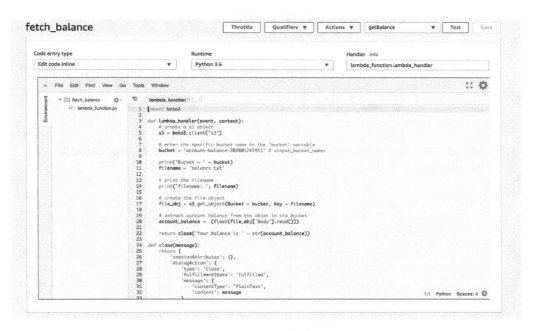

Figure 5.53: Function code for fetch_balance

10. First, we import the **AWS SDK** for Python (**boto3**) from http://boto3.readthedocs.io/en/latest/:

```
import boto3
```

11. Next, create a function that takes two parameters—**event** and **context**:

```
def Lambda_handler(event, context):
```

12. Next, create the **s3** client object:

```
s3 = boto3.client("s3")
```

13. Next, replace **<input Bucket name>** with the bucket you created (**account-balance-202001241911**, in my example):

```
# e.g." account-balance-202001241911"
bucket = "<input Bucket name>"
```

14. Next, assign the **filename** to a variable, and then print the filename:

```
filename = 'balance.txt'
print("filename: ", filename)
```

15. Next, create the file object by getting the **Bucket** and **Key**:

```
file_obj = s3.get_object(Bucket = Bucket, Key = filename)
```

16. Extract the account balance from the file:

```
account_balance =   (float(file_obj['Body'].read()))
```

17. Then, return the balance as a message:

```
return close('Your balance is ' + str(account_balance))
```

18. We need the **close** function for our bot, which requires a well-formed JSON response:

```
def close(message):
    return {
        'sessionAttributes': {},
        'dialogAction': {
            'type': 'Close',
            'fulfillmentState': 'Fulfilled',
            'message': {
                'contentType': 'PlainText',
                'content': message
            }
        }
    }
```

Remember to **Save** the function frequently:

> **NOTE**
>
> Use the **Test** button in the top-right corner to test and debug the code. You will see the results in **Execution Results** below the code pane.

19. Click the **Test** button on the top-right corner:

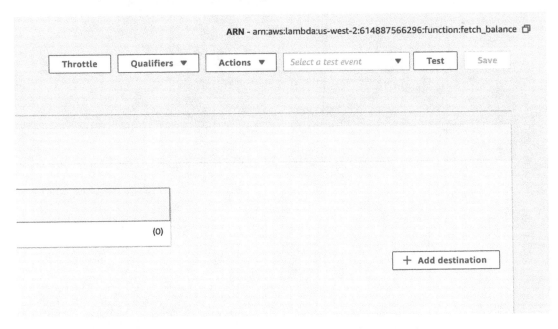

Figure 5.54: Test Button for testing Lambda function

20. For every test, we need to create at least one **Test Event**. If this is the first time you are running a test, you will see the **Configure test event** screen:

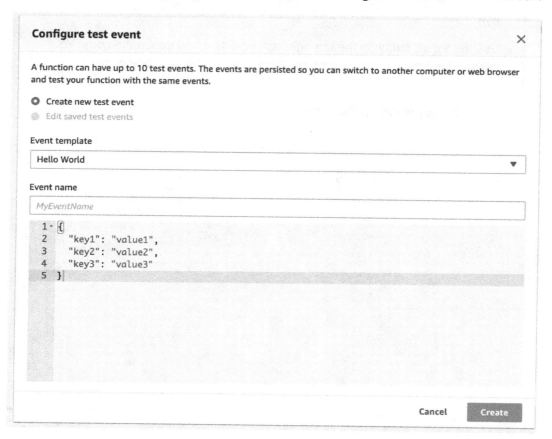

Figure 5.55: Configure Test Event to test a Lambda function

21. If the event expects values, for example a stock symbol or an account number, this is the place to create a valid JSON payload for the event. And, if you have multiple actions based on what the user asks for, you can have multiple events and then invoke the lambda with any of the events. In our case, to keep the interaction simple, we do not look for any information in the event payload. So just give the event a name – for example, type **getBalance** and then click the **Create** button.

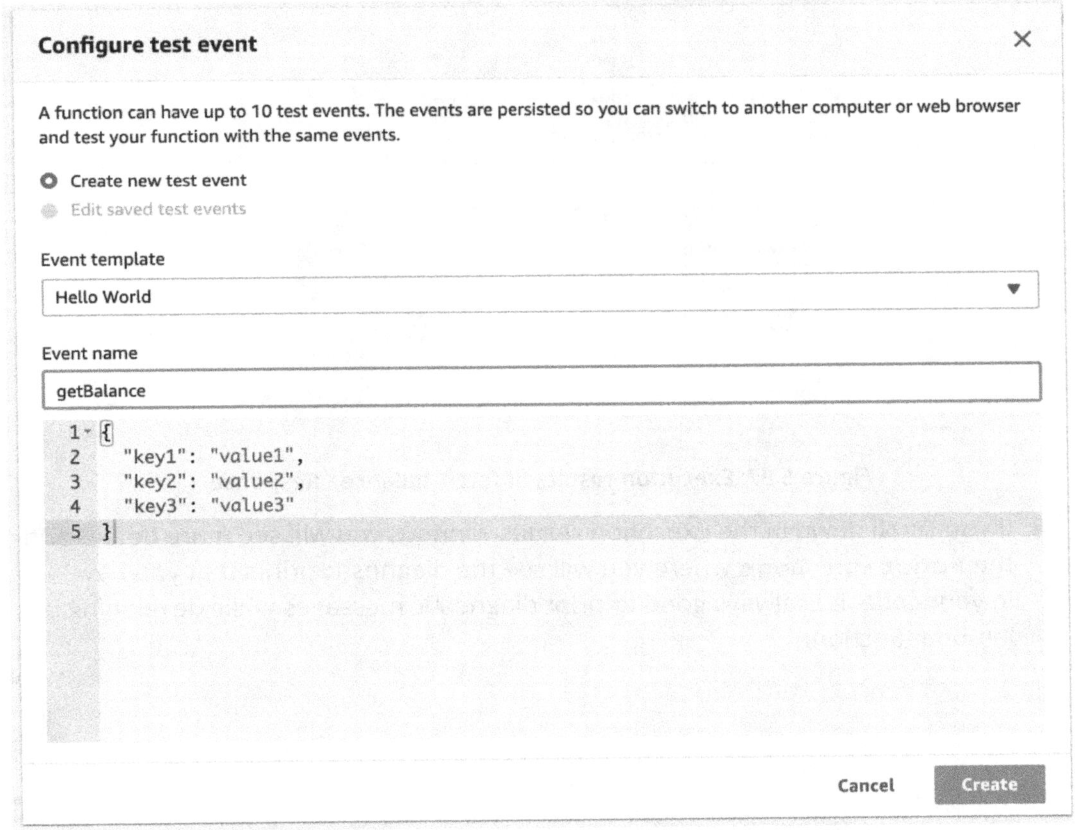

Configure test event   ✕

A function can have up to 10 test events. The events are persisted so you can switch to another computer or web browser and test your function with the same events.

◉ Create new test event
◯ Edit saved test events

Event template

| Hello World | ▼ |

Event name

| getBalance |

```
1 ▾ {
2      "key1": "value1",
3      "key2": "value2",
4      "key3": "value3"
5 }
```

                                                            Cancel   Create

Figure 5.56: Configure Test Event with name getBalance

22. You will see the results under the **Execution Results** tab:

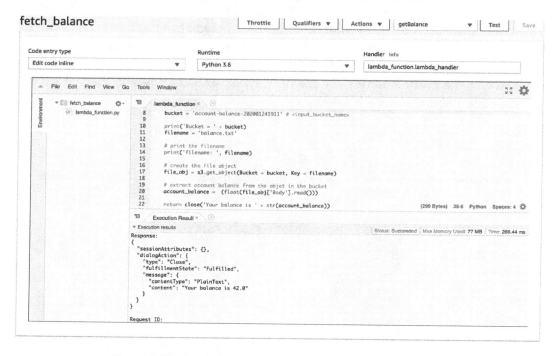

Figure 5.57: Execution results of fetch_balance - Response

23. If you scroll down in the Execution results window, you will see more details and the **Function Logs** where you will see the diagnostic prints that you have in your code. It is always good to print diagnostic messages while developing a lambda function:

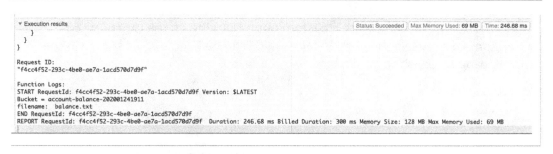

Figure 5.58: Execution results of fetch_balance – Function Logs

Step 3: Creating a Lex bot to get the balance using the Lambda function

1. The first step is to navigate to the **Amazon Lex** service within the AWS Console. You can do so by clicking on **Services | Machine Learning | Amazon Lex** or navigating to https://console.aws.amazon.com/lex.

2. The next step is to click on the **Create** button in order to get to the **Bots** creation screen:

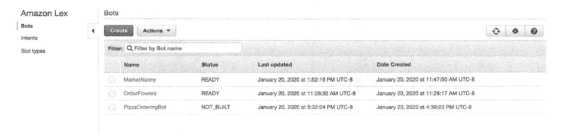

Figure 5.59: The Amazon Lex console

3. At this point, you can create a custom bot by clicking on the **Custom bot** option. This reveals the bot's details, which can be filled out, as shown in the following screenshot:

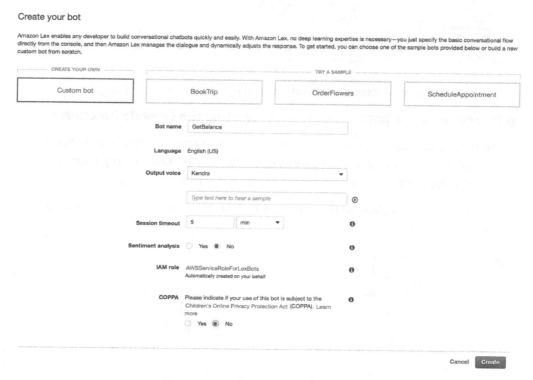

Figure 5.60: The Custom bot option

4. The **Bot name** field can be set to **GetBalance**. The **Output voice** field is set to any of the voices, for example, you can select **Kendra**. This is because we will be interacting with the bot using voice.

5. **Session timeout** can be set to the default of **5 min**. The **IAM role** field displays the name of the IAM role, which is automatically created by Lex for use by bot applications. Let's say **No** to **Sentiment analysis**.

6. Finally, the **COPPA** field pertains to the **Children's Online Privacy Protection Act**, which online applications must conform with. Choose **Yes** or **No** depending on whether you want to have someone under the age of 13 using your chatbot.

NOTE

A law was passed in 1998 to protect the privacy of children under 13. It states that online sites may not collect personal information from users who are younger than 13 years old without parental consent, among other provisions. You can learn more about COPPA at https://www.ftc.gov/ enforcement/rules/rulemaking-regulatory-reform-proceedings/childrens-online- privacy-protection-rule.

7. Finally, clicking on the **Create** button will create the chatbot and bring you to the bot's **Editor** screen. This screen will allow you to create and define an intent for the bot, as well as a slot with a custom slot type.

8. Click on the **Create Intent** button to bring up the **Add Intent** pop-up dialog window:

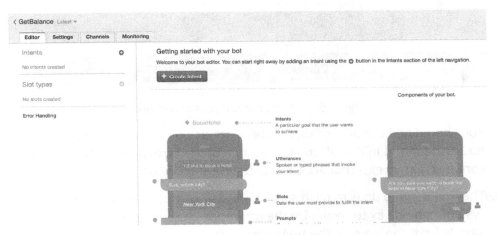

Figure 5.61: GetBalance bot's Editor tab

9. Conversely, if you already have an intent defined, you can create a new one by clicking on the **+** sign next to the **Intents** heading in the left-hand side menu on the screen.

10. The **Create Intent** window offers a few options to add an intent to the bot. The **Import intent** link allows you to import an intent from a **ZIP** file containing one or more **JSON** files with intents in the Lex format.

11. The search for existing intents allows you to reuse the intents that you may have defined or imported previously, as well as the built-in intents defined by Amazon Lex.

12. You should just click on the **Create Intent** link, however, to get to the following dialog box.

13. In the **Create intent** dialog box, name your new intent **Balance**. The bot will recognize this intent when you let it know that you are interested in a market quote. Click on the **Add** button to complete this step:

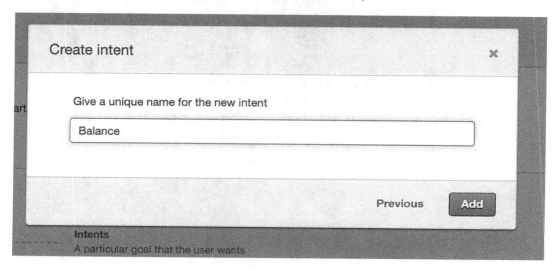

Figure 5.62: The Create intent dialog box

You should be back at the **Editor** screen at this point, and you should see the **Balance** intent in the left toolbar portion of the screen. The **Editor** screen also contains many fields that are used to define and customize the new intent.

14. The first thing to do is to fill in some **Sample utterances** to train the NLU system behind Lex to recognize the utterances you will provide to the bot as signals from the user for the **Balance** intent:

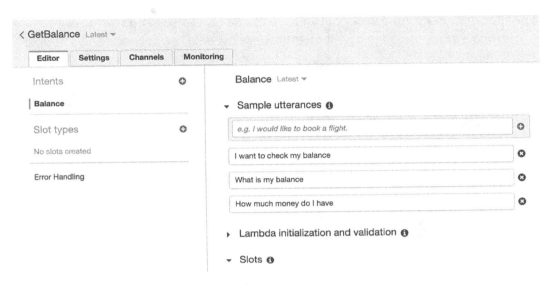

Figure 5.63: Creation of the new intent

15. After entering some sample utterances, you click on the **Build** button near the top of the page in order to kick off the training process for the bot:

Figure 5.64: Building the bot

16. There will be a follow-up dialog box with another **Build** button, which you should also click on:

Figure 5.65: Build confirmation

17. After this, you should wait until you see the **GetBalance build was successful** message box. It might take between a few seconds and a couple of minutes:

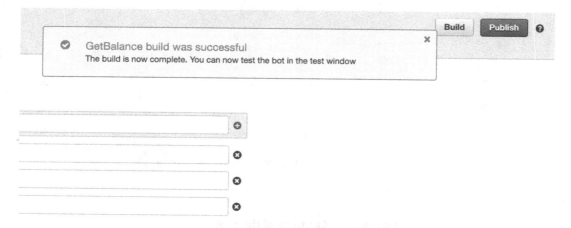

Figure 5.66: Bot build is successful

You can test your new intent within the bot in the **Test bot** pane, in the top-right corner of the screen.

> **NOTE**
>
> If the **Test bot** pane is not visible, you may have to click on the arrow button in order to expand it and make it visible.

Type utterances into the pane to verify that the bot is able to recognize the correct intent from the utterances:

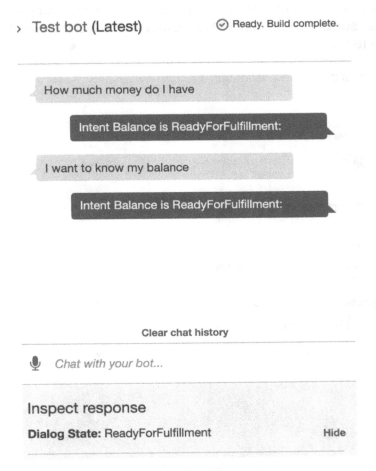

Figure 5.67: Test bot pane

You know that it has recognized the intent correctly when it returns the response: **Intent Balance is ReadyForFulfillment**. Feel free to experiment with different utterances, based on your sample utterances, in order to verify that the NLU engine is working correctly.

At this point, your bot does not do much, other than try to recognize the **Balance** intent and flag that it is ready for fulfillment.

18. Let's now connect our Lambda function and see whether it works. Select **AWS Lambda function** in **Fulfillment** and then select the **fetch_balance** Lambda function:

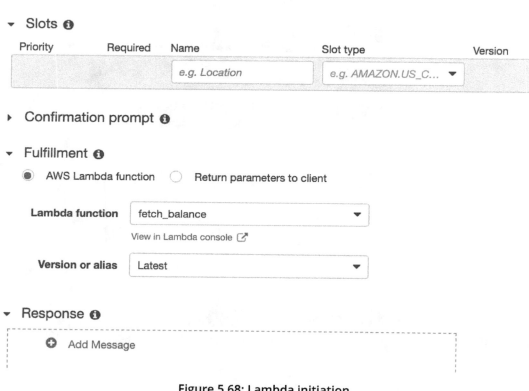

Figure 5.68: Lambda initiation

19. Click **Build** and then test again. Now it should show the balance:

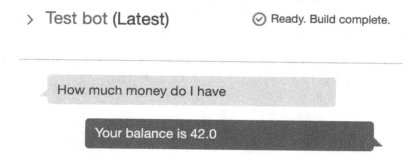

Figure 5.69: Testing the Lambda function

We are making good progress.

Step 4: Connecting the Amazon Connect call center to the GetBalance bot

We will extend the call center created in **Exercise 5.01** to add this **GetBalance** feature.

1. From the **My Account | AWS Management Console**, go to **Services | Customer Engagement | Amazon Connect**. Select the instance you have created (**jarvis42**, in our case):

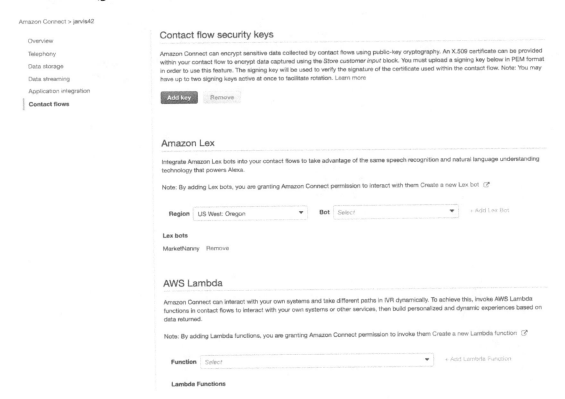

Figure 5.70: Amazon Connect contact flow configuration

We have two ways to connect — via Amazon Lex or AWS Lambda. We will use Lex, but feel free to try out Lambda.

2. Add the **GetBalance** bot:

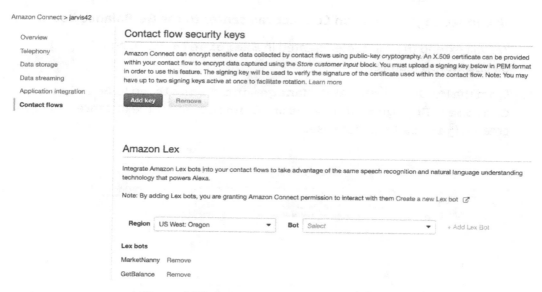

Figure 5.71: Amazon Connect contact flows

3. The next step is to create a contact flow. Go to the Dashboard, click **View Contact Flows** and **Create Contact Flow** in the upper-right corner:

4. Name it **GetBalance** and wire it as follows:

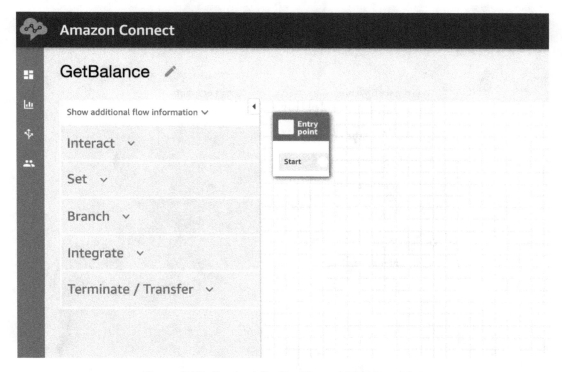

Figure 5.72: Contact flow editor—add entry point

5. Add **Get customer input** and a friendly message:

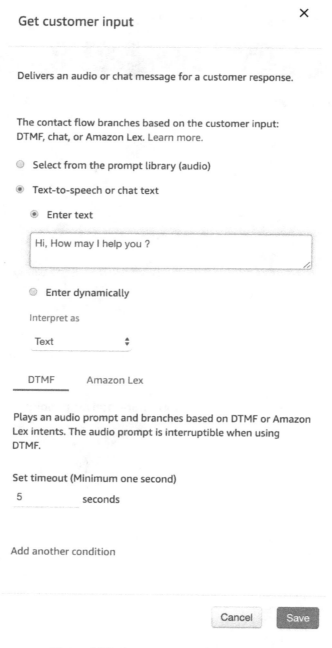

Figure 5.73: Get customer input details

6. Connect it to our **GetBalance** Lex bot and the **Balance** intent:

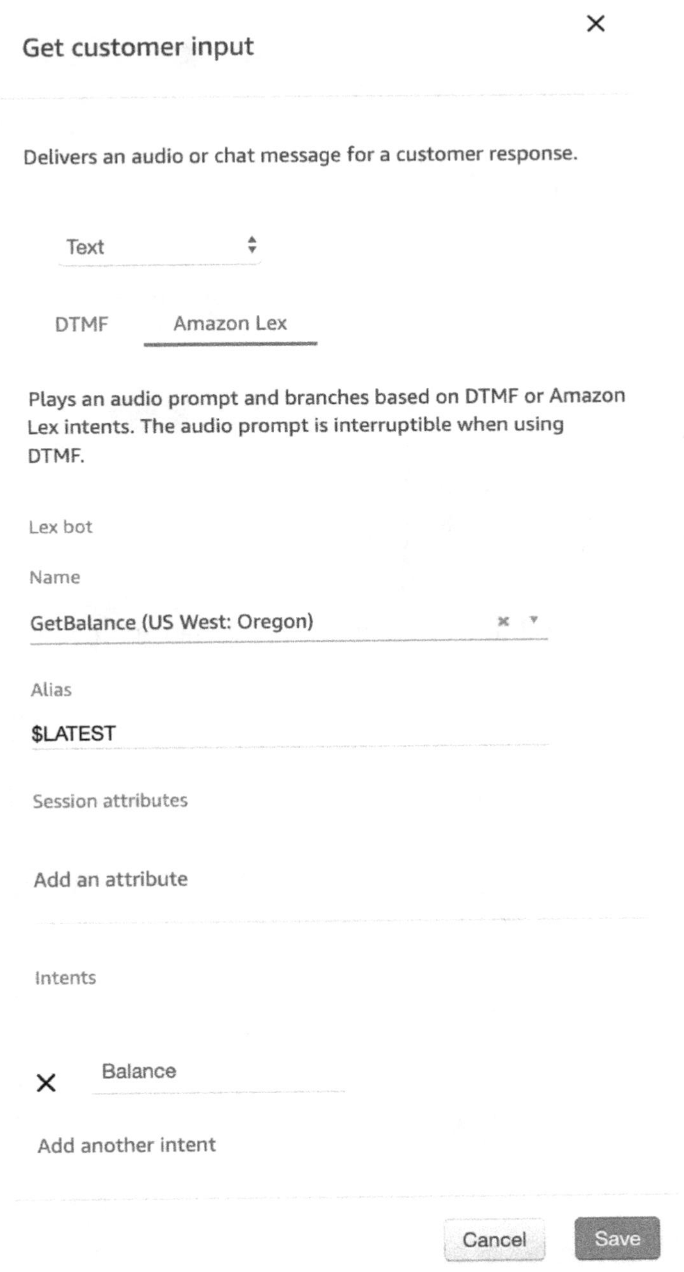

Get customer input   ✕

Delivers an audio or chat message for a customer response.

Text   ⬍

DTMF   Amazon Lex

Plays an audio prompt and branches based on DTMF or Amazon Lex intents. The audio prompt is interruptible when using DTMF.

Lex bot

Name

GetBalance (US West: Oregon)   ✕   ▾

Alias

$LATEST

Session attributes

Add an attribute

Intents

✕   Balance

Add another intent

Cancel   Save

Figure 5.74: Get customer input configurations

Then, connect all of them to hang up for now. It is a simple sequence. You can experiment with various flows:

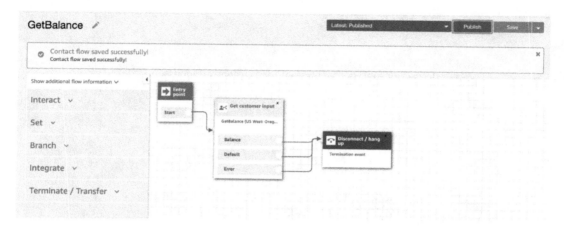

Figure 5.75: Add a hang up flow

Now that we have created another contact flow, let's rewire our phone number to answer this.

7. Go to **Overview** and click on **Login URL** and then enter your Amazon Connect credentials:

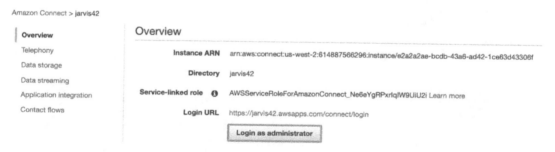

Figure 5.76: Overview screen

8. Click on **Routing** and **Phone numbers**:

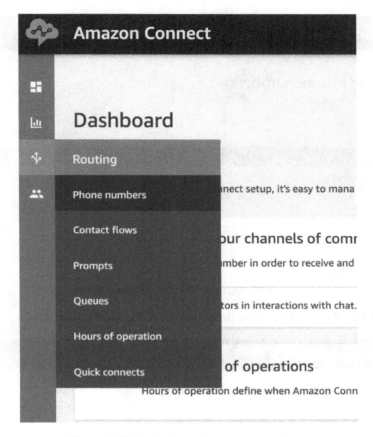

Figure 5.77: Selecting the phone numbers

9. Click on the phone number:

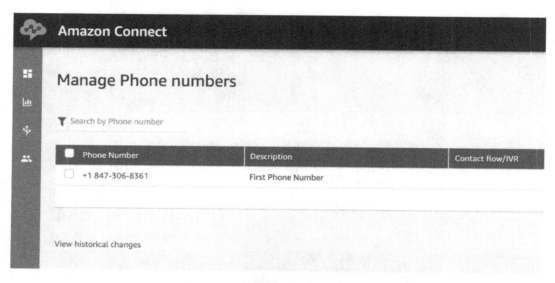

Figure 5.78: Manage Phone numbers screen

10. Select **GetBalance** from the drop-down list for **Contact flow/IVR**:

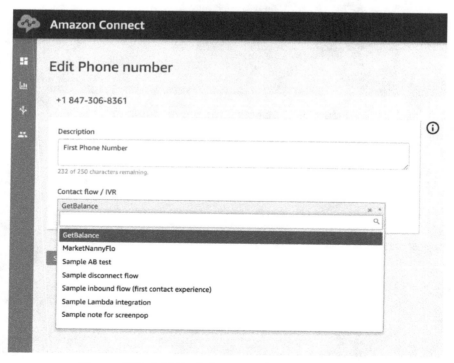

Figure 5.79: Add GetBalance to the phone number

11. Click **Save**. Now you have wired your bot to a call center.

12. Call the number. It will ask you **How may I help you?** You can say **How much money do I have?** and it will reply **You have 42.0!** Amazon has done a good job: when we activated the bot via the keyboard from the test console, it gave us a text message back. However, when we called it via Connect, it gave us a voice answer back.

This is a good time to play around with different questions and even different people—your friends, your spouse, and others. With relatively very little work, the voice bot will understand what they are saying and answer this simple question. You can try different prompts, maybe even add a dollar sign and see whether it says it the right way.

CHAPTER 6: COMPUTER VISION AND IMAGE PROCESSING

ACTIVITY 6.01: CREATING AND ANALYZING DIFFERENT FACES IN REKOGNITION

Solution:

1. Navigate to the Amazon Rekognition service from the Amazon Management Console and choose **Face comparison** from the left toolbar.

2. Upload the first set of images to Rekognition so that it can recognize and compare the faces, that is, https://packt.live/31X6IP6 and https://packt.live/2ZLseUd:

Face comparison

Compare faces to see how closely they match based on a similarity percentage.

Reference face

Comparison faces

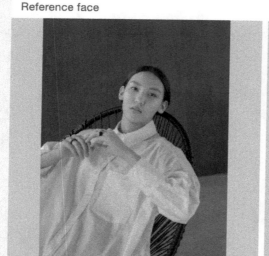

Figure 6.56: The first images provided for face comparison

Rekognition can recognize that the faces are of the same person with a **99.1**% degree of confidence, even with different angles, lighting, and shades:

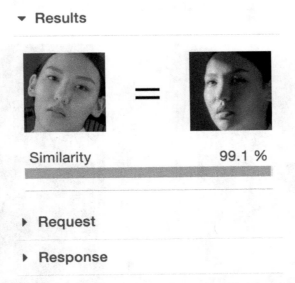

Figure 6.57: Results for the first images provided for face comparison

Additional Challenge

3. The second set of images are https://images.unsplash.com/photo-1526510747491-58f928ec870f and https://images.unsplash.com/photo-1529946179074-87642f6204d7:

Figure 6.58: The second images provided for face comparison

Once again, Rekognition recognizes the faces with a 99.4% degree of confidence, even at different angles:

▼ **Results**

Similarity   99.4 %

Figure 6.59: Results for the second images provided for face comparison

With those impressive results, we conclude this activity.

INDEX

CPSIA information can be obtained
at www.ICGtesting.com
Printed in the USA
FSHW020547281020
75180FS